UNDERSTANDING
SERGERS

Diana Davies

ACORN PRESS

The publisher offers discounts on this book when ordered in bulk quantities. For information about our products, write us at:

Acorn Press, P.O. Box 26333, Shoreview, MN 55126

Layout: Stewart Whiteside
Illustrations and Cover Art: Kathleen Koon

"Gathering Plate", "Tape/Piping Guide", "Piping Foot", and Cloth Guide" illustrations used by kind permission of Elna Inc., Eden Prairie, Minnesota

"Beading Foot", "Elastic Foot", "Blind Hem Attachment", and "Shirring Foot" illustrations used by kind permission of Pfaff American Sales Corp, Paramus, New Jersey

The following trademarks appear throughout this book: DMC, Decor 6, E-Z Thru Floss Threader, and Lycra

Library of Congress Catalog Card Number 92-070237

ISBN: Otabind 0-9634868-1-0

ISBN: Wire Bound 0-9634868-0-2

Third Printing

Printed in the United States of America

95 94 93   10 9 8 7 6 5 4 3 2

PREFACE

Sewing is a practical skill. In industry, knowledgeable operators can identify and solve problems quickly, and produce consistent high quality. With the increasing cost of ready-to-wear, more and more people are turning to home sewing as a means of getting the quality, fit and style they want at a price they can afford. At the same time, more and more people are pursuing the dream of a home-based or small business: sewing is a ideal way to achieve this.

Sewing also offers unlimited opportunities for artistic expression. This artistic expression can be turned into a business or career if desired. Sewing is an endless source of delight to those who know it, and the serger adds a whole new dimension!

Sergers, sometimes called overlocks, have been widely used in industry for decades. Now they are revolutionizing home sewing. At first glance these machines can appear strange and even intimidating. In fact, they are no more complicated than a conventional machine, just different. And they are wonderful! Here are some of the reasons people get _so_ excited about sergers:

A serger easily makes beautiful and durable edge finishes, whether decorative or just functional. Many people buy a serger for the narrow rolled edge. This is a dainty yet durable decorative edge for ruffles, napkins, handkerchiefs, scarves and garment edges. The serger is wonderful for securing the raw edges on the inside of the garment too: the most ravel-prone fabrics are secured, the lightest silkies are beautifully finished without puckering or tunneling. And if you want to get really fancy, you can finish an edge with just about anything that will go through your looper, such as metallics, fine yarn, pearl cotton or shiny rayons.

Sergers are unexcelled for sewing all kinds of knits, including swimsuit fabric, tricot, tee-shirt knits, polar fleece and fake furs. Knits are wonderful to sew with since garments generally have fewer pieces, fewer seams and little or no interfacing. Also, knit garments look great, are comfortable and require little care.

A domestic serger sews much faster than a domestic conventional machine making a straight seam. The difference is even greater when the conventional machine is making a complicated stitch, such as is used to finish raw edges or sew knits. Sergers also save much time in industrial settings.

The serger blind hem is both quicker and easier than the one on a conventional machine, it finishes the raw edge at the same time, and it stretches if you are hemming knits.

The serger can be used for a wide variety of decorative effects, including dainty heirloom sewing, pintucks, various piped and corded edges, and various types of flat-locking.

This book is addressed both to home sewers and to people in a commercial or industrial setting. This book describes stitches and techniques, most of which can be done on either an industrial or a domestic serger. There is also information specific to each type of machine. Most home sewers use domestic sergers, while virtually all commercial users have industrial sergers.

Little information is in print on industrial sergers. When time is money, it is essential to be able to solve problems quickly and properly. In addition to solving problems, this book will suggest many ways to improve quality, save time and provide unique decorative touches. Since sergers have been available to the home sewer for a relatively short period of time, few people are thoroughly familiar with them. The right information can save hours of frustration and improve quality, as well as make possible a much wider variety of garments and home furnishings.

This book is based on my experience teaching people how to use sergers, on what I have found is necessary and useful information. As a teacher I found the information already in print on sergers did not meet the needs of my students. Much essential information was not available. Also, there was no book designed to be used as a reference, where one could easily look up the answer to a variety of questions. So, I wrote a hand-out which I used in my classes. Since I had it on computer it was an easy matter to revise it and update it as I figured out new things or found things I had omitted. (Much of the material in this book is original.) It ended up being the book you are holding in your hand. Since I will not be there to go over the material with you, this book is also designed as a complete self-study course.

ACKNOWLEDGEMENTS

I first wish to thank my husband Stewart Whiteside, and our daughters: Heather, Kerry, Maya. They have been enthusiastic supporters of my sewing from my earliest awkward efforts. And now they have been patient with the insatiable demands of a book. They make it all possible and precious.

Many people have assisted me with this book, and it is a pleasure to acknowledge them. My husband spent many hours on the layout and formatting of this book, to make it as legible as possible. Virgil Abel has helped me in innumerable ways: information, introductions, suggestions, editing, enthusiasm. Thanks, Virgil. Kathy Koon is a friend and valuable critic, as well as a fine illustrator. Greg Koon contributed valuable advice and enthusiasm. My mother, Ida Davies, spent many days babysitting so I could sleep at night instead of writing. Louellyn Nestingen refined my English. Wanda Sieben of the University of Minnesota and Janet Salisbury also assisted me. A special thanks goes to Steve S and Larry D. A book takes a long time to complete, and longer than I thought: I owe a special thanks to the many people who would listen politely and not laugh when I kept saying, "Well, it's almost done." Seriously, many people were very supportive and encouraging, which meant a great deal to me.

The following dealers have generously helped me research this book: T. J. Elias of T. J. Elias Sales & Service in Minneapolis, Minnesota: Roger Kurtz of EWC in St. Paul, Minnesota; Tom and Darlyne Peters of Nationwide Sewing Centers in Minneapolis, Minnesota; Virgil Abel, Louellyn Nestingen and Mister "M" (Eldon Metaxas) of Round Bobbin Sewing Centers in St. Paul, Minnesota; Curt Kingsley of Valley West Sewing Center in Bloomington, Minnesota. Margrit Schwanck of Elna also helped me.

Finally, I wish to thank my students. They asked good questions, and were patient and enthusiastic as I learned how to answer them. This book would not exist without them. I have truly enjoyed meeting them and sharing their excitement about sewing.

TABLE of CONTENTS

APPENDIX A: TROUBLESHOOTING 159

APPENDIX B: DICTIONARY OF FABRICS 167

INTRODUCTION

This book is intended to give you a thorough understanding of sergers. In other words, you will _understand_ your machine and its settings, rather than memorizing. (This makes it easier to remember the material, and to adjust it for different circumstances.) Since I cannot be there leaning over your shoulder I have made the explanations as clear and complete as possible, especially in the beginning. Most of us learn something better if we watch it, and best if we do it. That is why this book is designed for self-demonstration. The easiest way to learn the material is to put the book beside your machine and follow it step-by-step, in most cases using scraps of fabric. At the beginning, the explanations are very thorough. As the book goes on the pace picks up, because I will assume you are familiar with the material in the earlier chapters.

In the first chapter you will learn how a serger works and how to operate it. This is really a complete basic course on sergers. If you are unfamiliar with sergers I recommend going through this chapter step-by-step, in the order it is written, with a machine in front of you. Chapter 2 describes blind hemming and other special stitches. Chapter 3 covers techniques for securing stitches. Chapter 4 describes how to use the serger on various types of fabric and in various situations. Chapter 5 covers the different kinds of thread you can use in the serger. Chapter 6 covers the wide variety of decorative effects possible on the serger. Chapter 7 covers special stitches available on some sergers. Chapter 8 covers industrial sergers plus some serger attachments. Appendix A is a trouble-shooting guide. Appendix B describes how to serge specific types of fabric. Appendix C offers suggestions on selecting a serger. Appendix D lists books and mail-order sources for supplies. Finally, there is a glossary and index.

There is a lot of information in this book, much of it in the form of little "obvious" tips. If you do each step on your machine as you read about it you will understand and remember these tips much better. This is particularly important for chapter 1. After going through the first chapter the remaining chapters can be read, then referred to as necessary while sewing. This book is intended to be used as a reference. There are many cross-references and many headings, making it easy to find an answer to any question. You can use either the table of contents or the index as a place to start. Please refer to the glossary at the back of the book for any unfamiliar terms.

This book is intended for both novice and expert users.

If you are considering purchasing a serger, read this book to learn what a serger is and what it can do. Sew on a friend's machine if you can. Refer to Appendix C: Selecting a Serger. Using all this information you can decide what kind of sewing you will probably do with your serger and which features will probably be important to you. Then when you are shopping you will know what to look for, and you will be able to actually sew on the various machines and play with their tensions. This is essential to properly evaluate a machine.

If you have a serger but are not comfortable with it, sit down in front of your machine with this book next to you. Go through the first chapter of the book, trying everything out on your machine as you go. Take the time to experiment and play. Read the remaining chapters. As you have time and inclination learn techniques from the other chapters in the same manner. (If you see it and do it you will learn it far better than if you just read it.)

If you are already proficient with a serger, it is still a good idea to go through the first chapter with your machine handy, but you will move more quickly. Some points and ideas probably will be new to you. Covering the information in a logical sequence is valuable: it makes it much easier to understand "why." Understanding how the machine works helps you to understand threading and tensions, and understanding tensions helps you to understand special stitches.

One final note: I have had many students who were scared of their serger, but every one has learned how to use and enjoy their machine. You can too!

CHAPTER 1

THE BASICS

This chapter is a complete basic serger course, as well as an important reference on serger essentials. In order to understand how to use a serger, sit down in front of your machine with this book next to you. Go through this chapter step by step, looking at everything and doing it on your machine as you read about it. It will help to go through the material in the order it is given, especially if you are not familiar with sergers. After you have covered the material in this chapter, you can read the other chapters so you know what is available. Then, when you wish to learn another technique or solve a particular problem, sit down with your machine and this book, and go through that section step by step. Once you understand the material in chapter 1 you will be able to understand the material in chapters 2 through 5. Understanding that material will enable you to understand the material in chapter 6. Use chapters 7 and 8, and the appendices as needed.

There are differences in the way sergers are put together. When appropriate this book describes these differences in detail, for example in the section on "Threading." It is helpful to mark the descriptions that relate to your machine, perhaps circling them with a pencil. If you cross out the non-relevant sections I suggest you do it with a pencil, in case you decide to upgrade to a new machine someday.

TYPES OF SERGERS AND STITCHES

Industrial sergers are designed for use in commercial settings where they may be used continuously for 8 or more hours a day. They are designed for speed, ease of use, quality stitching and durability. (refer to section on "Industrial Sergers," page 151, for more information) Domestic sergers are much smaller and less expensive.

There are several types of serger stitches available. Each machine offers one or a combination of these. The most commonly used stitches are the overlock (3- or 4-thread), 2-thread overedge stitch and 2-thread chainstitch. The overlock is the most common stitch: most domestic and many industrial sergers offer it. Some also offer a 2-thread chainstitch, and some offer a 2-thread overedge stitch. Other stitches are available only on specialized industrial sergers. Industrial sergers are not designed to be converted from one type of stitch to another. Some domestic machines can convert from an overlock to an overedge stitch.

Sergers are often described in terms of the number of threads they have, for example a "5-thread machine" or a "4/3-thread machine." This is a shorthand for describing which stitches are available on a given machine. The most commonly used serger stitches are the 3-thread and 4-thread overlocks. Many machines just offer a 3-thread overlock, or a choice between a 3- and 4-thread overlock. These are the "3-thread" or "4/3-thread" machines. The 5-thread machines produce a 2-thread chainstitch and a 3-thread overlock. Many domestic 5-thread sergers can make a 4-thread overlock if the 2-thread chainstitch is not being used. Industrial 5-thread sergers cannot be converted to make a 4-thread overlock. Some machines can also produce a 2-thread overedge stitch. On most domestic machines this is accomplished by converting the overlock loopers to produce the overedge stitch. These are the "4/3/2-thread" machines or the "5/4/3/2-thread" machines. Some machines produce a 2-thread chainstitch and a 2-thread overedge stitch. The first domestic sergers were of this "4/2-thread" type. This type of domestic machine is rarely sold now, but 4/2-thread industrial sergers are still available.

Most of the material in this book concerns the overlock stitch, either 3-thread or 4-thread. The 4-thread overlock is basically the same as the 3-thread overlock, except that there are two needles side by side instead of one. (The overlock stitch is described in the section on "The Serger Stitch" on page 29. The other stitches are described in chapter 7, "Stitches," page 141.)

HOW A SERGER WORKS

Sergers have a completely different mechanism for forming a stitch than conventional machines, and the stitch they produce is completely different. All serger stitches are produced through the action of needles and loopers: no bobbin is used. The needle never moves sideways, and the machine never sews backwards. In a conventional or lockstitch machine the needle thread is carried around the bobbin by the shuttle hook, catching the bobbin thread and pulling it up into the middle of the seam. On a serger, the needle thread is interlaced with threads carried by loopers, loop inside of a loop inside of a loop. Each looper has an eye at the end, through which its thread passes. Since loopers do not have to pierce the fabric they are thicker than needles and have a larger eye.

Here is a description of the sequence for making a 3 or 4-thread overlock stitch. Other serger stitches are formed similarly, as you will see if you look inside and watch the stitch being formed. If the threads are not white they are easier to see. It also helps if they are not the same color. Slowly turn the balance wheel on your machine with the front door open while you watch this process:

(Make sure you are turning the balance wheel in the proper direction. On Industrial sergers and older domestic sergers, the top of the wheel moves backwards. On newer domestic machines it moves forwards. Domestic machines have an arrow by the balance wheel indicating the proper direction.)

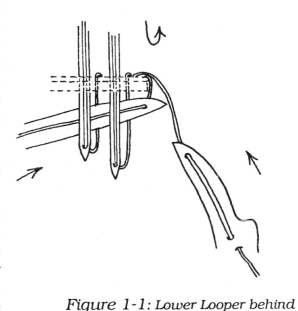

Figure 1-1: Lower Looper behind Needle Picks up Loops of Needle Threads

The needle(s) comes down through the fabric, and begins to rise.

The lower looper moves across from left to right under the needle plate, picking up a loop of thread from behind the needle(s). The lower looper continues toward the right, the needle(s) continues to rise (see Figure 1-1).

The upper looper moves upwards, catching a loop of thread from behind the lower looper (see Figure 1-2). The upper looper continues upwards, moving to the left over the top of the fabric. The lower looper begins moving back toward the left. The needle(s) continues upwards, reaching the top of its stroke (see Figure 1-3).

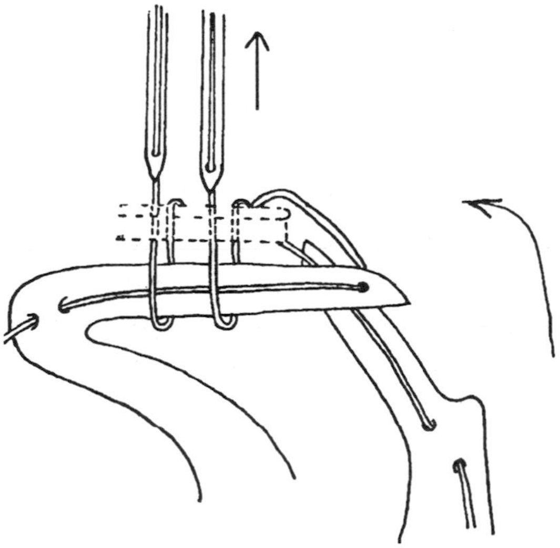

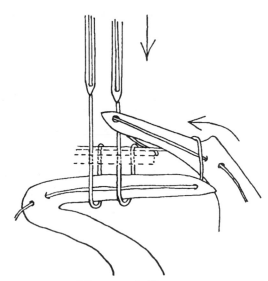

Figure 1-2: Upper Looper Picks up Loop of Lower Looper Thread

Figure 1-3: Upper Looper has caught Loop of Lower Looper Thread

The needle(s) start downward, catching a loop of thread from behind the upper looper (see Figure 1-4). The lower looper moves to the left as the upper looper moves to the right and down. The loop(s) of needle thread slip off the lower looper and the loop of lower looper thread slips off the upper looper.

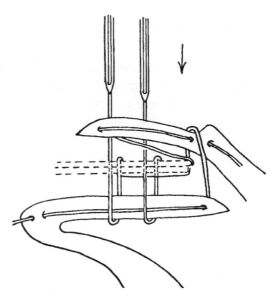

If you think about it, the serger stitch is really knitted; lower looper thread inside a loop of needle thread, upper looper thread inside a loop of lower looper thread, needle thread inside a loop of upper looper thread, and so on. However, because several threads are looped together in sequence, it cannot be pulled out as a chainstitch can.

Figure 1-4: Needles about to capture Upper Looper Thread

Another important point is that when the needles are up, their threads are always going down through the needle plate and around the lower looper. (More on this later, in the section on "Threading.")

Observe how the upper looper moves up and down, catching a loop of thread below the fabric then moving up and over on top of the fabric so the needle can catch its loop. Clearly the overlock stitch must be formed over the edge of the fabric, so the upper looper can connect with both the lower looper and the needle without touching the fabric. Therefore overlock (and overedge) sergers have knives, to cut an even edge. These knives have a scissor-like action. The upper knife moves up and down against the stationary lower knife. The knives are found in front of and slightly to the right of the needle, and partially block your view of it. (refer to section on "Stitch Width and Knives," page 37)

On a serger, it is important that the fabric feed straight from these knives to the needles. Therefore, sergers have longer feed dogs than conventional machines. This makes fabrics feed more evenly, which is nice if matching stripes or feeding slippery fabrics. However it also makes it more difficult to turn curves. You will find it necessary more often to raise the presser foot and turn the fabric slightly when sewing tight curves. Because of this, a serger is not as good as a conventional machine for detailed intricate sewing.

Finally, sergers have stitch fingers (see Figure 1-5). If you look at the needle plate of your serger (it may help to remove the presser foot) you can see that the needle goes through a narrow slot, open at the back. To the right of the needle is the stitch finger. These come in widths of approximately 1 to 3 mm. The stitches are formed _around_ this finger. This, along with properly set looper tensions, keeps the edge of the fabric from crumpling up because of the stitches. After the stitches form they remain on the finger for another 1/2 inch or so. This is another reason why it is more difficult to execute tight curves on the serger. Some machines have a skinny stitch finger on the needle plate and a wide one on the presser foot. Wherever it is located it functions the same way.

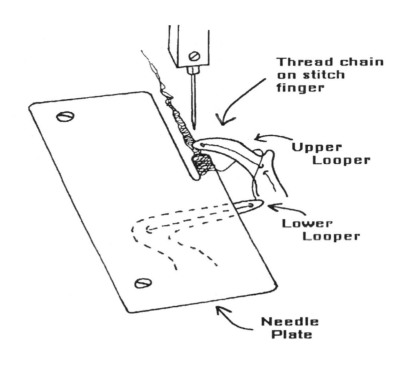

Figure 1-5: Stitch finger

NEEDLES

Some domestic sergers use the same kind of needles as conventional domestic sewing machines, and others use industrial needles. Industrial sergers use industrial needles. There are several kinds of industrial needles. Each has its own code, for example "DB x 1". Make sure you use the proper needles in your machine. You can get them from your dealer. If your machine uses the same kind of needles as your conventional sewing machine try to use the same brand that came with your machine. Your dealer carries them. Serger needles are not available in as wide a range of sizes as needles for a conventional machine. Even if your machine takes conventional needles it will probably not form a stitch with a very small needle. Use a size 11 or 12 (75 or

80) for light to medium weight fabric and a size 14 (90) for medium to heavyweight fabric.

Do _not_ use a damaged needle. A burr on the tip will damage your fabric, a bent needle may damage your lower looper. If in doubt remove the needle from the machine and examine it. A burr feels rough if you pull it across your finger tip. Check for a bent needle by sighting down it. When checking for a damaged needle rotate it so you are checking it on all sides. Anytime you hear a clicking sound when you sew, check for a bent needle. If you hear a "popping" sound when the needle is penetrating the fabric you may have a damaged needle. If your machine takes conventional needles and you are sewing on heavy fabric such as denim you can try a denim needle.

If the needle makes holes in your fabric, check for a damaged needle. If the needle is good, try a smaller size. You can also try using finer thread. I am usually blind hemming when I get needle holes. (refer to section on "Blind Hemming," page 44) Another option is a ballpoint needle. This needle has a rounded tip which pushes the threads of the fabric aside rather than piercing them. It is mostly used with knits. If your machine uses conventional machine needles you can buy ball point needles for it from your dealer. If your machine uses industrial needles and your dealer does not carry ballpoint industrial needles you may be able to mail-order them. (refer to Appendix D: Sources, page 189)

Make sure your needles are properly positioned in the machine. Both needles must have the long groove directly to the front. If your machine uses industrial needles which do not have a flat shank at the top, hold your thumb nail in this groove when you start inserting the needle to make sure the groove is facing forward. After you finish tightening the screw check to make sure the needle eye is facing directly forward. Make sure all needles are pushed up into the machine as far as they will go. For the 4-thread overlock stitch the left needle goes in a little farther than the right one. If you are using a 2-thread chainstitch its needle is in front of and to the left of the overlock needle. If you will not be threading one of the needles remove it from the machine. When you remove a needle from the machine tighten the set screw just enough so it will not work its way loose and fall out. If you get frustrated trying to insert a needle into your machine you can use tweezers. Pliers, especially the clamping kind, work better. Best is the needle insertion tool, a narrow piece of plastic with a hole at the end for the needle. If your dealer does not carry these you can order them. Refer to the section on "Supplies" in Appendix D: Sources, page 189.

Some domestic sergers use a special double needle to make a 4-thread overlock stitch. If your machine uses a double needle for the 4-thread overlock stitch, position it so the longer needle is on the right. If your machine has this type of needle, refer to the section on "The Serger Stitch," page 29, for more information.

THREADING

Sergers have a reputation for being difficult to thread, primarily because of the loopers. Sergers are somewhat slower to thread than conventional machines, but threading goes quickly once you know the tricks. Fortunately, in most cases you can simply tie the new looper threads onto the old threads and use the old threads to pull the new ones through the machine. When changing thread, cut the old looper threads about 8" above the machine. Tie the new looper threads onto the ends of the old looper threads, using an overhand knot rather than a square

Square Knot

Figure 1-6: Overhand Knot

knot (see Figure 1-6). Cut the old needle threads, lift the presser foot and run the machine slowly, pulling on the thread chain until the new looper threads are through the machine. You may find it helpful to loosen the looper tensions while pulling the threads through, or simply assist them through with your fingers as the knots come up to the tension disks. Thread the needles with the new thread. (On most machines it does not save time to tie on the new needle threads: the needles are much quicker to thread than the loopers and generally the knots do not go through the eye of needle.) After tieing on, check the looper thread guides to make sure a thread has not popped out of its guide.

When threading a needle on a serger I find it helps if I sit to the left of the needle, so the knife is out of the way of my right hand. It may help to open the front door. On a domestic machine it may also help to swing the upper knife out of the way, especially if the upper knife comes from above. (refer to section on "Stitch Width and Knives," page 37) Use the balance wheel to get the needle as high as possible, and lower the presser foot. If you have a snap-on presser foot, removing it may make it easier to get at the needle. I put the thread through the needle with my right thumb and forefinger then pinch it with my left thumb and forefinger, which are going around the presser foot shaft. I pull it a little way through and to the right with my left hand, pinch it with my right thumb and forefinger, then get my left hand around and pull a long tail through. It sounds awkward, but by now I can do it quickly. You may want to use a tweezer to grasp the thread as it emerges from the back of the needle. A needle threader may help also: use a large one if possible. Your dealer has these large needle threaders. (If you have trouble getting the thread through the needle threader, use the floss threader described below.) If you have a domestic 5-thread machine which can also do a 4-thread overlock, there are two threading paths for the left needle. One is used for the chainstitch needle, one for the left overlock needle.

When you purchase your machine it will have threads already on it, ready to tie on to the ends from the new cones of threads. If by chance your machine is completely unthreaded, you should thread it in the following order: upper looper, then lower looper, then needles. The following tips will make threading the loopers much easier when you cannot tie on (ie, when a thread has broken). Although these descriptions are for threading overlock loopers, they are also useful when threading loopers for other stitches.

1) Refer to the threading diagram in your manual or on the inside front door of your machine. Follow it step by step.

2) Use tools. The "Butler Floss Threader," available in the dental section of any drug store, greatly simplifies threading loopers. Put your thread through it and leave a generous tail, at least 6". Use it with or without a tweezer (see Figure 1-7). Use a needle threader as necessary. If using a needle threader, you can use the floss threader to get the thread through the eye of the needle threader: this is useful for threads like texturized nylon.

Figure 1-7: Threading Lower Looper with Floss Threader

3) When threading the loopers or needles use the balance wheel to position them for easy threading.

Position the lower looper at the far left for threading the left-hand end. Use the floss threader to pass the thread under the needle plate and through to the left side of the machine, threading any guides along the way.

On some domestic sergers the left-hand end of the lower looper has a slot or hook for the thread. Catch the thread into it, hold the thread in with a finger as you use the floss threader to pass the thread back to the right under the needle plate, then use the balance wheel to move the lower looper to the right. Position the lower looper so as to get the eye clear of the upper looper, and as high as possible so you can angle the floss threader up through the eye and grab it easily behind the eye. If necessary use a tweezer to pull the threader through. After you thread the right-hand eye pull at least 6" of thread through.

If the left-hand end of the lower looper has an eye, insert the floss threader partway into it, then turn the balance wheel to move the looper to the right, keeping the floss threader in the left-hand eye as you do. When the looper is at the right push the floss threader through until you can pull it from the right. If it is stuck pull it back a little to the left then push it through again. Pull it through and thread the right-hand eye as described above.

On some industrial sergers the left-hand eye of the lower looper must be threaded from back to front, a difficult operation even with a floss threader and tweezer. The solution is to take a two foot length of thread and thread the looper eye backwards, from front to back, using the floss threader with a tweezer to grasp it as it comes out through the eye. Then tie the appropriate end of the short piece of thread onto the end of the thread from the cone and pull the knot through the eye. A similar trick can be used if you finish threading a looper, only to realize you forgot one or more guides. Cut the thread near the guides, thread them with one end, knot the two ends together, then pull the knot through the looper.

Some domestic sergers are designed so you do not have to pass the lower looper thread through to the left side of the machine in order to thread the left hand end of the lower looper. These usually have a hook on the left end of the lower looper. On some the front part of the machine, including the knife assembly, swings out of the way. On some machines part of the lower looper is slid to the right so the thread can be caught in the hook at the left end, then the assembly is slid back to the left. Some machines simply allow enough clearance so the lower looper thread can be caught in the hook if the lower looper is all the way to the right. In any case, move the lower looper all the way to the right before beginning to thread it. Thread the left end as necessary then thread the eye.

Though much easier to thread, you still want to position the upper looper with the balance wheel so it is clear of the lower looper and so you can easily grasp the floss threader as you feed it through the eye. Some sergers have a vertical eye at the bottom of the upper looper. This eye is much easier to thread with the floss threader.

4) If you need to rethread either of the loopers, you can have problems with threads inexplicably breaking every time you start sewing. Here is the reason. The serger stitch is formed as a series of loops inside of loops. As you recall from the section on "How a Serger Works," page 16, the needle thread(s) form a loop around the lower looper, and the lower looper thread forms a loop around the upper looper. When rethreading either looper it is essential not to trap the loop of thread which is already around that looper, the needle thread(s) in the case of the lower looper or the lower looper thread in the case of the upper looper (see Figure 1-8).

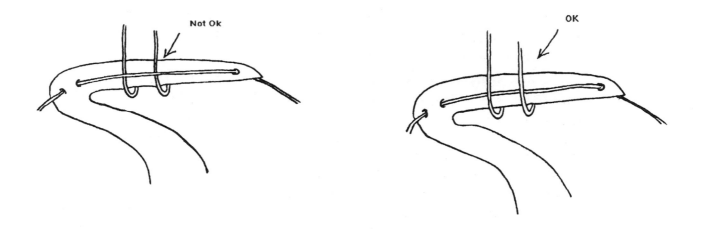

Figure 1-8: Lower Looper with Needle Threads

With the lower looper it is particularly difficult to see the loops of needle thread(s) around it, but if you peer into the machine from the side you can see them. You must get the lower looper thread _inside_ the loops of the needle thread.

On some machines you can clear the lower looper by moving the lower looper all the way to the right after threading the left-hand end, pulling the loops of needle thread off of it with a finger, then threading the eye. It is much easier to pull the loops of needle thread off the lower looper if you pull back and to the right with the loose threads or chain behind the needle.

Sometimes you can use the floss threader to run the thread inside the needle thread loops as you are threading the lower looper.

Another option is to just thread the lower looper and then clear the loops of needle thread by running something like a business card along the top of the needle plate to bring up the needle threads. (You may need to cut the chain in order to be able to pull the needle thread(s) free. Leave about 1 and 1/2" of chain when you cut it, then pull the needle thread(s) out of it before you run the card across. If necessary pull on the needle thread(s) to get a slightly longer end.) Loosening the needle tensions makes it easy to pull extra slack through. You want to make sure you have a long enough end on the needle thread(s) and looper threads so you can easily grasp them afterwards.

A fourth alternative is to cut the needle threads and rethread after the lower looper is threaded.

You can have similar problems with the upper looper, but in this case it is a simple matter to knock the loop of lower looper thread off of the upper looper before threading. An even quicker method is to rotate the balance wheel _backwards_ until the upper looper is clear. (Note: this is the _only_ time you should turn the balance wheel backwards. Major tangles result if you do this when the machine is completely threaded. There is an arrow on or next to your balance wheel indicating the normal direction.)

5) After threading the serger, grasp all the threads together under and behind the presser foot and pull them gently towards the rear of the machine while you make several stitches. This locks the threads together around the stitch finger so the upper looper cannot suck them down into the machine when you begin sewing. Make sure the chain is pulled back out of the way before you begin sewing. If you do not do this sometimes the threads will get tangled with the loopers and you will have to rethread.

If your machine has a tension release that releases both the needle and the looper threads, make sure you do this step after every time you use it. On most sergers, lifting the presser foot does not open the tension disks, as it does on a conventional sewing machine. Some machines have a tension release which opens all the tension disks so thread can easily be pulled through at the end of a seam. Sometimes it is operated by the presser foot lift, sometimes it is a separate control. Chaining off is the best way to end a seam, since the machine is left with the threads locked together and ready to begin the next seam. (refer to next section under "Beginning a Seam") Some tension releases just release the needle threads: these do not release an excessive amount of thread.

STARTING SEWING

The Sewing Area

Put the machine on a sturdy, vibration-free table of a suitable height. Find a chair of suitable height that allows you to sit erect comfortably. Your forearms should be just about horizontal when sewing. Use a footstool, cushion or something if necessary to raise your feet so your legs are comfortable. Sit down in front of the serger so that your body is centered in front of the needle. (Not all sewing cabinets are set up this way, but it is important for comfort and control.) Put the foot control next to your foot. If it tends to slide away on a slippery floor, put something under to secure it. Although you can buy "foot control stays," you can make one with a piece of carpet or a small no-skid type rug such as is used in the bathroom.

Make sure you have good lighting. In addition to overhead lighting and the built-in light in my machine, I have a long flexible arm light next to my machine. This way I can easily see my work as I position it for sewing. Make yourself comfortable so you can enjoy your sewing!

Consider having an extension made for your serger. Cut a piece of wood to fit around the left side of your serger. Give it a smooth finish so it does not catch on the fabric. Make it the proper height for your machine by putting legs on it. Put rubber feet on the legs to keep it in place. Make it so it can be moved out of the way when you need to open the left door.

If your machine does not have something to collect the trimmings you can rig one by putting the bill of a baseball cap under the front end of your machine. Choose a hat which does not have an opening in back.

Industrial sergers come in a cabinet that provides all these amenities except the chair.

Beginning a Seam

If you look beneath the front end of a serger presser foot, you can see the feed dogs extending a bit out from the end. Probably you have seen people stick fabric under the end of the presser foot without lifting it, and seen the feed dogs grab it and begin sewing. This works, but the feed dogs tend to catch the under-layer first, giving an uneven seam. One reason people do this is because the presser foot lift on domestic sergers is much more awkward to get at than on a conventional machine, since you cannot easily reach through to the right of the needle. The solution is to lift just the end of the presser foot with your right thumb, and use your left hand to position the beginning of your seam, under the presser foot and next to the knives. Industrial sergers have a knee or foot activated presser foot lift.

The serger seam allowance is about 1/4". If your garment pieces were cut with 1/4" seam allowances you will not be trimming fabric off, so the right-hand edge will be next to the knives. If your garment pieces include a 5/8" seam allowance you will need to trim about 3/8" off: position your fabric so that 3/8" is to the right of the knives. You may want to mark this distance on your machine if it is not already marked. A small piece of tape works fine.

You always want the knives to skim the edge of your fabric. If the edge of the fabric is somewhat to the left of the knives you will get a narrower seam allowance, and an insecure seam. (1/4" seam allowances do not allow a lot of margin for error.) This is why you always (almost!) watch where the knife is cutting rather than where the needle is sewing. If you make sure the edge of the fabric is next to the knife, the feed dogs will carry the fabric straight to the needle with a good seam allowance.

When you reach the end of the seam, continue sewing until there is about a 4" long thread chain between the fabric and the machine. Cut in the middle of this chain. It does not bother a serger to sew without fabric in the machine, although you need to pull gently on the chain to keep the thread from jamming up. Some decorative techniques use long lengths of chain. If you lift the presser foot before making long lengths of chain, you can keep the feed dogs from chewing up the bottom of your presser foot.

General Tips

Do not sew with the front door of your machine open. You will get lots of lint in your machine and you may jam it with a strip of fabric being trimmed off.

As you may recall from looking inside your machine, the lower looper passes just behind the needles. If you yank too hard on the fabric behind the needle while sewing you can bend the needle so it collides with the lower looper. This can mean burrs on your lower looper, a bent looper, and expensive service. At the least you will need to replace the needle(s). If you ever hear a clicking sound, take both needles out, run the machine and listen if the sound goes away. Most commonly it is a bent needle hitting the lower looper. If removing the needles eliminates the sound, check the lower looper for burrs. Move it all the way to the right with the balance wheel then run your finger along both edges to feel for any roughness. Smooth burrs with crocus cloth, available at a hardware store. After taking care of burrs, put in new needles. If you still get a clicking sound, take the machine in for service.

One final note: do not sew over pins. They kill the knives. For most sewing you do not need pins. When you do need pins you can remove them before they get to the knives: use this technique when sewing on ribbing or elastic. Use extra-long pins with large colored heads so you can easily see them sticking out. Another technique is to place pins parallel to the seam line and about 1" to the left of it: do this when blind hemming or couching wide trim. Or, use spring-type clothespins. (I guarantee you will not accidently sew over one of these!) They are particularly useful for bulky fabrics or fabrics such as ultrasuede. I also use them when sewing on elastic because they hold narrow elastic more securely and I do not have to stick pins through elastic. (Experienced sewers have a well-trained eye and rarely need pins. They can sew much faster once they get used to only using pins for such things as setting sleeves or applying ribbing. Beginning sewers benefit from using pins while they train their eye.)

MAINTENANCE

It is important to keep sergers clean and oiled. The knives generate a lot of lint which gets into the machine and soaks up the oil, preventing proper lubrication. This lint can also cause excessive wear on moving parts, particularly when sewing synthetic or metallic fabrics.

Always clean the machine before you oil it, or whenever the buildup becomes excessive. The most important areas to clean are behind the front door. Cleaning with a brush is usually sufficient. (Your machine is not going to stay perfectly clean for more than 30 seconds of sewing. It is more important to clean frequently than to clean thoroughly.) Pay particular attention to the lint around moving parts, namely the knife and loopers. You can use a squeeze bottle to "puff out" difficult to reach lint, or use a hair dryer on a warm setting. Also available are miniature vacuum cleaners, used to clean computers. Cans of "compressed air" are for sale, but many of them contain chemicals which destroy the atmospheric ozone layer. (The label clearly states if it does _not_ contain such chemicals.) Compressed air can chill your machine enough to cause condensation on it. It is best not to blow into your machine, because of the moisture in your breath. Be particularly careful about moisture or condensation if you have a humid environment.

Sergers run at higher speeds than conventional machines and therefore need more lubrication. Industrial sergers contain an oil reservoir. Check the sight glass to make sure there is enough oil. On domestic sergers you need to apply oil directly. Use only sewing machine oil. It evaporates so it does not leave a gummy residue. Since it evaporates you should also oil your machine if you have not used it for a month. If your machine starts running rough or noisy, stop and oil it immediately. Otherwise oil about every 8 hours of sewing. Turn the balance wheel with the door open so you can see where parts are rubbing together. Oil the friction points of the loopers (where one piece is rubbing against another) plus any other points your machine manual tells you to. If there are any accessible friction points on your knife mechanism oil those at the same time. Periodically open up the left door and oil the friction points there, too. One drop per friction point is enough, although you will not hurt it with more. Many domestic machines have oiling points, little holes on top of the machine where the oil soaks into a wick and is carried to various points inside the machine. Make sure you get enough oil into these points to thoroughly soak the wick: it takes a lot of oil. Here is a trick for oiling the needle bar. Turn the balance wheel until the needle is all the way down. Put a couple of drops of oil on your fingers and wipe them on the top of the needle bar. Turn the balance wheel so the part you oiled moves up and lubricates inside the machine. (This illustrates the need to take your machine in periodically for service, including lubricating parts you cannot reach.) Oil frequently, and your machine will run smoothly for a long time.

Tension disks need to be cleaned periodically on both industrial and domestic machines, especially if you are having unexplained tension problems. Lint builds up in them, as well as finishes from the thread. Loosen tensions completely, remove threads and brush out between the disks. Then take a soft cloth soaked in alcohol and "shoe shine" it between the disks.

The blades on serger knives need to be replaced eventually, or sooner if you sew over a pin. (Sewing over pins can leave notches in the knives.) It is time to change a blade when the knives start fraying the edge of the fabric. One blade is made of hardened steel, and probably will not need to be replaced. A replacement for the softer blade probably came in the attachment kit with your machine. Your manual tells you how to replace it.

THE SERGER STITCH

In the section on "How a Serger Works," page 16, we studied how a 3-thread or 4-thread overlock stitch is produced. Here we will analyze how this stitch works. The 3-thread or 4-thread overlock is by far the most common and versatile stitch. The 4-thread overlock stitch is converted to the 3-thread stitch by removing one needle. (If your machine uses a double needle for the 4-thread overlock, see below.) The other stitches are described in chapter 7, "Stitches," page 141.

By adjusting tensions the 3-thread overlock stitch produces a narrow rolled edge, flat-lock and other stitches. (Note that the word "stitch" refers both to how a stitch is produced, such as 3-thread overlock, and to how the tensions are adjusted, such as narrow rolled edge stitch. Sorry about the confusion, I did not invent it.) In this section we will be describing the "balanced" stitch. This is the stitch you will use most often.

If your machine is capable of making a 4-thread overlock stitch, one needle can be removed to make a 3-thread overlock. Generally it is the left needle which is removed, making a narrower 3-thread overlock. A wide stitch with just the left needle is not nearly as secure as one with both needles. The second needle produces a line of stitching down the middle of the stitch, preventing tunneling and providing extra security. If the fabric is free to move around inside the stitch it can fray, which can cause the seam to fail. By securing the middle of the stitch to the fabric, the 4-thread overlock prevents this movement and fraying even with a wide stitch. This is why, when a wide overlock is desired, a 4-thread overlock stitch is used.

Some machines use a double needle to make a 4-thread overlock stitch. When converting to a 3-thread overlock stitch the double needle is replaced by a single needle. This single needle is in the same position as the left needle of the double needle. As described above, the 4-thread overlock stitch is normally converted to a 3-thread overlock stitch by removing one needle, usually the left needle. Therefore, if your machine uses a double needle, you should reduce stitch width when converting to a 3-thread overlock.

Please have a sample of an overlock stitch in your hand. If the needle threads are a different color than either the fabric or the looper threads, it is easier to see things. If your sample is a 4-thread overlock, so much the better. Use a medium weight fabric, preferably not a stretchy knit. Do not worry if the tensions are not perfect, we are getting to that (see Figures 1-9 and 1-10).

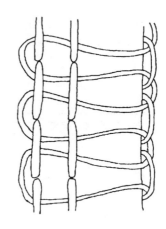

Figure 1-9: 4-Thread Balanced Stitch - Top

Look at the top of your stitch sample and identify the needle threads. They march in a straight line down the top of the stitch. The left-hand needle thread is on the left (inside) edge of the stitch, and the right-hand needle thread goes down the middle of the stitch. Together they secure the upper looper thread onto the top of the fabric. On the right-hand edge the upper looper thread loops together with the lower looper thread. If you now turn your sample over you will see the lower looper thread on the bottom of the seam, looping together on the right with the upper looper thread (see Figures 1-11 and 1-12). On the left-hand edge of the bottom of the seam you will see where the lower looper thread is held in place by the left needle thread, coming through the fabric from the top of the stitch. Ideally the needle thread is visible as a tiny dot of thread as it goes around the lower looper thread. If tensions are not properly set it may be a stretched out loop or it may be pulled up into the fabric. To the right of the left needle thread you should find a dot of the right needle thread. If you are looking at a 3-thread stitch everything is the same except that there is no right needle thread (see Figures 1-10 and 1-12). (Some machines produce a 4-thread overlock stitch in which the upper looper thread is only caught by the right needle: refer to the section on "Balanced Stitch," page 43.)

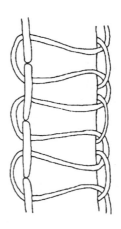

Figure 1-10: 3-Thread Balanced Stitch - Top

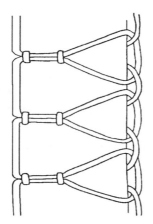 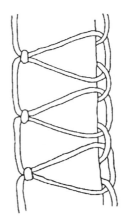

Figure 1-11: 4-Thread Balanced Stitch - Bottom   *Figure 1-12:* 3-Thread Balanced Stitch - Bottom

The most important threads in a serger stitch are the needle threads, and they are the most difficult to see. In a properly adjusted stitch the needle threads go all the way through the fabric, around the two strands of the lower looper thread, and back up through the fabric. The two strands of the lower looper thread should lie flat on the bottom of the seam, and the needle thread should form a small visible dot of thread as it goes around (see Figures 1-11 and 1-12). This is different from the lock-stitch seam produced on a conventional machine. There the bobbin thread and needle thread should loop together in the middle of the fabric. There are two reasons why this is not correct for a serger stitch. First, the needle thread is capturing _two_ strands of thread, rather than one. If the needle thread were tight enough to pull both of these strands up into the middle of the seam a stiff ugly seam would be produced. Secondly, the serger seam is often required to stretch, particularly when used to sew knits. If you look at the top of the serger stitch you realize that the needle threads lie in a straight line. _The only stretch in a serger seam comes from the vertical motion of the needle thread through the fabric._ If you make the needle threads too tight the seam will not stretch enough, and will break under stress. (The section on "Knits," page 67, covers settings for knits in detail.)

The looper threads should meet on the edge of the seam. If the joining between them is pulled to the top or the bottom, it is easier for loose threads to be snagged. If their joining is too far away from the edge they are not protecting the edge from fraying and they are again liable to be snagged. If they are too tight and are pulling up on the edge of the fabric, a stiff seam with poor drape results. (In these figures the looper threads are a little loose, so they can be seen clearly.)

ADJUSTING TENSIONS

Serger tensions can be intimidating: all those knobs while the books tell you "Tighten this or loosen that, tighten that or loosen this!" Tensions do need adjusting more often on a serger than on a conventional sewing machine, and there are more to adjust. However, with a little practice it goes quickly. If you have gone through the preceding sections, you know how the stitch is formed and how it should look. This makes adjusting tensions easy. In this section I will give you a step-by-step procedure for doing so.

Think of tensions as controlling how much thread goes into each stitch. For example, if the upper looper tension disk is squeezing tightly on the upper looper thread, it does not allow as much thread to pass through it as it would if it were more open. Therefore there will be less upper looper thread in each stitch, and it will pull on the other threads more. There is a separate tension disk for each thread. Unlike conventional machines, on most sergers the tension disks are not disengaged when the presser foot is lifted.

Most tension disks are numbered: the larger the number the tighter the tension. Some dials have both minus and plus numbers. On these the loosest tension is the largest minus number (for example "-5") and the tightest tension is the largest plus number (for example "+5"). If there are no numbers, turning the dial clockwise tightens the tension. Do not depend on numbers to tell you what the "right" settings are. Tensions change because of many factors, including the personality of the machine. Just look at the stitch, and adjust accordingly. It may help when adjusting tensions to label your tension disks: "LN" for left needle, "RN" for right needle, "UL" for upper looper and "LL" for lower looper.

Here is a general principal when adjusting needle or looper tensions: It is easier to see if it is too loose rather than if it is too tight; so loosen it until it is too loose, then tighten it until it is not too loose anymore.

In order to check your tensions, save the scraps from your garment as you cut it out. Use these to determine the best tensions, stitch length and stitch width for that garment. Here is the step-by-step procedure for adjusting tensions for an overlock stitch:

Procedure For Adjusting Tensions

1) Preliminary checks:

Make sure each thread is properly seated in its tension disk. It is not uncommon on many machines for a thread to be sitting on top of or beside the disks rather than between them. To make sure it is properly seated, grasp both ends of the thread and pull it into the disk. Sew a sample and look at it. Loosen any tensions which are noticeably too tight. Make sure your differential feed is set to 1 and that your stitch length is normal, about 2.5 to 3.0 for most sewing. (Both of these topics are covered in detail later.)

2) Adjusting needle tensions:

You always have to look at the _bottom_ of your seam to check your needle tensions. The loop of the needle thread should be visible as a dot on the lower looper thread. (This is easier to see with a contrasting color needle thread.)

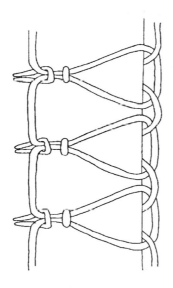

Figure 1-13: Left Needle Tensions too Loose (bottom of seam)

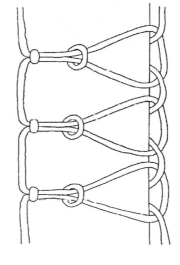

Figure 1-14: Right Needle Tensions too Loose (bottom of seam)

If the needle tensions are too loose, the needle threads form loops on the bottom of the seam. If the left needle thread is too loose the tension on the lower looper thread pulls loops of the left needle thread out toward the edge of the seam (see Figure 1-13). Also, the seam pulls open; this is more noticeable with longer stitch lengths. It is more difficult to see the loops of the right-hand needle thread when it is too loose (see Figure 1-14). Check for these loops on the bottom of the seam by pulling towards the edge of the seam with your fingernail to see if you can pull out loops of the right needle thread.

If either needle tension is too tight it makes dimples on the bottom of the seam (see Figure 1-15). If the needle thread(s) tensions are slightly too tight a dot of needle thread is visible in the center of the dimple. If the tension is even tighter no needle thread is visible at all. These dimples are easier to see on a thicker layer of fabric, although you can learn to spot them on a single layer of broadcloth. Use a double or triple thickness of fabric, or use a spongy fabric such as interlock. It helps to use a magnifying glass, at least until you know what to look for. Remember that the needle thread should go all the way through the fabric and that the lower looper threads should lie flat on the bottom of the seam. Finally, if the needle tensions are much too tight they will pucker the seam.

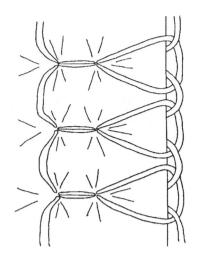

Figure 1-15: Needle Tensions too Tight (Bottom of Seam)

It is easier to see if the needle thread tensions are too loose than it is to see if they are too tight. Therefore loosen the needle tensions until loops form, then tighten them until the loops disappear. Then take the fabric out of the machine and pull the seam open, checking how much needle thread shows. Tighten the needle tensions slightly if necessary. Finally, check the stretch if sewing knits. If sewing on a knit, you must make sure the seam stretches as much as the fabric. Loosen the needle tensions as necessary. (refer to section on "Knits," page 67)

3) Equalizing looper tensions:

This means getting the joining between the upper and lower looper threads to lie on the edge of the fabric, pulled neither to the top nor the bottom. Generally you begin by loosening the looper thread which is tighter, ie shorter. Once you have loosened any overly tight looper tension, the loops will generally lie out from the edge of the fabric. Then it is easy to see which looper thread is looser by pulling the joining out from the fabric edge with your finger tips.

4) Adjusting edge of stitch:

If the looper tensions are too loose, their joining will be off the edge of the fabric. If they are too tight, they will pull up the edge of the fabric. Some woven fabrics will have protruding threads. Lighter fabrics will have wrinkles parallel to the edge of the fabric, or be folded over inside the stitch. When tensions are slightly too tight on a stiffer fabric, often the edge of the fabric will be curved slightly downward within the stitch. Sometimes it is easier to feel this than see it. Gently pull your fingers outward towards the edge of the stitch and see if you feel a curve.

Since it is easier to see if the looper tensions are too loose than if they are too tight, loosen them until they are too loose then tighten them until the joining between the loops just barely touches the edge of the fabric.

Further Tips On Tensions

Here again is the general rule for adjusting tensions: it is easier to see if it is too loose than if it is too tight, so loosen it until it is too loose, then tighten it until it is not too loose anymore.

You can save yourself frustration by checking your stitch on a scrap of your garment fabric every time you sit down to sew. You may have left your machine set up for another type of stitch and forgotten. Or your machine, with the infinite perversity of mechanical objects, may decide it needs more oil or does not like the barometric pressure. Some machines are more touchy than others.

When changing to thick or bulky fabrics you need to loosen tensions, particularly the needle tension. For very lightweight fabrics you may need to tighten them. For thick spongy fabrics you may need to adjust the needle tensions so there are slight dimples on the bottom of the stitch.

When increasing the stitch length you need to loosen tensions, particularly the needle tensions. For very short stitch lengths you may need to tighten them.

When increasing stitch width you need to loosen looper tensions on most machines. When decreasing stitch width you need to tighten looper tensions on most machines. Note that adding the left needle automatically increases stitch width and removing it decreases stitch width. (On some machines the stitch finger moves in or out as the lower knife moves when stitch width is adjusted. On these machines looper tensions can generally stay the same when stitch width is changed.)

Loosen the needle tensions slightly when sewing on knits (for more stretch).

Loosen tensions when using texturized nylon, fingering yarn or heavy pearl cotton. Experiment with other special threads.

If you have been pulling fabric from the back of the machine you may have a burr on your lower looper from nicking it with the needle. (refer to section on "Starting Sewing," page 25) Move the lower looper all the way to the right with the balance wheel and feel both edges with your finger. Use crocus cloth to smooth any roughness.

If your tensions are inconsistent, check to make sure all guides are threaded.

When tensions _suddenly_ tighten a thread is probably caught. Check each cone in turn. The most common cause is a thread slipping under a cone, and the solution is to use the thread nets provided with your machine. Fold them in half and put them over just the _bottom_ part of the thread on each cone (see Figure 1-16). The reason for folding them is so threads cannot catch on the cut edges. The reason for just cupping the bottom of the cone of thread is that these flimsy little nets will change thread tensions if they cover the entire cone. (This is a trick if you need to tighten up a thread tension more than your machine will allow. Just put one or more thread nets on the offending thread cone.) If you do not have any nets, you can make them by serging together pieces of old panty hose, making sure they are just barely tight enough.

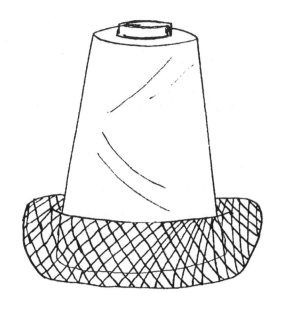

Figure 1-16: Thread Net

Another option is putting a disk of fiber fill under the cone, large enough to extend to the edge of the cone and thick enough so it touches the entire bottom of the cone. This keeps the thread from slipping down under the edge of the cone.

Another possible problem is thread not feeding evenly. If you are using spools of thread make sure you use the spool caps supplied with your machine (see Figure 1-17). Make sure all cones of thread are straight and vertical and that the thread telescope is fully extended. Make sure nothing is touching any cone of thread, including the base of the thread. If the cones are too large for your machine and are sitting on the table, you may need to use a cone thread stand (refer to section on "Basic Thread," page 89). (You will want one of these anyway so you can use your serger thread on your conventional machine. Since it is a slightly finer thread it is better for lightweight fabrics and for blind-hemming.) Some machines do not have a large enough base to keep even small cones of thread from slipping off the edge and tipping sideways: this is

Figure 1-17: Spool Cap

usually a problem with the end cones, the left needle and lower looper cones on a 4-thread machine. The solution is to take a small disk of cardboard or a plastic lid and make a hole in the middle to fit over the thread spindle. Put this over the spindle then put the cone on top.

Finally, there is a _Tension Gremlin_, who sometimes comes along and inexplicably changes tensions. One possible cause is changing humidity affecting the thread. Another possible cause is build-up in the tension disks, which can be cleaned as described in the section on "Maintenance," page 27. Uneven tensions can also be caused by incorrect threading, usually by missing one guide. If all else fails, your machine may be out of adjustment. Bring the machine in for service and explain the problem.

STITCH WIDTH AND KNIVES

There are two arrangements of knives in sergers. Industrial and some domestic machines have the upper knife coming from above the lower knife (see Figure 1-18), some domestic machines have the upper knife coming up from below (see Figure 1-19). In either case the term "upper knife" refers to the movable knife, which does indeed stick up above the lower knife. On industrial machines there is another blade set perpendicular to the back edge of the knife: this helps keep lint and bits of trimmed fabric from getting inside the machine. On most domestic machines the upper knife is held against the lower knife by spring pressure: on industrial machines the lower knife is held against the upper knife by spring pressure. (On a few domestic machines both knives are fixed in position.)

On some domestic machines the cutting action can be disabled by swinging the upper knife out of the way. On machines with the upper knife coming from above, push to the right on the upper knife then swing it out of the way. On some machines with the upper knife coming from below you cannot disable the cutting action without a screw-driver. On other machines there is a small handle on the left side of the machine that you can push to the right and use to swing the knife out of the way. When I am sewing I almost never move the upper knife out of the way. I like to have it there as a guide, even when I am

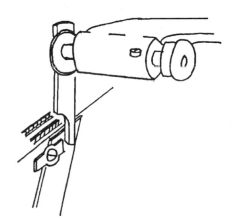

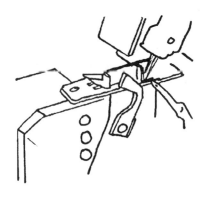

Figure 1-18: Upper knife coming from above   _Figure 1-19:_ Upper knife coming from below

carefully guiding fabric just to the left of it. This way I get an accurate seam allowance. More important, I make sure I never get the fabric too far to the right so it collides with the upper looper. That can do real damage to a machine. If you do disable the cutting action make sure you follow some sort of mark or line so you can guide accurately to the left of the path of the upper looper. (refer to section on "Guiding Fabric," page 104)

On many machines the knife can be moved to the right or left. This has the effect of increasing or decreasing the width of the seam allowance, sometimes referred to as "bight" or "stitch width." On some domestic machines you can change stitch width by turning a knob. On others a set-screw must be loosened before stitch width can be changed. On still others the only control over stitch width is by using or removing the left needle. Some domestic machines which have an adjustment for stitch width have a numbered dial or indicator. On these machines the numbers generally represent width in millimeters from the right needle. On some 5-thread machines there are two width indications, one for the overlock stitch alone and one for the chainstitch. On some 4-thread machines the smallest number represents the width as measured from the right needle whereas the largest number represents width as measured from the left needle.

On some domestic machines there is a set-screw to lock the upper knife for sewing heavy or bulky fabrics. Normally the upper knife is spring loaded against the lower knife. This set screws locks it so it cannot move sideways. This makes it more stable for cutting heavy or bulky fabrics. Loosen the set screw as soon as you are done with the heavy fabrics. You will have to loosen it to change stitch width.

In general, use the wider stitch width for heavier or more ravel-prone fabric. The narrowest widths are best for lightweight, non-raveling fabrics such as lace or tricot.

Some machines offer three needle plates, each with a different width stitch finger. Use the most slender stitch finger for the narrow rolled edge. Use the medium width for narrow cutting widths and the wide one for wide cutting widths.

Sometimes you want to sew a very narrow seam, for example when French seaming or sewing nylon tricot. (refer to the section on "Woven Fabrics," page 76 and the section on "Lingerie," page 82) Use a 3-thread overlock with the right needle only, the narrowest cutting width and the narrow rolled edge stitch finger. (refer to section on "Narrow Rolled Edge," page 46) If you cannot adjust cutting width on your machine, you can guide the edge of the fabric between the knives and the needle. (refer to section on "Guiding Fabric," page 104)

STITCH LENGTH

As on conventional machines, stitch length controls how far the feed dogs move the fabric for each stitch. Some domestic machines have a knob on the outside of the machine to change stitch length. On most domestic sergers however, it is not as easy to change stitch length as it is on a conventional machine. On some domestic sergers a lever or button must be depressed on or inside the left side of the machine. While depressing the lever or button the balance wheel is turned until the lever or button "locks in." Still depressing the lever or button, the balance wheel can now be turned to change stitch length. Then the lever or button is released. On some domestic sergers there is a knob inside the left door: you hold the knob then turn the balance wheel to set the stitch length. The numbers that show up in the window on the knob indicate stitch length. On other machines there is a curved piece of metal with a slot down the middle. A knob is loosened so it can slide along this slot, then tightened next to the number indicating the desired stitch length. On industrial machines the control is often under the front end of the cloth plate, the piece of metal the fabric moves across. Refer to your manual for detailed instructions. (It used to be worse, some domestic machines used to require a screw driver to change stitch length.)

Stitch length is measured in millimeters. Normal stitching is done with a length of 2 to 3. Heavy or bulky fabrics take a longer length, very stretchy or lightweight fabrics take a shorter length. Fabrics subject to raveling require a shorter stitch length. A seam subject to stress requires a shorter stitch length. Refer to the section on "Knits," page 67, for a discussion of stitch length for knits.

The ideal stitch length depends on the thread as well as the fabric. Finer threads generally take a shorter stitch length whereas heavier threads take a longer stitch length.

PRESSER FOOT PRESSURE

Most sergers provide a means of adjusting how hard the presser foot pushes on your fabric. Generally it is a little knob on top of your machine over the presser foot. Sometimes it is inside a little door above and to the left of the needle. Generally you loosen it for spongy knits, and tighten it for thin firm fabrics. Normally it does not need adjustment except to control rippling and get proper feeding of sweater knits: loosen if necessary. Increasing presser foot pressure can help reduce puckering. It can be tightened for lettucing or loosened for gathering. If you do not have differential feed it can be adjusted so that long panels of fabric, such as used for draperies, will feed more evenly. Do some samples to determine the proper setting.

DIFFERENTIAL FEED

This is an optional feature available on some machines. The distance the feed dogs travel for each stitch is set by the stitch length control. When a machine has differential feed, the distance the back half of the feed dogs travel is still set by the stitch length control. The differential feed controls the difference (or ratio) between how far the front half of the feed dogs moves and how far the back half moves. This means that the front half of the feed dogs can be set to move a greater or smaller distance than the back half. (This may sound a little like a centipede trying to decide which leg to move next, but it is really quite useful.)

Differential feed is usually changed with a knob or lever, often on the outside of the machine. Sometimes it is set with a curved piece of metal having a slot down the middle, as described in the section on "Stitch Length," on page 39. After using differential feed remember to set it back to 1. Otherwise, the next time you sit down to sew you may get unexpected results.

You can demonstrate to yourself what differential feed is doing. First, remove the presser foot from your machine. A long stitch length makes it easier to see what is going on.

Begin with the differential feed set to 1. As you turn the balance wheel watch the space between the front and back half of the feed dogs: you will see that it remains the same.

Now move the differential feed to less than 1, and watch the space again. When the feed dogs come up above the level of the needle plate to begin moving the fabric back, the front and back halves are close together. As they continue moving back the space between them increases (get bigger) because the front half is not moving as far as the back half. The back half is trying to pull out more fabric than the front half is releasing, causing the fabric to be stretched as it is sewn.

Now move the differential feed to greater than 1, and watch the space again. When the feed dogs come up above the level of the needle plate to begin moving the fabric back, the front and back halves are far apart. As they continue moving back the space between them decreases (get smaller) because the front half is moving further than the back half. The front half is forcing in more fabric than the back half is releasing, causing the fabric to be gathered or eased as it is sewn.

If you wish you can try the same process with shorter and longer stitch lengths. Changing the stitch length setting changes the distance the feed dogs travel (and how far they move the fabric, and the stitch length) for every stitch, but the difference between the front and back halves of the feed dogs is controlled by the differential feed.

The numbers on the differential feed control are ratios. If the differential feed is set to 2 and the stitch length is set to 3, the back half of the feed dogs will move 3 millimeters for each stitch and the front half will move 6 millimeters (2 times 3 millimeters). If the differential feed is set to .7 and the stitch length is set to 3, the back half of the feed dogs will move 3 millimeters for each stitch and the front half will move 2.1 millimeters (.7 times 3 millimeters). Similarly, with a stitch length of 3 and a differential feed setting of 1.5, the front half of the feed dogs will move 4.5 millimeters for each stitch.

Here is a summary of what the differential feed settings are used for:

Feed set for less than 1, sometimes called negative feed: The front half of the feed dogs is not moving as far as the back half, basically stretching the fabric as it is being sewn.

❑ use for fabric that puckers, such as lightweight silkies: wonderful when doing a narrow rolled edge, as this stitch tends to pucker the fabric

❑ use for creating a lettuce edge, with the narrow rolled edge setting (refer to section on "Lettucing," page 123)

Feed set for greater than 1, sometimes called positive feed: The front half of the feed dogs is moving further than the back half, basically scrunching the fabric together (easing it) as it is being sewn.

❑ use for gathering lightweight fabrics while finishing the raw edge at the same time: this provides a maximum of 2:1 gathering, when the dial is set at 2. (refer to section on "Gathering," page 126, for other gathering techniques)

❑ use for stretchy knits to prevent rippling of the seam: useful for most knits, but particularly sweater knits, interlock, and tee-shirt knits

Differential feed is also useful when sewing long panels of fabric, such as when making draperies. There is often a tendency for the lower layer to feed faster than the upper, so they do not end up even. If the lower piece is ending up shorter, move the differential feed control to a smaller number (negative feed). Experiment to determine the proper setting.

CHAPTER 2
SPECIAL STITCHES

The special stitches described in this chapter are all variations of the overlock stitch. They can also be produced from the overedge stitch. The narrow rolled edge is produced by changing the tensions and using a different stitch finger. Blind hemming is done with a blind hem foot or attachment and a properly adjusted stitch. The flat-lock, wrapped stitch and blanket stitch are primarily used for decorative purposes. There are many other types of stitches, which are described in Chapter 7. (refer to chapter 7, Stitches, page 141)

BALANCED STITCH

This is a overlock stitch, either 3-thread or 4-thread, with the tensions adjusted for normal sewing. It is the "basic" serger stitch. This is the stitch that was described in the section on "The Serger Stitch," page 29. In the section on adjusting tensions, page 32, this is the stitch that was produced. This is by far the most commonly used stitch, for finishing edges and making seams. Before changing tensions for any special stitch you should begin with a properly adjusted balanced stitch.

If the same thread is used in both the upper and lower looper this stitch looks the same on both sides.

On most machines a 4-thread overlock stitch is converted to a 3-thread stitch by unthreading and removing one needle. _Whenever you are converting to a 3-thread overlock stitch, make sure you remove the unthreaded needle from the machine._ (refer to section on "4-thread or 3-thread Stitch?" on page 83) In most cases, the left needle is removed for a 3-thread overlock stitch. If your machine uses a double needle for the 4-thread overlock stitch, convert to the 3-thread stitch by inserting a single needle: in most cases you will also reduce stitch width.

On most 4-thread overlock stitches the upper looper thread is caught by the left needle thread. Some machines produce a 4-thread overlock in which the upper looper thread is only caught by the right needle thread. This limits the use of the machine for decorative techniques. Most decorative threads are used in the upper looper, and do not show up as well with the narrower upper looper thread. Also, the right needle cannot be removed for a left needle flat-lock, a left needle wrapped edge, or any other left needle special stitch.

However, the upper looper uses somewhat less thread when making seams. (refer to chapter 7, Stitches, page 141 for more information)

BLIND HEMMING

Industrial sergers have a special attachment for blind hemming. On domestic sergers blind hemming is done with a blind hem foot (refer to section on "Special Attachments," page 153). Use the longest stitch length. Use a 3-thread balanced stitch (see above), right needle only. Normally you use a stitch width of about 3.5 to 4, increasing it if necessary for ravel-prone fabric. Measure and pin up your hem, placing the pins parallel to the edge and about 3/4" from it. In industrial settings the hem is commonly pressed in place before hemming rather than pinned. In order to reduce bulk, turn serger seam allowances the opposite direction at the edge of the hem, so they are not lying on top of each other in the hem (see Figure 2-1). Position the fabric as you would for a blind hem on a conventional machine (see Figure 2-2). Sew a sample on a scrap of your fabric, adjusting the guide on the foot so that the needle just nips the edge of the fold and catches one or two threads. The guide needs to be moved slightly to the right for heavy or bulky fabrics, and to the left for lighter fabrics. You must guide the fabric consistently and accurately: a little fold of fabric riding up on the side of the blade will make a difference. Set the guide so the fold just touches it.

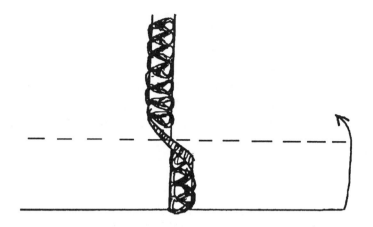

Figure 2-1: *Blind Hem*

Turn seam allowances in opposite directions before pinning up hem to reduce bulk in fold.

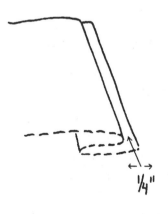

Figure 2-2: *Preparing fabric for Blind Hem*

Fold hem to right side so 1/4" of raw edge is extended past fold.

Note: This really is a cross section, as almost all blind hems are sewn in a circle.

Use the techniques for sewing in a circle. (refer to section on "Sewing in a Circle," page 62) Sometimes the pins get caught in the feed dogs, so it helps to remove them just before they get to the presser foot.

The closer the needle is to the edge of the fold, the more inconspicuous the blind hem will be. In addition to setting the guide properly and guiding the fabric properly, here is another tip for getting a fine blind hem. Look down on top of the foot as you are sewing so you can watch where the needle is sewing: pull in or out slightly on the fabric to the side of the needle so the needle just pierces the edge of the fold.

Loosen the needle tension some: it makes the hem lie flatter and stretch more, and makes it less noticeable if the needle nips a slightly wider fold of fabric. If you loosen the needle tension quite a bit, for example when blind hemming a stretchy knit, tighten the lower looper tension part way so the stitch lies closer to the raw edge and protects it better from fraying.

If your needle tension is properly adjusted a serged blind hem will stretch as much as your fabric. This is important for knits because the hem is usually on the crossgrain, the direction of greatest stretch. The serged blind hem is the best blind hem for knits. It is acceptable on spongy wovens that can hide the stitches. Otherwise serge the edge and blind hem on a blind hem machine, conventional machine or by hand. (refer to section on "Flat-Locked Hemming," page 55, for a flat-locked blind hem)

Sometimes when blind hemming you can have problems with needle holes. This occurs most commonly on interlock, a fine spongy knit. The first thing to check for is a damaged needle: replace it if it is damaged. (refer to section on "Needles," page 19) The next thing to check is needle size, shift to a smaller size if possible. You can try a ballpoint needle. If the needle is good the problem is due to the needle clipping the edge of the folded fabric and cutting it as it moves past. Loosen the needle tension somewhat and move the guide slightly to the right. Something else to try is washing the fabric using fabric softener: it makes the threads more flexible so they can more easily move out of the way of the needle.

For casual garments an alternative to blind hemming is top-stitching on a conventional machine with either a zig-zag or a double needle. Commercially, a cover seaming or coverstitch can be used: these are described in chapter 7, on pages 145 and 147. The zig-zag finish is easy and durable, and it is easy to make sure the stitch has enough stretch. Generally a 2.5 by 2.5 zig-zag is about right. The double needle duplicates the effect of the cover seaming stitch: two parallel lines of straight stitching show on the right side with a joining thread on the back. Make sure you use a wide enough double needle, use a 3.0 or 4.0 width needle. (On double needles the first number indicates the distance between the needles, the second indicates the needle size.) If using a double needle on knits check stretch, and loosen the needle and/or the bobbin tension as necessary. Sew the double needle hem with the garment right side up and the zig-zag with wrong side up. In both cases make sure the hem stitching encloses the raw edge of the fabric. There are two ways to get the twin needle stitch to enclose the raw edge of the hem. First, you can leave a wider hem, stitch between the raw edge and the fold, then trim the raw edge to the stitching. Another technique is to feel with your fingers on the bottom of the fabric, so you know where the raw edge is. Guide it just to the left of the left needle of the twin needle.

Some fabrics have a tendency to curl or roll up at the edges, especially when washed. The most common offenders are single knits, such as tee-shirt knits, sweater knits and velour. Twill weaves, such as denim and many other bottom weight fabrics, will also curl. A narrow hem also tends to curl up on garments made from these fabrics. The solution is to make the hem wide enough so it cannot curl. Hems should be turned up an inch or more, depending on how determined the fabric is to curl. Flared hems also tend to curl: the solution is the faced hem described in the section on "Woven Fabrics" under "Serger construction techniques for wovens," page 77.

NARROW ROLLED EDGE

The narrow rolled edge, sometimes called a rolled hem, is a very durable yet dainty finish for lighter weight fabrics. It will not work on anything heavier than a mid-weight fabric. Generally it is used as a finish for exposed edges of fabrics, but it can also be used for a nearly invisible seam on lightweight sheers. It is a wonderful finish for the edges of circular skirts in sheer fabrics, ruffles and flounces such as jabots. (refer to section on "Decorative Narrow Rolled Edge," page 125, for decorative techniques) Most machines with an overlock stitch can be converted to produce this stitch. It is done with a 3-thread overlock stitch, removing the left needle if necessary. Some machines have a slightly different threading path for the rolled edge. There may be a checkspring by the lower looper tension disk. Or, there may be an additional tension disk for the lower looper thread. Check your manual.

Domestic overlock machines which can also produce a 2-thread overedge stitch can do a 2-thread narrow rolled edge. The 2-thread narrow rolled edge is somewhat finer and softer than a 3-thread narrow rolled edge. Tighten the needle tension. This does not work as well with very short stitch lengths. (refer to section on "2-Thread Overedge," page 141)

The narrow rolled edge is done over a special stitch finger which is very slender. On most machines a special needle plate and/or presser foot is used which has the narrow stitch finger. On some domestic machines part of the stitch finger itself is slid out of the way or removed, leaving a narrower stitch finger. Some domestic machines have a slender stitch finger on the needle plate and a wide stitch finger on the presser foot. When converting to the narrow rolled edge another presser foot is used without the wide stitch finger.

The lower looper tension is tightened, generally as much as possible. This pulls on the upper looper thread, which pulls on the edge of the fabric so it folds under, wrapping around the narrow stitch finger. The edge of the fabric should fold under completely so it is lying next to the line of the needle thread. This leaves a smooth edge with the threads looped together on the underside. The lower looper thread should be scarcely visible (see Figures 2-3 and 2-4).

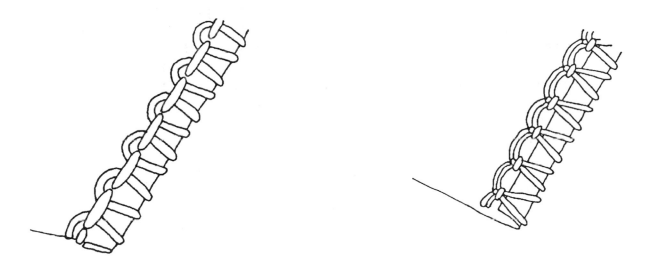

Figure 2-3: *Narrow Rolled Edge - Top*   **Figure 2-4:** *Narrow Rolled Edge - Bottom*

Typically a very short stitch length is used. Generally you will use a stitch length of 1 to 2. Start with a stitch length of 1.5, then shorten it if necessary to get a good stitch. A shorter stitch length produces a more defined edge, a longer stitch length produces a softer edge. On soft fabrics which do not ravel easily a long stitch length can be used to produce a scalloped edge. If the stitch length is greater than 1.5 the fabric edge will not be protected as well from raveling: use on non-raveling fabric or when the garment will be dry-cleaned only. Experiment with your fabric to determine the best setting. Any stitch length from 1 to 4 can produce a beautiful narrow rolled edge on the right fabric.

It is easier to get a beautiful narrow rolled edge if the edge is parallel to the cross or lengthwise grainline.

Setting up the machine for narrow rolled edge

1) Begin with a properly adjusted 3-thread (right needle only) balanced stitch and a medium stitch width. Note that if you have just converted from a 4-thread overlock stitch you probably need to adjust your looper tensions.

2) Set up machine with the narrow rolled edge stitch finger (see above). Shorten the stitch length. Change lower looper threading path if necessary for your machine.

3) Adjust the lower looper tension. The lower looper thread should lie in a straight line in the bottom of the stitch, between the needle thread and the upper looper thread. It should be scarcely visible. Begin by tightening the lower looper tension almost completely. If it is too tight the seam will pucker. If it is too loose the lower looper thread will not lie in a straight line. (The general principal, as explained in the section on "Adjusting Tensions" is this: it is easier to see if tensions are too loose than if they are too tight, so loosen them until they are too loose then tighten them until they are not too loose anymore.) If you cannot eliminate puckering without the lower looper thread being too loose, refer to the trouble-shooting guide below. If the lower looper thread is not forming a straight line with the lower looper tension disk fully tightened, use the following techniques until it does form a straight line.

On machines with beehive type tension disks you can wrap the lower looper thread twice around the lower looper tension disk. Loosen tension completely, wrap twice, then gradually increase tension as you make samples. Remember to return to normal as soon as you finish doing the narrow rolled edge.

You can put thread nets one by one on the lower looper thread cone, until the stitch looks good. You can also use tubes stitched together from old pantyhose.

Another option is to put texturized nylon in the lower looper. (refer to section on "Texturized Nylon," page 93)

4) Once the lower looper thread is tight enough, you may see loops of the needle thread on the lower side of the fabric. They look like tiny "V's" between the fabric and lower looper thread. You may need to pull the line of stitching away from the bottom of the fabric with your fingernail in order to see these "V's". (You may think I am overly fussy here, but a properly adjusted needle tension makes the stitch lie flatter and the edge drape better.) Tighten the needle thread tension slightly and sew another sample. If the needle thread tension is too tight your edge will pucker. If you cannot eliminate puckering while still getting a good looking needle thread, refer to the trouble-shooting guide below.

5) Occasionally you need to tighten the upper looper thread. Sometimes on heavy or stiff fabrics the edge of the fabric will not be rolling over completely so that it is next to the needle thread on the bottom of the seam. If you have this problem try tightening the upper looper tension. If tightening the upper looper tension does not fix the problem refer to the trouble-shooting guide below. Sometimes on very light fabrics loops of upper looper thread show up on the bottom of the seam to the left of the needle thread. Other thin soft fabrics may not roll completely over because they take up so little

space. Just tighten the upper looper tensions slightly. If you began with a properly adjusted balanced stitch, the upper looper tension is unlikely to require adjustment.

A narrow rolled edge can also be produced with a balanced stitch. Shorten the stitch length and set up the machine with the narrow rolled edge stitch finger. Tighten both looper tensions equally so the fabric folds over within the stitch. The stitch should end up with the stitch width about half the cutting width, as it is for a conventional narrow rolled edge. Similarly, a 2-thread narrow rolled edge can be made by tightening both needle and looper tensions equally: this stitch has a great deal of stretch but does not secure a ravel-prone fabric as well as a normal 2-thread narrow rolled edge.

If your machine permits, you can do a 4-thread narrow rolled edge. (refer to section on "Decorative Narrow Rolled Edge," page 125)

Trouble-shooting guide for narrow rolled edge

If puckering occurs, use differential feed if you have it. Set it to 0.7 or 0.5, whatever is the smallest number you can set it to. Try a slightly shorter stitch length if your stitch length is fairly long. Otherwise, try loosening needle and/or lower looper tensions. Increase presser foot pressure. If this does not fix the problem without making a poor quality stitch try gently pulling on the fabric in front of the needle. You may be familiar with "taut sewing," the technique of stretching the fabric both in front of and behind the presser foot. This is tricky on the serger because it can cause the serger needle to hit the lower looper, as described in the section on "Starting Sewing," page 25. Besides, you cannot do it next to corners.

Control rippling by lengthening the stitch length.

On a very lightweight and fragile fabric, such as china silk, too short a stitch length may cause the stitching to pull away from the fabric. Increase stitch length slightly. If you can on your machine, also increase stitch width slightly.

Some loosely woven fabrics have stiff threads which will protrude from between the stitches of the rolled edge. An example would be a metallic fabric, although many cottons and linens have the same problem. Try increasing stitch width slightly. You may need to loosen the upper looper tension slightly when increasing stitch width. Shortening the stitch length may help. Texturized nylon in the upper looper helps cover the edge. Loosen upper looper tensions when using texturized nylon in the upper looper so it spreads out to cover the edge. (refer to section on "Texturized Nylon," page 93) An almost sure cure is to put a strip of sheer tricot on top of the edge of the fabric, being careful not to stretch the tricot. Sew normally, allowing the tricot to be trimmed by the knives and rolled into the hem. Then trim the other edge of the tricot flush with the stitching. You can use strips of water soluble stabilizer instead of tricot. It does not have to be trimmed after stitching, but the threads may poke out again after washing. (refer to glossary under "Sheer Tricot," page 198, and "Water Soluble Stabilizer," page 200, for more information) Another technique is to fold the edge of the fabric and do the rolled edge stitch over the fold, trimming the raw edge to the stitching after serging. (The section on "Guiding Fabric," page 104, tells how to guide the fold accurately between the knife and the needle.)

Tightly woven fabrics with stiff threads may make the rolled edge appear irregular, with some stitches longer than others. Usually the problem is corrected by shortening the stitch length, until it is close to 1. If this does not solve the problem try texturized nylon in the upper looper. You can also try increasing stitch width, or using the other techniques described in the preceding paragraph.

It is difficult to properly roll thicker fabrics, particularly if they are also stiff. The first thing to try is increasing stitch width to allow for the "turn of cloth." Although you generally need a tight upper looper tension when rolling stiff heavy fabric you may need to loosen it slightly when increasing stitch width, especially if your fabric is more bulky than stiff. Experiment. If your machine cannot change stitch width but can do a rolled edge with the left needle, try doing a rolled edge with just the left needle. (refer to section on "Decorative Narrow Rolled Edge," page 125) You can also try a shorter stitch length, texturized nylon in one or both loopers, even the sheer tricot as described above. If these techniques do not work, here are some alternatives:

Try doing the rolled edge over a _fold_. Fold and press the fabric before you put it into the machine, then guide the fold to the left of the knife. (refer to the section on "Guiding Fabric," page 104) Trim the raw edge after stitching.

Use a balanced stitch with a short stitch length, or the wrapped stitch. (refer to section on the "Wrapped Stitch," page 57)

Another option is the serged and top-stitched hem. This is a wonderful finish for bulky wovens such as corduroy, and curved hems such as on shirt-tails. Finish the raw edge with a balanced stitch, fold up a narrow hem, and top-stitch on a conventional machine. I often use this finish on wovens before applying trim to the edge, when I cannot do a narrow rolled edge.

Many fabrics will only roll properly on the straight of grain. If texturized nylon or sheer tricot do not hide ugly stitches, consider the alternatives mentioned above.

FLAT-LOCKING

Flat-locking is primarily a decorative technique. It works best with mid- to heavy weight fabrics. For light fabrics which do not ravel use a right needle flat-lock. (see below) It is primarily done on domestic sergers, imitating the effect of the coverstitches, described on page 147. Flat-locking does not produce as secure a seam as a coverstitch, although the top-stitching technique described below secures the seam well. (refer to section on "Decorative Flat-Locking," page 106, for information on decorative uses for these techniques)

Remember, in the section on "Tensions," about when the needle thread gets too loose the seam pulls open? When the needle tension is loosened enough the seam can be pulled completely open and flat after sewing: this is flat-locking. On one side of the fabric the upper looper thread is visible, with the needle thread and lower looper threads scarcely visible along its edges. On the other side a "ladder" of needle thread is visible (see Figures 2-5, 2-6 and 2-7). Either side can be used as the right side. If you sew with wrong sides together, the upper looper thread will end up on the right side. If you sew right sides together, the needle

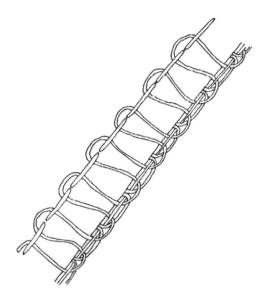

Figure 2-5: *Top of Flat-lock*

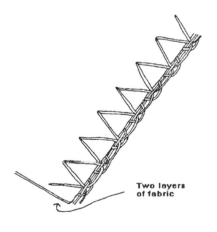

Two layers of fabric

Figure 2-6: *Bottom of Flat-lock
before pulling flat*

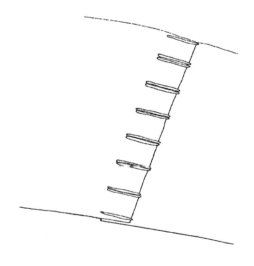

Figure 2-7: *Bottom of Flat-lock
after pulling flat*

thread ladder will end up on the right side.

The flat-locked seam is usually done with one needle, generally by removing the right needle and making a 3-thread overlock with just the left needle. This gives a wider stitch: this is more decorative, and flat-locking is usually used for decorative effect. Use a normal stitch length, generally about 3. To flat-lock, tighten the lower looper tension and loosen the needle tension until the loops of needle thread on the bottom are at the edge of the fabric and the lower looper thread is forming a straight line. If the needle thread is not loose enough with the tensions loosened completely you may need to remove it from the tension disk. Make the lower looper tension just tight enough so the lower looper thread lies in a straight line: if it is too tight the seam will pucker and the lower looper thread may pull out of the stitch as you remove it from the machine. If it will not lie in a straight line even with the tension fully tightened, refer to step 3 in the section on the "Narrow Rolled Edge," page 48.

After sewing the seam you must pull it flat. Holding the upper layer of fabric with your left hand and the lower layer with your right hand, pull the seam apart. After the seam is pulled flat there may be a small fold of fabric left on the ladder side of the seam. To get rid of this fold hold your fingers right next to the seam on the two pieces of fabric, left hand on the upper piece and right hand on the lower piece. Gently jerk down and to the left on the right-hand (lower) piece of fabric as you pull up and to the right on the left-hand piece. If this does not do it, gently jerk the two pieces of fabric back and forth as you pull up on the left piece and down on the right piece. Do this section by section. If your fabric is bulky it may not pull completely flat. In this case loosen the upper looper and/or needle tensions slightly and sew another sample. Remembering that the upper looper thread is on top and the needle thread on the bottom, you can generally tell by looking at your sample which is too tight. If the fabric is too soft, for example a tee-shirt knit, it will be difficult to get rid of this little fold.

If you have a 2-thread overedge stitch on your machine you can use it for flat-locking. Generally you do not need to change tensions. A 2-thread flat-lock has virtually unlimited stretch. (refer to section on "2-Thread Overedge," page 141)

All through this book I refer to a "wide flat-lock," or a "narrow flat-lock." Most machines form a 4-thread overlock stitch with two needles, a left needle and a right needle. A wide flat-lock is produced by dropping out the right needle and a narrow flat-lock is produced by dropping out the left needle. Some machines use a double needle to produce a 4-thread overlock stitch. On these machines, a wide flat-lock is produced with a single needle and a wide stitch width, while a narrow flat-lock is produced with a single needle and a narrow stitch width. For those of you who have these machines, remember that a "wide flat-lock" simply means a wide stitch width and a "narrow flat-lock" means a narrow stitch width. You generally want a wide flat-lock when using a decorative thread.

Securing the Flat-Lock Stitch

Because of the loosened needle tension a flat-locked seam ravels out easily. Do not cut the thread chain without securing the stitching with 3/4" of straight stretch stitch on a conventional machine. If crossing a flat-locked seam with another seam use the following technique: put the two pieces of fabric together with the flat-locked seam on top. When the flat-locked seam gets close to the presser foot pull its thread chain gently to the left, enough to ensure none of the threads get cut by the knife. When the seam is past the knives continue sewing normally. (for an illustration demonstrating this technique, see Figure 3-1 on page 48).

Sometimes the lower looper thread will pull out of the stitch as you are removing it from the machine, leaving a row of empty loops. If this occurs on your sample try loosening the lower looper tension to see if you can get a good stitch with a looser tension. Another trick is to simply pinch or knot the thread chain as you begin sewing, and continue pulling on it until you have removed the fabric from the machine. Stretch the seam then knot both thread chains next to the fabric.

Flat-locking does not produce as secure a seam as a normal or "balanced" stitch. Because the stitch is wide without an extra needle thread going down the center, strands of thread are more liable to be snagged, and raw edges are not secured as well from fraying. After pulling the seam flat it can be top-stitched on a conventional machine to make the seam more secure. Use a wide long zig-zag for stretchy knits or to make the top-stitching less apparent. Invisible thread will also make the top-stitching less apparent.

There is another way to secure the seam if you do not want a line of top-stitching down the middle of it. In this method fusible thread is zig-zagged to the right side on one edge of fabric, then fused after the seam is flat-locked and opened. This technique is not as secure or as quick as the top-stitching but it does not show. (refer to section on "Fusible Thread," page 94) Put the fusible thread in the bobbin of a conventional machine and zig-zag the edge of one piece of fabric, putting the fabric in the machine upside down so the fusible thread ends up on the right side. If you want the upper looper thread on the right side after flat-locking, put the zig-zagged piece of fabric next to the feed dogs, right side down. When you pull the seam flat the fusible thread will be in the middle of the seam and can then be fused to secure it. If you want the needle thread ladder on the right side, put the zig-zagged piece of fabric on top, with the fusible thread down. Flat-lock, pull flat and fuse.

Fusible web can be used to secure flat-locking. One technique is to lay a sheet of fusible web between the layers of fabric and flat-lock. Holding the fusible web against the upper layer of fabric, pull flat, trim away extra fusible web, and fuse. Another possibility is fusing a strip of fusible web to the wrong side of one seam allowance, then fusing the seam after it is pulled flat. Cut a 1/4" wide strip of paper-backed fusible web. Fuse to the wrong side of one seam allowance, remove paper, then position the pieces for flat-locking as described above.

You can produce the appearance of a flat-locked seam without the problems. Using a balanced stitch, serge the seam with wrong sides together. Then, top-stitch the seam allowance flat on a conventional machine. This is somewhat bulkier than a true flat-lock.

Raw edges are exposed on the right side of the flat-locked seam, where any fraying will show. If non-raveling fabrics are used this is not a problem. If using a fabric which ravels, serge each raw edge with a balanced stitch. Press a fold on each fabric edge about 1/2" deep. Flat-lock over the two folds, being careful not to cut them, and pull the seam flat. If you wish you can top-stitch each edge flat on a conventional machine, perhaps with a decorative stitch. Or, you can flat-lock each raw edge flat. Flat-lock the raw edges with the technique described in the section on "Flat-Locked Hemming," page 55.) Since the flat-locked seam is a decorative accent anyway, you may choose to thus accent it further. Another possibility is to make a flat-locked French seam. Serge the two edges together with a narrow 3-thread balanced stitch (refer to section on "Stitch Width and Knives," page 37), then flat-lock over the previous seam. Use the techniques for flat-locking over

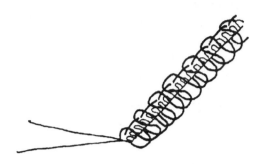

Figure 2-8: *Flat lock French seam: First line of serging out.*

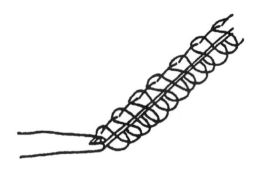

Figure 2-9: *Flat lock French seam: First line of serging folded in.*

a fold. (see below) While flat-locking, the seam can be exposed, or folded inside as you would do for a normal French seam. Either side of either type of flat-locked french seam can be used as the right side (see Figures 2-8 and 2-9). If the seam is folded inside while flat-locking, as it would be when making a normal french seam, the ladder side of the flat-lock will cover the previous seam. If the seam is exposed while flat-locking, the upper looper side of the flat-lock will cover the previous seam.

4-Thread Flat-Lock

A 4-thread flat-lock seam is done with both needles. This cannot be pulled completely open, as both raw edges end up on the looper side. This can be an advantage for ravel-prone fabrics. Also, with the right needle thread going down the middle of the stitch, it is somewhat more secure. Both needle threads are loosened and the lower looper thread tightened until the needle thread loops are at the right-hand edge of the stitch. Sew, then pull open. It pulls open easily. This will not work well on heavy stiff fabric, because one edge of fabric must be able to fold and lie flat within the stitch.

Flat-Locking Over a Fold

Flat-locking can also be done over a fold then pulled flat to produce a line of decorative stitching wherever desired without raw edges (see Figure 2-10). Tensions must first be adjusted for a normal flat-lock. When flat-locking over a fold, position the fold so that it is halfway between the needle and the knife, or slightly closer to the needle for bulky fabrics. It is important to guide this fold accurately so you can pull the stitching completely flat. If you have a blind hem foot that permits you to use the left needle, use it to guide the fold. Generally you want the fold to come just to the right of where the right needle would be. This is where the guide will normally be set for blind hemming. If you cannot

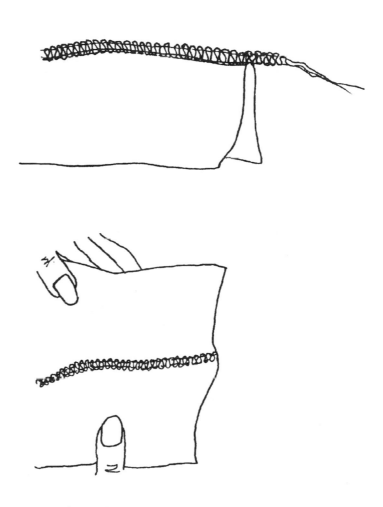

Figure 2-10: *Flat-locking over a fold*

use a blind hem foot, refer to the section on "Guiding Fabric," page 104 for various techniques. In order to position the flat-locking where you want it on the garment, mark the fold on the fabric with a line of chalk, or secure it with pins parallel to the edge and about 1" in from it.

Flat-Locked Hemming

A flat-locked blind hem lies flat, even when the needle nips more than one thread of the fold. (refer to section on "Blind Hemming," page 44) Set up machine for a right needle flat-lock and long stitch length. Use the blind hem foot. Position fabric for blind hemming and sew a sample to check guide placement and stretch. If the hem does not have enough stretch you will need to loosen the lower looper tension and tighten the upper looper tension so the joining between the looper threads lies in the middle of the looper side of the stitch. The needle thread will still join with the lower looper thread on the edge of the stitch (refer to Figure 6-6 on page 95). When you pull the seam flat the hem will be about 1/4" shorter than what you pinned up: allow for this when pinning up the hem. If you want the ladder side out fold up hem and fold back as if blind hemming, then flat-lock (see Figure 2-11). If you want the upper looper side out, fold raw edge _inside_ the fold and flat-lock, using the techniques for flat-locking over a fold (see Figure 2-12).

This technique can be used to secure seam allowances so they lie flat. Make sure you leave wide enough seam allowances to work with. Position as you would for blind hemming.

A decorative thread is often used with this technique. If the decorative thread is in the needle, fold as for normal blind hemming. If the decorative thread is in the upper looper, fold the opposite way with the raw edge inside the fold. If using a decorative thread you may choose to do a wide or left-needle flat-lock to get a more prominent stitch: serge the raw edge with a right needle 3-thread balanced stitch in a matching thread before flat-locking if necessary to prevent fraying.

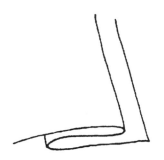

Figure 2-11: *Flat-lock ladder side out*

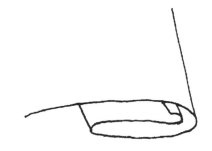

Figure 2-12: *Flat-lock looper side out*

When to use a Flat-Lock

Flat-locking is functional when a very flat seam is desired on fabric that does not ravel. A good example is lingerie made of nylon tricot. Use a narrow (right-hand needle only) flat-lock. Flat-locking is also nice for attaching elastic or lace to tricot. Flat-locking is the best seam for many fake furs. (refer to section on "Fake Furs" in Appendix B: Dictionary of Fabrics, page 170) Flat-locking can also be used wherever seam irritation is a problem, such as exercise wear (shirts for runners), underwear and baby clothes.

WRAPPED STITCH

With this stitch the upper looper thread wraps completely around the edge, and the lower looper thread is scarcely visible. It appears the same from both sides. It looks very much like a wide narrow rolled edge (see Figures 2-3 and 2-4). Begin with a 3-thread balanced stitch, then loosen the upper looper and tighten the lower looper tensions. The lower looper thread should lie in a straight line on the bottom of the stitch. You may need to tighten the needle tension slightly. Generally it is done with a short stitch length, which may need to be lengthened for heavier threads. Either needle can be used, depending on the desired effect. When doing a left needle (wide) wrapped edge you will want to narrow the stitch width somewhat; this helps control snagging or tunneling and makes it easier to get the upper looper thread to wrap completely around. Use the left needle (wide) wrapped edge on heavy firm fabric only. A heavier thread such as yarn or serger ribbon can be used in the upper looper. You probably need to remove heavier threads completely from the tension disk. (refer to section on "Special Threads," page 90 for other tips) If you have problems getting the lower looper thread tight enough, refer to step 3 in the section on the "Narrow Rolled Edge," page 48.

The wrapped edge can be done with a 2-thread overedge stitch. Tighten the needle tension and loosen the looper tension. This looks somewhat finer since there is no lower looper thread. It may be difficult to get the looper thread loose enough if converting an overlock machine to do the overedge. (refer to section on "2-Thread Overedge Stitch," page 141)

This stitch makes an attractive decorative edge. It is also nice for seaming or finishing the edges of sweater knits; a lightweight matching yarn can be used in the upper looper, and the lower looper and needle threads will not show if a matching color is used in both of them. Especially when done with the right needle, the wrapped edge can be used as a decorative edge finish on fabrics which are too heavy for a narrow rolled edge.

BLANKET STITCH

A blanket stitch is produced from a balanced 3-thread overlock stitch by loosening the needle tension, and tightening both looper tensions. Stitch length can vary but is usually medium to long. The needle thread shows on both sides and the looper threads form a line along the edge. The blanket stitch is used as an edge finish only. It is primarily decorative and does not provide much protection from fraying. It appears the same from both sides. It can be done with either the left needle or the right needle (wide or narrow blanket edge). It can be difficult to get the needle thread loose enough and the looper threads tight enough for this stitch.

Because the needle tensions are loose this stitch ravels out easily. Do not cut thread chains without securing the stitching. Secure by sewing over the edge of the stitch with 3/4" of a narrow short zig-zag on a conventional machine.

Because both looper tensions are tight this stitch has a strong tendency to pucker. You can reduce puckering by shortening the stitch length and by using a firm fabric. If you have differential feed set it to less than 1. You can also try increasing presser foot pressure.

The blanket stitch produced with the 2-thread overedge stitch has less tendency to pucker. If using a 2-thread overedge stitch, loosen the needle tension and tighten the looper tension. (refer to section on "2-Thread Overedge Stitch," page 141)

The left needle (wide) blanket stitch looks best with a prominent thread in the needle. Unfortunately this can make it even more difficult to get a properly adjusted stitch. You may need to take the needle thread completely out of the tension disk in order to get it to work. A narrower stitch width works better. It is difficult to get the looper tensions tight enough for both of them to form a straight line. (refer to step 3 in the section on "Narrow Rolled Hem," page 48) Use this stitch on firm non-raveling fabrics such as coating.

On fine fabrics you can use the right needle (narrow) blanket stitch, with the narrow rolled edge stitch finger and normal stitch length. This makes a light fine rolled edge which is not as secure as a conventional rolled edge. Hand wash only and treat gently, unless the fabric is something like tricot or coated fabrics which will not ravel. Some industrial sergers are set up to do a 2-thread narrow rolled edge blanket stitch, which is used for such things as finishing the edges of vinyl tablecloths.

The blanket stitch has limited uses. It cannot be used as a seam, plus it provides little protection from fraying. It is primarily decorative yet any decorative thread must go through the needle, which limits the choice of decorative threads. It has a strong tendency to pucker unless a short stitch length is used, at which point it looks much like a balanced stitch. However, it may work fine on your machine.

CHAPTER 3
SECURING STITCHES

This chapter covers techniques for securing the ends of the serger stitching. Use these techniques when making seams or finishing raw edges, when doing a balanced stitch or special stitches. Some special stitches require special techniques.

Many of these techniques involve sewing on top of a previous line of stitching. When overlapping stitching on a narrow rolled edge, align fabric so the needle is sewing right on top of the left edge of the previous stitching. (There will be a space between the edge of the fabric and the knives.)

Flat-locking and the blanket stitch ravel more because of their loose needle tensions, and so need extra securing. If the flat-locking thread chain must be cut, secure the seam ends on a conventional machine with 3/4" of straight stretch stitch in matching thread. If the blanket stitch thread chain must be cut, secure the ends with 3/4" of a short narrow zig-zag over the edge of the stitch. Securing the stitches on a conventional sewing machine is quick, secure and neat. A thread sealant can change the appearance of the fabric, and make it scratchy when worn next to the skin.

Some of these techniques involve sewing over a chain and enclosing it in a seam. Before sewing over a chain, pull your fingers along it to pull out the slack looper threads and make it thinner.

With these techniques you frequently have to "clear the stitch finger." The stitch finger is the narrow tongue of metal around which the stitches are formed. (see Figure 1-5, page 7) The stitches remain on this finger for about 3/8" behind the needle. In order to get the stitches off the stitch finger stop stitching with the needle in the upper-most position. On some machines you can simply pull backwards on the chain or fabric to get the stitches off the stitch finger. On other machines you have to pull slightly on the needle thread(s) to give it some slack. (The looper threads already have enough slack.) Each machine is a little different so you will need to find the best place on your machine to do this. On domestic machines you can often stick your finger on top of the needle threads just to the right of the take-up lever and pull down slightly. Another place to pull some slack is directly above the needle, between the guides on the needle bar and the take-up lever: put your finger under the needle threads and pull out slightly. Lift the presser foot and pull the fabric or thread chain gently to the rear of the machine until it is clear of the stitch finger. Reposition fabric as directed in the sections below. If necessary, pull up a little more slack on the needle thread(s). If you have too much slack, pull up on the needle thread(s) just above the tension disk(s) after positioning the fabric. Excess slack can cause ugly loops, especially when turning corners. (see below) For this reason, I do not generally recommend using a tension release control if your machine has it: it is too easy to release too much thread. Some tension releases just release the needle threads. Since the looper threads are still held, this type of tension release generally will release just enough thread without excessive loops. Use it to "clear the stitch finger," then pull up on the needle threads if necessary after repositioning fabric.

SECURING SEAMS

It is not uncommon to see the ends of serger seams pulling out. The most common places are the ends of the shoulder seams and the bottom of the armscye. These are all places where one serger seam is crossed by another. When the second serger seam is sewn the thread chain from the first seam is cut, leaving the end of that seam to pull out. Even if the ends are carefully finished as described in this chapter under "Corners," it is still easy to cut a thread when sewing the second seam. Here are two techniques to eliminate the problem. Sew the first seam normally, leaving thread chains at both ends.

If you are not trimming anything off when you sew the second seam you can put the two sections of fabric under the presser foot. It is easier to see what you are doing if the section with the previously sewn seam is on top. When the first seam gets close to the presser foot, grasp its thread chain and pull gently towards the left with it, enough to pull its threads clear of the knives (see Figure 3-1). Once that seam is past the knives complete the second seam normally.

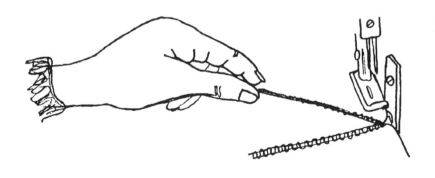

Figure 3-1: *Securing Seams:*

Pull Chain to left of the seam firmly enough to clear the knives

If there are seams on both the top and bottom sections, make sure the two seams line up. Turn the seam allowances in opposite directions. When the seams get close to the knives, lift the corner of both layers so that you can pull the bottom chain to the left. The pressure of the fabric will hold the bottom seam clear of the knives as you pull on the top chain. Later, trim thread chains to 1". (If you want to conceal the chain completely you can enclose it in the seam. Pull the chain out of the way of the knives, as described above. As soon as it is clear of the knives lay it along the edge of the fabric on top of the seam line so the stitching can enclose it. After enclosing about 1" of chain let the knives cut off the remainder.)

Sometimes you need to cut off the end of a serger stitch. Perhaps you need to trim a garment edge, for example to get a proper sized neck or proper length sleeves. Your pattern may have 5/8" seam allowances, which require trimming as you serge. Or, you may want to secure your seams before blind hemming. You can secure the cut end of the seam by sewing over it, with either a serger or a conventional machine. If using a serger, cut the seam, begin serging at the end of the seam (overlapping the previous stitching),

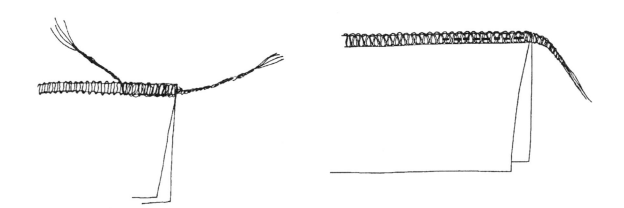

Figure 3-2: *Securing the end of a seam after cutting off a section: Serger method.*

Figure 3-3: *Re-enforcing Stitches in Seam Allowance on conventional machine*

then serge for a couple of inches before ending as described below under "Ending Sewing in a Circle." When making the crossing seam pull on the chain of the stitching you just made, as described above (see Figure 3-2). If using a conventional machine you do not have to cut the seam before securing. Sew for about an inch in the serged seam allowance with a straight-stretch stitch around where the seam will be cut (see Figure 3-3). (Since the stitching is in the seam allowance, thread color need not match.) Then cut off the end of the chain so you can see at a glance that you have secured the end of that seam.

SEWING IN A CIRCLE

These techniques are used frequently, for sewing on ribbing, blind hemming, finishing oval placemats, etc.

Beginning sewing in a circle

Clear stitch finger and lift presser foot. It may help to pull the chain back and to the right before inserting fabric. Place fabric in position under needle and next to the knife, pull chain to left on top of fabric and under presser foot (this keeps the chain from getting sucked into machine when you begin to sew), drop presser foot and sew. If you will be trimming off fabric as you serge, you will need to cut a notch with scissors before you start sewing. At any point along the edge, cut out a rectangle which is the length of the presser foot and the depth of the amount you will be having the knives trim off. When you start sewing put this cutout portion under the presser foot.

Ending sewing in a circle

Cut off beginning chain with knives. Being careful not to cut stitches, sew over beginning stitching for about 1/2". Clear the stitch finger. Lift presser foot, pull fabric back out of the way and chain off. Cut chain next to fabric.

If sewing with heavy decorative thread in upper looper, do not trim off the beginning chain. Pull it to the left out of the way of the knives. Sew just until end of stitching meets beginning of stitching. Lift presser foot, pull fabric out of way and chain off. Pull chains apart, pull threads into stitching for about 1" and trim. Use a crochet hook or a blunt needle, such as a yarn or tapestry needle, to pull the thread ends into the stitching. Another useful tool is one of the slender latch hooks, sold for turning spaghetti straps. (Refer to section on "Spaghetti Tubing" for an easier method of turning spaghetti tubing.)

SERGING CORNERS

The techniques for beginning and ending at a corner are mostly used for decorative techniques, for example lettucing and pintucks. (refer to section on "Securing Seams" for techniques to use on construction seams) The technique for turning corners is used frequently, for finishing rectangles such as napkins, handkerchiefs and scarves, and for finishing raw edges on garment pieces before construction.

Beginning at a corner

Let the needle make one stitch into the fabric. Clear stitch finger, lift presser foot, pull thread chain diagonally across fabric to knives, drop presser foot and continue sewing. Many industrial sergers are set up to do this automatically.

Ending at a corner

Let the needle take one stitch off edge of fabric. Clear stitch finger, lift presser foot and pull fabric off stitch finger. Flip fabric over so you are sewing over stitching just completed. Being careful not to cut stitches, sew about 1/2" over previous stitching. Clear stitch finger, lift presser foot, pull fabric out of way and chain off. Cut chain next to fabric.

Turning outside corners

Sew until next stitch will fall off edge. Clear stitch finger, lift presser foot, turn and place fabric so next stitch will be at beginning of next edge, drop presser foot and sew. (On many machines you can pull a 3-thread stitch off the back of the stitch finger without having to pull more slack in the needle thread.) If you will be trimming off fabric as you sew the next side, you will need to cut a slash with scissors well before the corner gets up next to the presser foot. Make the slash the length of the presser foot and as deep as the amount you will be trimming off.

Serging squares or rectangles

Begin at any corner, without bothering to secure beginning chain. Turn the four corners as described above, cutting off the beginning chain on the last corner. Sew about 1/2" after turning the last corner, then end as described above under "Ending Sewing in a Circle." If using a heavy decorative thread, begin and end in the middle of a side as described in the section on "Circles."

Serging inside corners and slashes (two methods)

Continuous sewing (works better on corners than slashes): sew normally until slash or corner is next to knives. Pull fabric firmly to the right then pull it taut so that it lies in a straight line. (Do not pull fabric straight until the corner is next to the knives. By this time the feed dogs are gripping the fabric so you can pull it straight without the point of the slash or corner pulling too far to the left. Pulling it to the right before pulling it straight gets the point of the corner closer to the right so you get a more secure stitch around the corner.) Continue sewing, allowing a slightly narrower seam allowance at point of corner or slash if using a 4-thread stitch. This method is easier and more secure than the method described next. However it does not lie as flat.

Sewing in two sections (use to finish slash and for stiff fabric or wide stitch): sew until slash is next to knives. Fold fabric out of way as shown. Being careful not to cut the fold which is next to the knife, sew until the next stitch will fall on the other fold of fabric. Clear stitch finger. Fold first part of fabric out of way and position second part for stitching. Drop presser foot and sew, pulling back on the first section sewn to keep it clear of the upper looper. The point of the corner or slash is not secured with this method. If it will be subject to wear it should be secured on a conventional machine with a bar-tack or straight-stretch stitch (see Figure 3-4).

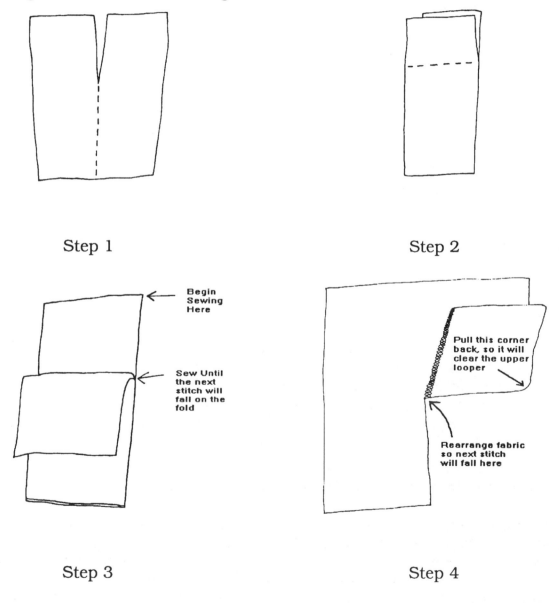

Step 1   Step 2

Step 3   Step 4

Figure 3-4: *Sewing slashes in two sections: Fold on dotted lines*

SERGING CURVES

Inside curves

Pull fabric straight and sew normally. If you have differential feed, increase it slightly.

Outside curves

These can be difficult to get even. Watch where the needle is sewing and sew slowly, trying to get an even stitch width. It is difficult to get the edges even on tight curves if you are trimming the edge with the knives: use scissors to do any trimming before serging. Depending on how tight the curve is you may need to lift the presser foot periodically to reposition the fabric.

SERGING CYLINDERS

Here is a technique for seaming a cylinder and finishing the end of it without removing it from the machine: the seam allowance is sewn flat so it is less noticeable from the right side. Although not a common problem, this technique may prove useful to you. For example, I was making puppets: I seamed the body then finished the bottom edge in one operation. Make the seam, ending with the last stitch on the fabric. Lift the presser foot, clear the stitch finger and pull the fabric back off it. Open the seam so it lies flat and place the raw edge next to the knives with the end of the seam under the needle. Drop the presser foot and serge the edge, using the techniques for sewing in a circle. If crossing another seam use the techniques for securing seams.

Sometimes you want to finish both ends of the cylinder, for example when making a sash. Begin by serging across one edge before making the lengthwise seam. When you get to the end of the first edge, clear the stitch finger and turn the fabric as if turning a corner. Fold the fabric and place the corner with the beginning chain on top, so you are ready to make the cylinder seam. Use the techniques for securing seams to secure the beginning chain as you begin making the seam. Finish the other end as described above.

COLOR BLOCKING

It is possible to sew two pieces of fabric together so that one fits into a corner of the other. (See Figure 3-5 for details on how to cut the pieces.) Sew the first seam as illustrated in Figure 3-6, making sure the knife does not cut the fold. Sew until the next stitch would fall on the edge of the folded piece of fabric. Lift the presser foot, clear the stitch finger and rearrange the fabric so you can sew the second seam. Drop the presser foot and continue sewing (see Figure 3-7). (If you are having trouble "getting" this technique, practice "Serging Inside Corners and Slashes," sewing in two sections. This technique is basically the same, except there are two pieces of fabric rather than one, and you are making a seam rather than finishing an edge.)

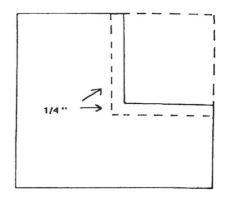

Figure 3-5: Allow 1/4"
Overlap for Seam Allowances

For color blocking this technique can also be used to produce exposed seams. Sew wrong sides together, perhaps with a decorative thread in the loopers. This technique can also be used to make square armholes. Piping can be incorporated in the seam. This technique works better on knits: on woven fabrics, sew the seam on a conventional machine and use this technique to finish the raw edges

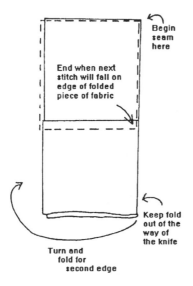

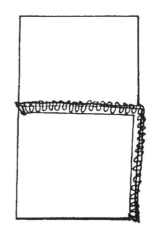

Figure 3-6:
Positioning the First
Seam

Figure 3-7: Second Seam

CHAPTER 4

FABRICS AND CONSTRUCTION METHODS

This chapter covers basic techniques for serging both woven and knit fabrics. For additional information on specific fabrics, refer to Appendix B: Dictionary of Fabrics. This chapter also includes construction techniques using the serger, plus some general information.

KNITS

When sewing very stretchy knits, several problems can occur. If the seam has sufficient stretch it can pull open or ripple. If the seam has insufficient stretch it can pucker, hang crooked or even split open under stress. These problems can be corrected, but it may require some experimentation for difficult fabrics. Experiment on scraps of your fabric. In a properly formed serger seam, the needle thread has some stretch in it because for every stitch it goes down through the fabric, around the lower looper thread and back up through the fabric. This is the only stretch it has, unlike a zig-zag stitch on a conventional machine. For this reason, it is important to make sure needle tensions are not too tight on a stretchy fabric. However, if they are too loose the seam will tend to pull open. The closer together the stitches are the more stretch the seam will have, and the less apparent it will be if it pulls open slightly. However, closely packed stitches can cause the seam to ripple. This may sound dreadfully complicated, but here is a procedure for setting tensions for knits:

Setting Tensions for Knits

Knit fabrics do not have the same amount of stretch in every direction. On most knits the lengthwise grain has little stretch. Swimsuit, exercise wear and other Lycra fabrics stretch in both directions, but generally more in the lengthwise direction. The pattern pieces are always laid out on the fabric so the greatest amount of stretch goes around the body. With most knits the

67

vertical seams will need to stretch only a small amount. At the same time they are most likely to pull apart, especially in tight fitting garments. For most knits a setting suitable for the crossgrain will also be acceptable for the lengthwise grain, but in some cases you may wish to tighten needle tension(s) slightly for vertical seams. Experiment if necessary. Make sure you notice which grainline you are using to set your tensions.

1) Set the stitch length to about 2 to 2.5, or as short as possible without making the seam ripple. Swimsuit fabric will often accept a stitch length of 2 or even less without rippling whereas interlock may need 2.5 or even more.

2) Begin with a balanced stitch as described in the section on "Adjusting Tensions," page 32. Loosen the needle tension(s) just enough to allow the seam to stretch as much as the fabric. In most cases you will be checking your tensions on the stretchiest grain of the fabric. If your stitch looks good you are done. In order to get sufficient stretch on very stretchy knits you may have to accept the seam pulling apart slightly. If the stitch length is short enough the pulling apart will scarcely be noticeable.

Controlling Rippling

There are several techniques to control rippling. These can enable you to use a shorter stitch length so the needle tensions need not be excessively loose.

The first technique to try is differential feed. Use it with a setting of greater than 1. Experiment to find the proper setting. If your machine does not have differential feed hold your finger on the fabric just behind the presser foot to scrunch it up as it comes out from under the presser foot. Check the stretch after correcting rippling. These two techniques will control rippling on most fabrics unless the seam is stretched to its limit. If the seam ripples when stretched the rippling may disappear when the seam is pulled apart, as it will be when the garment is worn. If pulling the seam apart does not correct rippling use one of the following techniques.

You can try a slightly longer stitch length, but you may need to loosen needle tension(s) in order to get sufficient stretch. Experiment, checking how much the seam pulls apart.

Spongy bulky knits such as sweater knits tend to get hung up between the presser foot and feed dogs, and not feed properly. They will feed better and ripple less if the presser foot pressure is reduced. Since proper feeding on these fabrics will result in a longer stitch length, be sure to check stretch after correcting rippling. Be careful how you are holding these fabrics in front of the needle: it is easy to stretch them while serging, and this too will affect rippling and stretch. (refer to the section on "Sweater Knits" in Appendix B: Dictionary of Fabrics, page 174)

If you really want to control rippling without losing stretch you can incorporate narrow elastic (preferably the new clear elastic) into your seam, guiding it under the needle. Experiment to determine how much, if any, to stretch the elastic. Use an elastic foot or guide if you have one. Otherwise a foot with a tape guide will help position the elastic. (refer to the section on "Special Attachments," page 153, or the section on "Guiding Fabric," page 104)

Another option is to use texturized nylon in the needle, since this is an elastic thread.

Finally, depending on fabric, you can often narrow your seam width so the rippling is less apparent.

Types of Seams in Knits

With most knit fabrics a good stitch can be achieved with steps 1 and 2. Some fabrics are difficult. Here is a list of types of seams, and strategies for dealing with each one, if your fabric is difficult. Again, the two methods of incorporating stretch into a seam are shortening stitch length and loosening needle tensions. However, too loose a needle tension will cause the seam to pull open, and too short a stitch length will cause the seam to ripple.

Vertical Seams (for example, side seams and sleeve seams): these are the easiest seams to deal with. Following steps 1 and 2 should be sufficient in most cases. Most fabrics do not stretch appreciably in the vertical direction. The two-way stretch fabrics with Lycra, such as swimsuit or exercise wear fabric, usually accept a short enough stitch length so that an attractive seam can be produced. Since pulling apart would be noticeable, make sure needle tensions are not too loose. If necessary, incorporate clear elastic in the seam or use texturized nylon thread in the needle to control rippling.

Shoulder Seams: these can be stabilized as described below under "Constructing Knit Garments."

Ribbing Seams (for example, necks and cuffs): sufficient stretch is critical for these seams. Fortunately the ribbing, being elastic, helps control rippling. Therefore a slightly shorter stitch length can be used if necessary.

Blind hem seams: these must stretch. Fortunately, the blind hem works best with a slightly loosened needle tension, which can be loosened as much as necessary to provide sufficient stretch.

Other horizontal seams (for example, color blocking seams): these are the most difficult. They have a lot of stretch, yet pulling apart or rippling is noticeable. Using texturized nylon in the needle or incorporating clear elastic in the seam are the two best strategies. If you change the design lines to diagonal seams, they will have less stretch than horizontal seams.

Another option is to make a virtue of necessity: sew wrong sides together and lettuce the seam. (refer to section on "Lettucing," page 123)

Constructing Knit Garments

Since knits are always sewn with the greatest amount of stretch going around the body, horizontal seams on knits tend to stretch out of shape if they are under stress. This is because horizontal seams are sewn on the cross-grain, the stretchiest direction. The worst offenders are shoulder seams, though crotch seams can also be a problem. (Crotch seams can stretch out of shape on wovens too, especially loosely woven ones, because they are cut on the bias. Stabilize as described below.) Saggy seams are much more of a problem if the knit is stretchy with poor recovery or "memory," for example sweater knits. Also, the heavier the weight of the garment the more the shoulder seams will tend to stretch. This means a dress will have more of a problem than a shirt, a man's shirt more than a child's, and a sweater knit top more than a tee-shirt knit top. If you think the shoulder seams might sag, stabilize them by sewing a non-stretchy something into them, guiding the something under the needle. (refer to section on "Guiding Fabric," page 104) Possible "somethings" include selvedges from lightweight wovens (guide the selvedge a little to the left of the needle with the raw edge to the right), narrow twill tape, strips of sheer tricot or lace seam-binding (nice because they are so non-bulky and have a small bit of stretch), even lightweight elastic (the new clear elastic is very lightweight). You can use folded strips of self-fabric, cut on the lengthwise grain, but this is more bulky. Do not depend on a non-stretchy stitch to stabilize a shoulder unless the garment is lightweight and will have light wear: the stitching can break under stress. If the fabric is very stretchy, it tends to stretch even while you are sewing on something to stabilize it. Before making the seam, you need to mark on the stabilizer how long the seam should be. Lay the stabilizer along the shoulder seam on the pattern and mark on the stabilizer how long the seam should be. <u>Do Not Cut off</u>. Begin sewing, and stop when the needle has started sewing into the fabric. Stretch your stabilizer and line the mark up with the other end of the seam. Ease the fabric as necessary so the stabilized seam ends up the proper length. Cut off the excess stabilizer.

Ordinarily neck openings are stabilized by their finish, whether ribbing, collar, facing or binding (knit or woven). On very firm fabrics which do not ravel garment edges can be finished by simply serging over the edge, usually with a decorative thread. Experiment, checking both cross and lengthwise grains if using a knit. Most fabrics require more stabilization than just a serged edge. Especially for hems and armholes, sometimes it works to fold the edge over and serge over the fold with a 4-thread stitch, trimming the excess fabric afterwards. The neck can be stabilized when doing a serged edge by sewing something into the stitch as described for shoulder seams. If possible, fold the edge over before serging to cover whatever is being used. Otherwise, place it slightly to the left of the knife so it does not show from the right side. An easy finish is to serge trim, such as a lace ruffle, onto the neck edge, stabilizing and finishing in one step. With neck openings it is important to remember they must fit over the head unless there is some type of closure. If you stabilize the neck by serging over elastic you will have some stretch for fitting over the head. Make sure the needle sews into the elastic rather than guiding it to the right of the needle.

Patterns for knits are designed for fabrics with a certain amount of stretch. Generally this is specified on the pattern envelope in the section on recommended fabrics. Stretch is measured in the direction of greatest stretch, usually the crossgrain. When measuring stretch, fold the fabric and measure stretch along the fold (see Figure 4-1). If working with a 2-way stretch fabric such as swimsuit fabric, the minimum amount of stretch in each direction will be given. If a 4" piece of fabric will stretch comfortably to 5" it has 25%

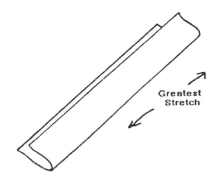

Figure 4-1: *Greatest Stretch*

stretch or "moderate" stretch. If it stretches to 6" it has 50% stretch: stretching to 7" would indicate 75% stretch and to 8" would indicate 100% stretch. If your pattern called for fabric with 25% stretch you would generally use one size smaller if making it up in a fabric with 50% stretch unless the fabric had very good recovery, and one size larger than normal if making it up in a fabric with little stretch such as most sweatshirt fleece. Recovery, the ability of a knit to "spring back" when stretched, is also important. In the example above, for a knit with poor recovery such as a sweater knit you would use one to two sizes smaller, depending both on its stretch and its recovery. It is easier to use a pattern drafted with 1/4" seam allowances.

Because of their structure knits are much more subject to shrinkage than wovens. All washable fabric should be washed before sewing, but knits with any cotton in them should be washed twice. (refer to section on "Prewashing Fabric," page 84)

Because the seam allowances on knits are only 1/4", the sleeves in knit garments are sewn onto the bodice before the side seams are sewn. Here is the construction sequence for a simple knit shirt:
    Sew shoulder seams
    Finish neck, for example with collar or ribbing
    Sew sleeves to bodice, if shirt has sleeves
    Sew side seams, sewing bodice and sleeve in one step
    Finish sleeve edge and bottom edge, for example with ribbing or blind hem

RIBBING AND ELASTIC

Not all ribbing is created equal. When selecting ribbing, make sure it has 100% stretch and good recovery. If the ribbing has some Lycra in it, it will generally have better recovery. In order to get a good color match I sometimes use self-fabric, especially for the wrist where little stretch is needed. Interlock works well as ribbing for lighter weight fabrics, since it has 100% stretch and good recovery. Cotton/Lycra fabric is wonderful for lightweight ribbing. Use lighter weight ribbing for lighter weight fabrics and heavier ribbing for heavier fabrics. If necessary you can use a double thickness of lightweight ribbing for heavier fabrics.

Do not pre-wash your ribbing before sewing.

For variety, you can also use ribbing with woven fabrics, for example as a sleeve finish for a casual shirt or a wide waistband for a lightweight dress. Ribbing can also be lettuced. (refer to section on "Lettucing," page 123)

How long should ribbing be? For a crew neck or turtleneck opening, the unstretched ribbing should be about the size of the neck and the stretched ribbing must fit over the head. For more scooped necks make ribbing about 2/3 as long as the neck opening. If ribbing has a finished width of more than 2", make it slightly shorter so the inner edge will lie flat. For V-necks cut a strip of ribbing, stretch onto back portion of neck opening as you would for a scoop or crew neck, stretch very slightly onto V portion, overlap or miter at bottom, and cut off excess. Wrist ribbing should be slightly smaller than the wrist measurement. When using ribbing or elastic for a waistband, make it comfortably snug, generally about 2" to 4" smaller than the waist. For pants or a skirt, make sure it will fit over the hips when stretched. For a top, make sure the wearer can get it on over their head. If the bottom edge will ride on the hips, make the band about 2" to 4" smaller than the hip measurement.

For turtlenecks or crew necks, the stretched opening on the garment must fit over the head. If the fabric has little stretch it may be necessary to trim the opening slightly. Increase the width of the ribbing to fill in the space. Be conservative when trimming: trimming off 1/4" all around increases the neck opening by about 1 and 3/4".

Sewing Into A Circle

It is best to sew ribbing or elastic into a circle before applying it to the garment. For elastic, you can overlap the ends about 1/2" and secure them with one of the stitches on your conventional machine. I usually use a 3-step zig-zag or smocking stitch for securing the ends of elastic. For narrow elastic which is difficult to overlap and sew accurately you can sew a 1/4" seam on the conventional machine, then flatten the seam allowances and top-stitch to secure, using a stitch like the smocking stitch. This is also a nice finish for stretch lace or wide decorative waistband elastic, since both raw edges end up on the inside.

Ribbing can be sewn into a circle on the serger. If you do this turn the seam allowances the opposite directions at the raw edge when folding wrong sides together (See Figure 2-1 on page 31). A much nicer method is to seam the ribbing on a conventional machine then finger press the seam allowances open. Use an ordinary straight stitch. When constructed this way, the ribbing both looks nicer and wears better. It wears better because there is no hard lump of seam allowance to push the edge of the fabric out and cause it to fray.

Attaching To Garment

To apply elastic or ribbing, quarter your elastic or ribbing and quarter your opening. To quarter the ribbing or elastic, put pins at the seam, midpoint, and halfway between seam and midpoint. Quarter the garment opening the same way. For a neck opening start out with center front and center back, then find the points halfway between: the quarter marks will lie forward of the shoulder seams (see Figure 4-2). (This is because the front half of the neck opening is longer than the back half, and the ribbing is stretched equally all around on a crew or turtleneck.) For a waistband, put four more pins halfway between the quarter pins, so you have eight pins in all. Pin elastic or ribbing to opening, matching your quarter marks. With the ribbing or elastic on top and using the techniques for sewing in a circle, begin sewing between two pins, stretching

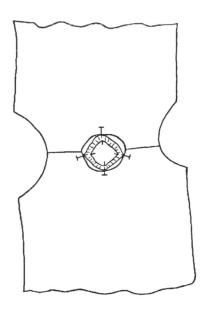

Figure 4-2: *Attach Ribbing at quarter marks*

the ribbing or elastic as you sew and *removing pins before they get up to the knives*. It is best to stretch only a short section at a time, about 2" to 3". Use a long stitch length: you are sewing while the elastic or ribbing is stretched, and the stitches will be a lot closer together when the seam is no longer being stretched. Make sure your stitch has sufficient stretch.

When attaching ribbing, make sure all three edges of fabric are caught in the stitching, the two layers of the ribbing plus the garment. Check the edges of the fabric in front of the presser foot as you go along. Generally you will apply ribbing to the right side of the garment edge unless you want an exposed seam.

There are several methods for applying elastic to waistbands.

A common method is to fold over the edge of the garment, enclosing the elastic. This works well unless the pants or skirt are very full. It is done in two or three steps (see Figure 4-3).

The first step is to sew the elastic to the wrong side of garment edge. In order to reduce bulk use as long a stitch length on the serger as possible or zig-zag on a conventional machine. A 2-thread overedge stitch is useful for this step since it has so much stretch and is somewhat less bulky than the overlock stitch.

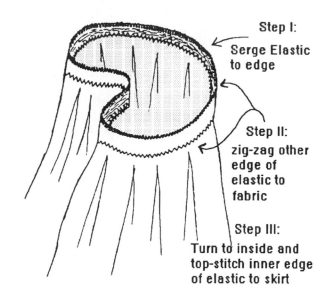

Step I:
Serge Elastic to edge

Step II:
zig-zag other edge of elastic to fabric

Step III:
Turn to inside and top-stitch inner edge of elastic to skirt

Figure 4-3: *Applying elastic to waistbands*

Step two secures the elastic so it cannot fold over inside the casing. Zig-zag the unstitched edge of the elastic to the garment before turning, to prevent rolling. Pin before sewing and stretch the elastic as you sew. This is not necessary if you are using non-roll elastic.

In the third step, the edge is folded to the wrong side and sewn to the garment. An easy and secure way to do this is to top-stitch with a medium width and length zig-zag, stretching elastic as you sew. Sew with the inside of the garment on top so you can easily guide the stitching along the edge of the elastic. Some people like to use a twin needle for top stitching. If you do, check the stretch: you may need to loosen the bobbin tension slightly as well as needle tension, especially for the wider twin needles. Sew with the garment right side up. From below feel with your fingers where the edge of the elastic is so you can guide the fabric accurately. Another option is to blind hem the edge in place rather than top-stitching: set up the machine for blind hemming, fold the edge back and blind hem.

A separate casing reduces bulk on a full cut garment. Cut a strip of fabric long enough to go over the hips plus two seam allowances. If the casing will be a knit fabric cut it so the greatest amount of stretch is going around the body, and make it long enough so it will fit over the hips when stretched. Make the casing twice the width of the elastic plus 3/4" (two 1/4" seam allowances plus 1/4" ease). Join the ends. Fold wrong sides together. Quarter the opening and the casing then add four more pins as you would for a waistband. Pin the casing to the garment. Serge together, leaving a 2" opening. Determine your waist size, for example 28". Subtract 2" to 4" from this, depending on what your personal preference is, how stretchy the elastic is and how heavy the garment is. Measure this distance from one end of the elastic, say 25". Make sure this will stretch enough to go over the hips. Mark a line at this point: this is the finished length of your elastic. *Do not cut off.* Using a bodkin or large safety pin, thread the elastic through the casing. After the elastic is all the way through pull out both ends. Cut off near the mark, leaving about 1/2" for overlapping the ends. Sew the ends together on a conventional machine. Pull elastic into casing and serge together the opening you left for the elastic. Stretch and release the waistband several times all around to distribute fullness evenly, then topstitch at front, back and side seams to prevent the elastic from twisting within the casing.

Exposed elastic shows on the right side, with the skirt or pants attached to the bottom edge of it. Wide decorative elastic is available for this purpose.

> If you cannot find the color you want, consider buying white elastic and painting it with textile paints. You can paint it a solid color or paint on a design. The paints must be thin enough so you can brush them on and have them soak into and through the fabric: dilute with water if necessary. If the paint is too thick the repeated stretching of the elastic will soon cause it to flake off. If the colors are not bright or dark enough, do a second coat. Heat setting is recommended for many types of textile paints to make them completely washable. After the paint has dried for 24 hours, tumbling in a hot dryer for an hour should set the paints, with less damage to the elastic than the normally recommended ironing. If you cannot find such paints locally you can order them. (refer to Appendix D: Sources, page 189)

> As an alternative, a separate strip of fabric can be folded around wide elastic, top-stitched on a conventional machine, then joined to the garment. A soft lightweight fabric makes a less bulky waistband. Make sure both the elastic and the fabric strip are long enough to fit over the hips with some ease. Make the fabric strip twice the width of the elastic plus 1/4" so it can fold over and cover both sides. Sew both fabric strip and elastic separately into circles before pinning them together. Use the quartering techniques for pinning the fabric strip to the elastic, using at least eight pins as described for waistbands. Make sure you stretch the elastic while you are top-stitching, so the stitching will stretch enough.

> After your elastic band is finished, quarter the elastic and garment opening then pin together. Sew elastic to the garment, using a 4-thread stitch for security and sewing right sides together. If the garment opening is too big you may need to gather it slightly before attaching the elastic. (refer to section on "Gathering," page 126)

It can be difficult to sew on wrist ribbing, especially on a child's garment. I often use three pins instead of four. I turn the sleeve inside out, pin the ribbing into place, and sew with the ribbing on top. Stretch the ribbing to fit the garment fabric. If the sleeve is very full the ribbing may not stretch enough. Refer to the section on "Gathering," page 126 to gather sleeve before sewing on ribbing, or to gather the sleeve while sewing on the ribbing.

WOVEN FABRICS

A serger is wonderful when sewing home furnishings. Use a wide 4-thread stitch for wovens, or a 5-thread stitch if you have it.

There are two ways to use a serger when making garments from woven fabrics. One method is to finish the raw edges on the serger then construct the garment on a conventional machine. The other method is to do virtually all construction on the serger.

Constructing the garment on the serger does go much quicker. This is how most ready-to-wear is made. Generally you will use as wide a 4-thread overlock stitch as you have, or a 5-thread stitch if you have it. (This refers to a 2-thread chainstitch plus 3-thread overlock, as produced by a 5-thread serger.) Do not use a 3-thread overlock stitch to construct garments from woven fabric. You will be trimming off some fabric, since most patterns for wovens are designed for 5/8" seam allowances. After trimming off this fabric you will have no fabric for letting out any seams, or extra insurance in a seam under stress. Unless you are using a 5-thread stitch, reinforce crotch and armscye seams (ie, any curved bias seam or seam under stress) with a straight stretch stitch on your conventional machine, or a straight stitch with a short stitch length. The serger seam is a better construction method for garments which will be washed and not pressed, because the seam is less bulky than an unpressed seam made by a conventional machine. If the seam is pressed to one side and top-stitched it will lie even flatter and be more secure. This is wonderful on the outseam of washable pants, because it reduces bulk and adds a slimming vertical line. Curved seams usually lay flat without clipping if they are a serged seam. Not only is this method much quicker than a clipped conventional seam, it is more secure in ravel-prone fabric. I like to use this seam on princess seams (after checking the fit!), and I often top-stitch the seam allowance flat.

Another alternative is to finish the raw edges with the serger and then construct the garment on a conventional machine with a 5/8" seam allowance. Because this seam can be pressed open, it is preferable where a smooth flat appearance is desired, for example the bodice of a dress or a tailored jacket. (Sometimes I use this seam on the bodice of a washable dress, but I use the serger seam on its full skirt. Because both ends of the bodice seams are secured by crossing seams, they lie flat after washing without being pressed. This is not true of the longer seams in the skirt.) It takes little time to serge around the raw edges of the garment pieces, and construction on a conventional machine goes quickly because just about all of it is straight stitch. When completed the seams lie nice and flat, have some room for letting out, and are more secure. If you wish you can put fusible thread (refer to section on "Fusible Thread," page 94) in the looper and then fuse the seam allowances flat. Here is the sequence for this method:

> Mark all notches in the seam allowance with a washable fabric marking pen, before taking the pattern off the fabric. These marks will show up after

you have serged the edges (and neatly trimmed off or covered up any notches you might have cut).

Fuse any fusible interfacing you may be using. (The heat can set the marks from the washable marking pen but these are not usually under the interfacing. In any case, the marks are in the seam allowance.)

Serge all the raw edges, going around every piece.

Finally, construct the garment on a conventional machine, except for when trimming seam allowances (for example when turning facings). Do this trimming on the serger, using a narrow stitch width.

For casual garments which will be washed and not pressed, the serged seam, as described above, works well. Here are two alternative techniques. With the first technique, you sew the seam on a conventional machine with a 5/8" seam allowance. Then you serge the two raw edges together, with about 3/8" seam allowance. If you just have a 3-thread or 4-thread machine, this gives a wider and more secure seam allowance. The second technique is to serge the seam allowances before sewing the seam on the conventional machine, but put fusible thread in one looper while serging. Sew the seam on a conventional machine with a 5/8" seam allowance, then fuse the seam allowances flat. (refer to section on "Fusible Thread," page 94) This seam has many of the advantages of both types of construction

---

Serger construction techniques for wovens

(refer to "Decorative Construction Techniques," page 100, for more ideas)

A French seam is easily made with a serger (see Figures 4-4, 4-5, and 4-6). Wrong sides together, sew as narrow a seam as possible, using a medium length balanced stitch and the narrow rolled edge stitch finger. (refer to section on "Stitch Width and Knives," page 37) Turning right sides together and enclosing the previously serged seam, sew seam with straight stitch on conventional machine just beyond edge of serging. This makes a dainty finish for seams in sheer wovens, yet is more secure than a plain serged seam.

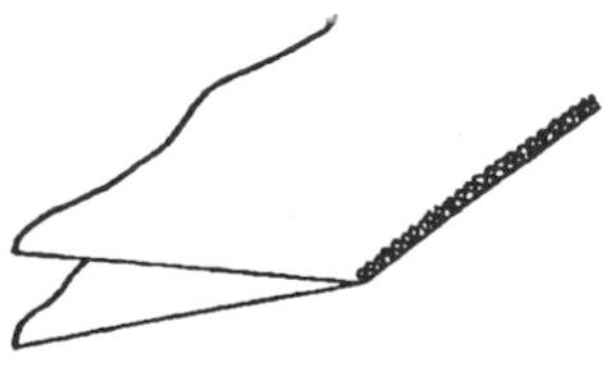

Figure 4-4: *Narrow rolled edge serged with wrong sides together*

Figure 4-5: *Folded for second seam*

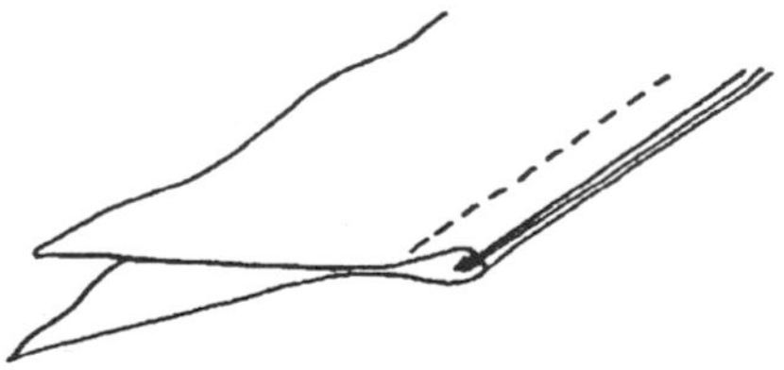

Figure 4-6: *French Seam (second seam)*

The serger makes it easy to line or face bodices, although binding the edges is another option when a light effect is desired. The narrow seams at the neck and armhole are sewn and trimmed in one step, and are more secure in ravel-prone fabrics. I usually line a bodice rather than use facings for the neck or armholes. A lining stays in place, looks and wears better than facings, and is just as quick to complete. Often you can eliminate interfacing. For summerwear choose a light absorbant fabric such as cotton batiste. To make the edges turn under, trim 1/8" from the neck and armhole edges of the lining. (You can eliminate this trimming at the neck if applying a collar, and at the armhole if applying sleeves.)

If the bodice has set-in sleeves sew shoulder seams separately on lining and shell. Then complete the neck finish, treating the lining as a facing. Then sew side seams separately on both lining and shell. Generally you treat the shell and lining as one layer when setting in sleeves. In sheer fabric serge/trim armscye seam allowances to 1/4" and secure with sheer tricot seam binding. Another alternative if only the sleeves are sheer is to set the sleeve into the shell fabric, serge/trim all the armscye seam allowances to 1/4", turn under the lining armscye seam allowance, then slip-stitch the lining in place.

If a sleeveless bodice is open down the front or back you can use the following sequence: sew shoulder seams on both shell and lining with conventional machine, join the lining to the shell by serging the armholes and the neck edge (unless applying another finish to the neck edge), turn right side out through the shoulders, then sew side seams on conventional machine (see Figures 4-7 and 4-8).

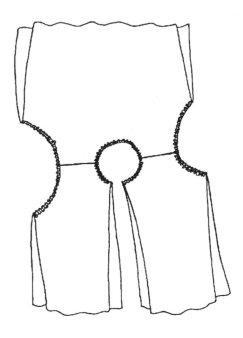

Figure 4-7: *Sleeveless Bodice with neck and armholes serged*

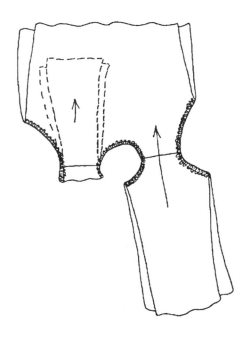

Figure 4-8: *Same Bodice turned right side out through shoulders*

With a lined bodice I like to sew the skirt to the shell fabric of the bodice, then turn the bodice wrong side out and sew the right side of the lining to the skirt side of the seam just completed. The skirt must be open along the seam that matches the opening on the bodice, generally center front or center back. It is easier to attach the skirt this way before setting in sleeves: if the bodice is sleeveless, finish the armholes as described in the previous paragraph before attaching skirt. This technique encloses the waist seam and keeps it flat, and it does not require much more time. If you prefer, you can attach the skirt to the bodice shell by machine, then slip stitch the lining to the waist seam. Another option is to sew the skirt to the bodice shell, turn under and press a seam allowance on the waist edge of the bodice lining, pin in place on top of the waist seam, then stitch in the ditch to attach.

If lining a bodice with princess seams, the seam allowances can be tacked in place onto the lining, eliminating unsightly lumps along the princess seam. These lumps are caused by the seam allowances turning the wrong way and are most common over the bust.

When the edge of a curved piece of fabric must be finished, such as the hem on a circular skirt, there is a tendency for the edge to curl to the right side unless the fabric is lightweight or a very narrow hem is used. (An example is denim skirts: the twill weave of denim has a tendency to curl to the right side anyway, a problem compounded by the extra fabric in the hem.) If a serged or bound edge is not suitable the best way to avoid the curling is to line small pieces to the edge and face large pieces. Because the serger stitch is narrow it is easy to get the edge to lie flat. Face a circular skirt hem by cutting another piece of fabric curved like the skirt edge and about 2" wide. Serge the facing to the skirt, right sides together. Turn and press, then blind hem the other edge of the facing to the skirt. The edge of a ruffle or flounce can be finished with a narrow rolled edge or by lining. If lining, place right sides together, serge the lining to dress fabric, then turn and press. When lining or facing, make the edge turn under by trimming 1/8" from the facing or lining edges which will be serged to the outer fabric.

When facing garments, serge the facing on, right sides together. In one serger-quick step you have made the seam, trimmed the seam allowance and finished the raw edges.

When you are underlining, serge the underlining to the garment pieces, joining them and finishing raw edges in one step.

If you end up trimming off a section of a partially constructed garment (for example a hem), make sure the seams are pressed flat then serge around the entire edge.

If cutting out an extremely unstable or ravel-prone fabric, mark your cutting line on the fabric and do the actual cutting on the serger, serging around it and securing the edge as you go. (refer to the section on "Serging Corners," page 62, for directions on trimming off fabric when turning outside corners)

MATCHING STRIPES OR SEAMS

Be sure to start your seam by lifting the presser foot, either as described in the section on "Starting Sewing," page 25, or with the presser foot lever. For stripes, start your layers of fabric so that they match. Every few inches look at the edges of your fabric in front of the presser foot and pinch them together so they match, then hold them together until your fingers get up to the presser foot. Then repeat. If matching seams, start the seam with the two ends of the fabric and sew until they reach the needle. Then stretch out the unsewn pieces of fabric and pinch together the seams that should match. Take additional "pinches" between this point and the presser foot as necessary. Hold them with your fingers, clothespins or regular pins. Keep sewing, releasing pinches as you go. (refer to section on "Starting Sewing," page 25, for information on _not_ sewing over pins) (refer to section on "Securing Seams," page 60, for securing the seams)

INSERTING ZIPPERS

Zippers are actually quite easy to insert with a serger. They are not top-stitched as a conventional machine would do, although the conventional machine can be used to add top-stitching after the zipper is serged on. Because the serger tends to feed difficult fabric more evenly than a conventional machine, zippers go in easily. The zipper teeth will be exposed, not hidden by a placket or small fold of fabric. Therefore, this type of application is more suited to casual or sporty garments.

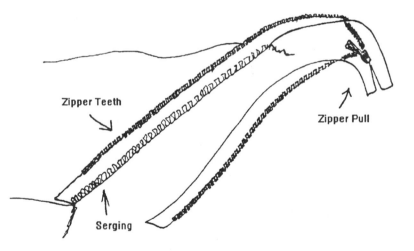

Figure 4-9: Inserting a Zipper

In one type of application, the zipper is serged to the edge of one garment section (see Figure 4-9). If the fabric is cut with 1/4" seam allowances, match the edge of the zipper tape to the raw edge of the fabric and serge, right sides together, without trimming anything off. If the garment section has 5/8" seam allowances, place the edge of the zipper tape 3/8" from the edge and serge, trimming off 3/8" of fabric. If the zipper is not enclosed between two layers of fabric, it should be top-stitched on a conventional machine after serging (see Figure 4-10). This keeps the zipper teeth facing the right direction.

Often the zipper is sandwiched between two layers of fabric. These two layers would typically be an upper and lower collar, or a garment section and facing. It is much easier to see what you are doing if both layers of fabric have 1/4" seam allowances so you can match edges. Place the right side of the zipper to the right side of the garment section or the right side of the under collar. Lay the right side of the upper collar or facing on top, sandwiching the zipper. Serge together.

When selecting a zipper for a garment I always like to get a zipper a few inches too long. This way I can sew it in without having to sew around the zipper pull. I cut off the excess zipper tape after setting in the zipper. This is particularly important when using a serger because a serger does not have a zipper foot. If the zipper will be closed at the bottom (non-separating), use the following procedure:

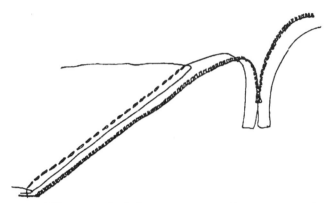

Figure 4-10: *Top-Stitched Zipper Application*

Open the zipper and serge one side of the zipper to the garment, as described above.

Close the zipper. You want the two garment sections to meet at the bottom, plus at any intersecting seam lines (see Figure 4-11). Mark the unsewn side of the zipper with a pin, chalk or pencil where the match points are.

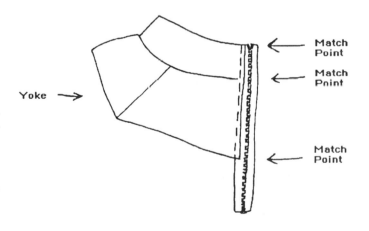

Figure 4-11: *Zipper Match Points*

Unzip the zipper and serge the other side of the zipper to the garment, with all due respect for the match points.

Close the zipper and check your match points. Sew across the bottom of the zipper several times with a conventional machine. Cut off the excess allowing 1/4" seam allowance. Serge the edge to protect it from fraying, or fold a scrap of fabric over the end and sew it on.

If the zipper is a separating zipper, use the above procedure but leave the excess at the top of the zipper. Before trimming the excess from the zipper, fold it so the raw edge is hidden in the seam. Especially if the zipper teeth are large, you may want to remove them from the portion you fold in. Use a pliers or nail clipper, being careful not to cut the zipper tape.

LINGERIE

Lingerie is quickly made on a serger. Use a right needle balanced stitch and a very narrow seam allowance on nylon tricot. (refer to section on "Stitch Width and Knives," page 37) Use flat-locking for the smoothest possible seam: lace and elastic can also be applied with flat-locking. Many fabrics can be used in lingerie besides nylon tricot. What about _nice_ cotton panties? Look for a fine silky cotton knit, perhaps with a bit of a lace pattern knitted in, then finish with stretch lace. Make a matching camisole. You can also buy silk jersey. (Use spray starch if you have problems handling it.) Another nice fabric for panties or camisoles is cotton/Lycra, such as is used for exercise wear. It is more durable than 100% cotton, fits beautifully, yet still has the softness and absorbancy of cotton. You can buy 45" wide stretch lace: this could be nice as a camisole or the bodice of a nightgown. Or use it as a yoke on panties, slips or camisoles. Woven fabrics can also be used, although they are often used on the bias. (refer to the section on "Bias" in Appendix B: Dictionary of Fabrics, page 167, for more information) Since lace does not ravel it is very easy to work with: any piece of lace can be placed on top of another, zig-zagged together, and the raw edges trimmed. For more lingerie ideas refer to the chapters on "Thread" and "Decorative Techniques," or look at expensive ready-to-wear. Lingerie is one place you can let your imagination go free. (refer to Appendix D: Sources, page 189 for mail ordering lingerie supplies)

OUTDOOR WEAR

Much effort has been made to design high performance outdoor clothing which is comfortable and functional. Initially many items were designed for specific sports such as skiing, backpacking or hunting. However, their functional design has made these garments popular for general use. Many patterns and fabrics designed for this market are available to the home sewer. (refer to Appendix D: Sources, page 189) Appendix B: Dictionary of Fabrics discusses specialized techniques for several of these fabrics, such as coated fabrics and bulky fabrics (including polar fleece). By sewing your own you can save money, ensure a proper fit, and get a customized design. These are wonderful fabrics: attractive, durable and functional. They can be used in a variety of styles, not just the ultra-practical styles commonly shown. Have fun!

RIPPING OUT A SERGER STITCH

Ripping out a serged seam ("As you sew so shall you rip.") is as easy or easier than ripping a conventional straight-stitch seam. On some fabrics you can simply pull out the needle thread. If your fabric is too thick or spongy for this, first run a seam ripper under the upper looper thread, cutting all its loops. Then look at the bottom of the stitch and catch a loop of the lower looper thread. Pull on this loop, and the lower looper thread will pull out of the seam. Then it is easy to pull out the needle thread, and there are just a few pieces of upper looper thread to pick off. If you have a decorative thread in the upper looper which you do not want to cut, you can cut the lower looper threads instead. Pull on the left needle thread to pull out the lower looper threads then the seam will come apart. It is somewhat more difficult to pull out than when the upper looper thread is cut, because the needle thread must pull the cut pieces of lower looper thread up through the fabric.

4-THREAD OR 3-THREAD STITCH?

The 4-thread overlock stitch is wider and stiffer than a 3-thread overlock stitch, but it is also more secure. If the fabric is free to move around inside the stitch it can fray, and cause the seam to fail. By securing the middle of the stitch to the fabric so the fabric cannot move around inside the stitch, the 4-thread overlock can be wider while still producing a secure stitch. I use a 4-thread stitch when finishing the edges of very ravel-prone wovens. I also use it whenever constructing anything out of a woven fabric unless I am using a 5-thread stitch. I also use a 4-thread overlock for bulky fabrics, or knits prone to raveling such as sweater knits. I use a 3-thread overlock or narrow 4-thread overlock for finishing the edges of most wovens, and for seaming most knits. A 3-thread stitch will generally stretch a little more than a 4-thread stitch with the same tensions. A narrow 4-thread is nice for swimsuits and exercise wear, because it helps to keep the Lycra threads from pulling out of the seam allowance. The narrowest 3-thread is best for tricot lingerie. A wide 3-thread overlock should not be used except for some decorative serging techniques. If your machine uses a double needle for the 4-thread overlock, use a narrow stitch width when using a single needle. If your machine uses two single needles for a 4-thread overlock, use just the right needle for a 3-thread overlock. If not using a needle always remove it from the machine.

PREWASHING FABRIC

Washing fabric before sewing removes finishes that can interfere with sewing. Prewashing helps ensure the garment will not shrink after you make it up. If any selvedges have puckered or rippled as a result of prewashing, you can cut out the garment without using those selvedges. You also know how the fabric will wash before you invest your time in a garment. If you are wondering whether a particular fabric is washable, serge around a small piece of it and wash it to see how you like the results.

Wash as you intend to wash the garment, or more. If you normally use a warm wash and dry, prewash with a warm or even hot wash and dry. If the fabric shrinks a lot when washed the first time, wash it a second time to remove residual shrinkage.

For prewashing fabric, serge the raw ends before washing. Not only does this prevent raveling, you can also tell at a glance whether a piece of fabric has been pre-washed. (Now I know that none of you ever "stash" fabric, but I am telling you this just in case you might need to someday. You know, the one of a kind piece or the great price.)

If the fabric is subject to curling, fold in half crosswise and serge the three open sides together. Most single knits will curl: this includes tee-shirt knits, lighter weight cotton/Lycras, sweater knits, cotton velours and stretch terries. Also, some wovens such as twills (denim, many bottom weight fabrics) will curl when prewashed. After washing cut off the serged seam and open out before laying out pattern pieces.

Knit or woven woollens can be steam shrunk, by you or by a dry-cleaner. To preshrink wool, get a bedsheet wet in as hot water as you can stand and wring it out, or run it through a short hot wash and spin cycle in the washing machine. Roll the wool in it and let sit several hours, wrapped in plastic. Unroll the wool and lay it out to dry. A plastic covered bed works well. Or tumble in a dryer on the air cycle, no heat.

FLAT CONSTRUCTION

One method for assembling garments is called "flat construction." This means finishing garment edges before all seams are made, so that no circular sewing is required. Edge finishes, ribbing, elastic and hems are all done this way. For example, one shoulder seam would be sewn, a strip of ribbing would be sewn onto the neck edge, then the other shoulder seam would be sewn, including the ribbing (see Figure 4-12). The ribbing ends up with an external seam which shows from the right side, and the end of the seam is likely to pull out (we have all seen it happen). Elastic is similarly applied flat then sewn into the seam, and we have all seen the ends of elastic pulling out of seams. I feel the ribbing or elastic should be sewn together into a ring, then sewn into a circular opening. Hems and edge finishes should be made _after_ all seams are made, using the techniques described for sewing in a circle. Flat construction may require somewhat less skill but it does not save much time and it produces a poorer quality garment. Of course, for some applications it is appropriate.

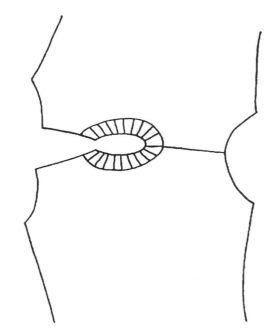

Figure 4-12: *Ribbing Sewn into Neck*

SOME IDEAS

I use the serger to make dress tights for my daughters out of swim-suit or exercise-wear fabric, or stretch lace yardage. They are more durable and warmer than purchased tights, plus my girls prefer the appearance. Use a pattern for exercise tights and add feet.

Any tights will fit better if the greatest stretch is going around the body, but they will fit a growing girl longer if the greatest stretch is going lengthwise.

For an adult, with the greatest stretch going around the body, the length of the tights should be slightly less than the distance from the wearer's waist to where the bottom of the tights will fall. The pattern is probably drafted for the greatest stretch going lengthwise, so you need to check the width at critical points if making this change: it may need taking in.

For a child, with the greatest stretch going lengthwise, measure across the pattern in the hip and thigh areas and adjust if necessary so the tights will be slightly smaller than the child. (Remember to double the hip measurement, and to subtract seam allowances. On the pattern measure the hip above the widening for the crotch.) Make the child's tights slightly less than the distance from waist to where the bottom edge of the tights will fall. For dress tights this will be the distance from the waist to the tip of the pointed toe.

Some fabric stretches more than other fabric, so the best gauge is to take a length of fabric and stretch it "some" until it feels about right, then measure how long it is before and after stretching. This will give an idea of how much smaller the pattern should be than the equivalent body measurement. Measure stretch in both directions.

If you want feet on the tights you have to modify a pattern for exercise tights. These come to the ankle, with or without a stirrup. The exercise tights are meant to fit snug over the ankle and not fit over the heel. Since the dress tights will have to fit around the heel you will probably want to make them somewhat wider through the heel. If you want to be accurate you can measure around the wearer's heel, subtract about 25% for the stretch of the fabric, and make the tights that width. (see Figure 4-13)

If you want comfortable, well-fitting tights that do not pull in the crotch, make sure the back crotch length is enough longer than the front. Many patterns are not

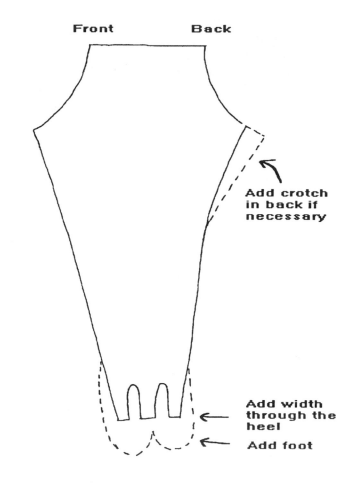

Figure 4-13: Changing pattern for stirrup tights to pattern for footed tights

drafted this way. See Figure 4-13 for the necessary correction. Also check the crotch depth and crotch length, if you normally change these when making slacks. Knits are, of course, much more forgiving than woven fabrics.

If making tights which end at the ankle, a nice touch is to finish the ankle edge with a 2" to 4" wide strip of stretch lace, shortening the pattern as necessary to allow for the width of the lace. This is the same type of lace used for waistbands on fine lingerie, and is available where lingerie supplies are sold. (refer to section on "Supplies," page 189).

Napkins and handkerchiefs are easily made with a rolled edge finish. (refer to section on "Narrow Rolled Edge," page 46) Often the purchased ones are made of non-absorbant polyester, despite the fact that both napkins and hankies are much more effective if they are an absorbant fiber such as cotton. Napkins work better if they are made from a slightly heavier weight fabric than broadcloth. Paper napkins are expensive and non-ecological, and nowhere near as nice as cloth ones. If you have enough cloth napkins you can toss them in whenever doing the laundry: then if you fold them right out of the dryer they do not need ironing. Another nice "luxury" is cloth hankies. They are much more gentle than paper: the red noses that people get when they have a cold or allergies are primarily from rubbing their noses with the wood fibers in paper tissues. Again, make enough to last from one washing to another. Use handkerchief linen or 100% cotton broadcloth. For a woman's hankie you can zig-zag on a lace edging after you do the rolled edge, butting the lace against the rolled edge (see Figure 4-14). Use about a 2 by 2 zig-zag. (If your machine has a 2-step zig-zag this is a good place to use it.) Leave the lace long enough to overlap in the corners. After the lace is applied to the four sides, zig-zag diagonally out from each corner to the edge of the lace, then trim lace to stitching. 100% cotton interlock makes an unconventional but nice fabric for handkerchiefs: you can even use it double thickness. Napkins and handkerchiefs make nice presents too, expensive to buy and easy to make.

Step I

Zigzag each strip of
Lace to Hankie

Step II

Zigzag out from each
corner

Step III

Trim Lace at corners to
the stitching

Figure 4-14: *Lace Edging for Hankies*

If you have two identical pairs of panty hose, each with one bad leg, cut off the two bad halves and serge the two good halves together with a narrow stretchy stitch. It will ripple, just like the original.

Fake fur (refer to section on "Fake Fur," page 170) is great for warm winter accessories. Make a scarf from 1/4 yard of fake fur. Serge the long edges together to make a cylinder and turn right side out. Use the techniques for beginning and ending at a corner (refer to section on "Serging Corners," page 62) to secure and conceal your chains. Leave the ends of the cylinder open so it will lie flat no matter how it is twisted. Fake fur is also wonderful for lining hats and vests, or making sweaters.

Receiving blankets for newborns work much better if made from a knit fabric: they do not come unwrapped as readily. Look for a 100% cotton fabric. If the fabric is suitable they can double as towels. Use two layers if desired. Serge around the four sides, perhaps with a soft pretty pearl cotton. (refer to section on "Cotton Threads," page 96) Cotton velour tends to curl, but what about two layers, serged wrong sides together? You could also add a hood. A handy thing to have is a baby's bath towel, generous sized, with a hood on one long edge (see Figures 4-15 and 4-16).

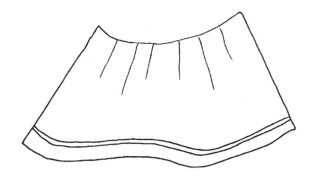

Figure 4-15: *Baby Towel Step I:*

Pleat along long edge of towel

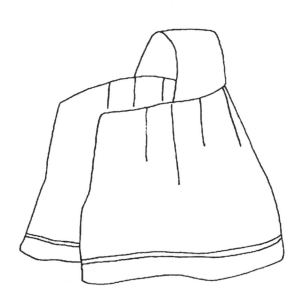

Figure 4-1: *Baby Towel Step II:*
Add hood over pleats

CHAPTER 5

THREAD

A large variety of threads can be used in the serger, both practical and decorative. These threads also come in a variety of forms, including large and small cones, spools and tubes. Most serging is done with regular serger thread.

BASIC THREAD

Although a wide variety of threads can be used in a serger, most of your sewing will be done with regular serger thread. This is somewhat finer than the thread you normally use on a conventional machine. It also has a special finish because of the high speed that sergers operate at. It comes cross-wound on cones, which hold more thread and facilitate proper feeding. Since serger thread is finer than conventional sewing thread, I like to use it on my conventional machine when sewing lightweight fabrics. I use a cone thread stand to hold the cone. It is also nice when blind hemming by hand or machine. As always, good quality thread works better. Good quality thread is smooth with little fuzz, and has a subtle sheen. Old thread can become brittle and break easily.

It is important that thread feed evenly and smoothly when serging. If you use spools of conventional thread on your serger you must put a spool cap on top (see Figure 1-17 on page 24). These come as accessories with your serger, and look like little frisbees with holes in the middle. They ensure the thread feeds properly, without dragging on the edge of the spool. When using tubes of thread remove the cone holders from the thread spindles. When using larger cones turn these cone holders upside down, so the wider part is on top.

For very lightweight fabrics you will get a finer edge or seam with extra-fine thread, sometimes sold as lingerie thread. Nylon lingerie thread is sold on cones and polyester lingerie thread is sold on spools. The nylon thread is stronger but the color choice is more limited.

If your needle tension is proper, the only thread that shows from the right side of the garment is the needle thread, or the left-hand needle thread if you are using both needles. Therefore, use a properly matched thread in the needle. This can be a spool of conventional machine thread, since the needle uses relatively little thread. In the loopers, use a thread that is "close enough." Buy the thread for the loopers on large cones, since loopers use a lot of thread and you will only be needing a few basic colors.

Many home sergers have a very narrow base to support the bottom of the cones. Consequently the base of the cone tends to slip over the edge so the cone is not vertical and thread does not feed properly. This problem usually occurs with the left needle and the lower looper cones, since they are at the ends of the thread stand. Some machines come with clear plastic circles about 3" in diameter, with a hole in the middle. One of these is placed over each of the pins that holds the thread, after removing any cone holders. You can easily make a similar device yourself from cardboard or light weight plastic. Another option is to put a small hole in the middle of a plastic lid, such as comes on soft margarine containers or fast food soft drink containers.

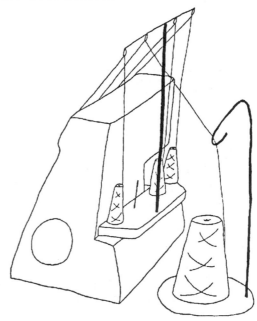

Industrial sergers can accept larger cones of thread than home sergers. If you should happen to get some cones which are too large to fit on your domestic serger, put them on the table directly behind your machine. Feed the ends of the thread into your telescope as you would normally. If you are having trouble getting the thread to feed properly, put the offending cone on a thread stand. (see Figure 5-1) This will ensure the thread feeds properly off the cone. Then you can take the thread end from the top of the thread stand and feed it into your machine's telescope. Make sure the cone of thread for the needle is out of the way of fabric as it comes out the back of the machine. If you have it on a cone stand you can move the stand slightly to the right. Often you can get one or two cones up

Figure 5-1: Thread Stand

on the machine even if all will not fit. If so get the needle thread cone up out of the way.

SPECIAL THREADS

One of the exciting things about a serger is the wide variety of threads you can use with it. Since the eye of a looper is larger than the eye of a needle, it will easily accept such things as fine yarn, crochet thread and metallics. The basic serger thread is the easiest to use. You will probably need to experiment with stitch width, length and tensions when using other threads. Remember to sew more slowly when using special threads in your machine: it will perform better. In this section I discuss some basic kinds of thread and how to use them. In the next chapter on "Decorative Effects," you can find many ideas for using these special threads.

Many of these decorative threads are heavier than regular serger thread. The rule of thumb is that if you can get it through the looper eye with your floss threader (refer to section on "Threading," page 21) you can probably sew with it in the looper. For thicker, heavier threads you will need a longer stitch length, and probably a wider stitch width.

Heavier threads also require looser tensions. Here are some suggestions if the thread is still too tight after loosening the tension disks completely. On most machines there is an "invisible" tension disk where the thread first comes into the machine. On some machines it is squeezed between the handle and a piece of foam. Bringing it over the top of the handle may make the difference in getting a certain thread to work. On some machines the thread comes off the telescope into a hole through a piece of metal. Then it wraps around and goes through another hole in the same piece of metal. Rethreading it so it goes through only one hole will put less tension on the thread. Sometimes it goes through a little pinch guide after it comes off the telescope: remove it if necessary. Sometimes you need to remove the thread entirely from both the "invisible" tension disk and the regular tension disks. On machines with beehive tension disks simply remove the thread from the tension disks but leave it in the guide it would normally go into after the tension disks. With vertical tension disks you will probably have to put something over the top of the disks to keep the thread from going into them. Although you can use tape, I like to put something like a 6" ruler over the top of the tension disks to keep the heavy thread out of its tension disks. If your machine has a separate needle plate for the narrow rolled edge this stays in place well when you put it on top of the tension disks. (The other threads are underneath and unaffected by whatever you are using.)

Most of the decorative threads work best in the _upper_ looper. If you look inside your machine you will see that the thread path for the upper looper is shorter and straighter than the thread path for the lower looper. You can use flat-locking or the wrapped stitch to display the upper looper decorative thread. A rolled edge works well with the finer decorative threads, such as metallics, rayon and the finer cottons. Sometimes you can get a balanced stitch to work with decorative threads in both loopers, especially if you sew slowly. Make sure your stitch is long enough.

Variegated thread is available, particularly in the cotton threads. This gives bands or strips of color. Fine variegated threads can be combined for a richer effect.

You can combine any of the finer threads. For example, texturized nylon gives coverage and a metallic or rayon gives sheen. You can combine threads to get the color you want, or combine variegated threads to get a more beautiful effect. Combining threads can give better coverage, particularly for the narrow rolled edge. Loosen the looper tension slightly. You will probably need to increase stitch length, and may need to increase stitch width. Make sure that the combination of threads is not too heavy for your machine. You may need to use one or more thread stands to handle multiple threads. Put each thread on a separate stand or on the stand that is part of the serger. Feed the threads together into the serger telescope and through the machine.

Some of these decorative threads are very slippery, particularly the rayons, invisible thread and some metallics. They tend to slip down and get caught under the bottom of the cone. The solution is to use the thread nets which came with your machine. Fold one in half and put it over just the _bottom_ part of the cone, making a sort of cup for the cone to sit it. (see Figure 1-16 on page 24) The reason for folding it is so the thread cannot catch on the cut edges. If using thread nets on large cones of thread you may not be able to make a cup with the thread net. If so, make sure you get the lower edge of the net tucked under the cone so the thread will not catch on the edge of the net and pull it off the cone. If you do not have any nets, you can make them by serging together pieces of old panty hose. Make them just barely tight enough because any pressure will change tensions. Another option is to put a disk of fiber fill underneath the cone, large enough to extend to the edge of the cone and thick enough to touch the entire bottom surface of the cone.

Needle lube reduces fraying and kinking of decorative threads, particularly metallics. Put it on the cone of thread. Needle lube is a silicon based lubricant: it comes as a clear liquid in a small bottle. Use by running it lightly over the thread, making multiple vertical stripes.

Many decorative threads do not come on crosswound cones, and yet the thread must feed smoothly and evenly to make a beautiful stitch. So, you may need to improvise. You can take an empty cone and wind it yourself. By getting on the phone with the yellow pages in front of you, you may find a place which serves industrial customers or machine knitters and can wind cones for you. (Appendix D: Sources, page 189, has a source for cone winders) For many threads you can use a yarn winder, available from places that supply machine knitters. You can pull out a few yards of your thread, run your machine until it has used it up, then pull out some more. You may be able to put some balls of thread into bowls, skeins of yarn into glasses or jars, tubes onto your thread stand. You may need to use your fingers to gently pinch the thread just before it goes into the machine to prevent kinks. You will have good stories to tell.

I find my machine is more tolerant of a variety of threads when I am just using one needle. Some machines are much more fussy about such matters than others. Generally, a machine with good solid tensions will handle a variety of threads well. Still, experimentation is the key to success.

Many of these threads can be difficult to find. Some sewing machine dealers carry an excellent stock of decorative threads. Other sources are yarn stores, fabric stores and stores which carry embroidery supplies. Stores which supply machine knitters will also have some good stuff. Also check craft stores. Some of these threads can be mail-ordered. Refer to Appendix D: Sources, page 189.

The finer decorative threads can be used in the needle as well. If your machine uses conventional needles, (Refer to the section on "Needles," page 19) you can use a top stitching needle in your machine. This needle has a larger eye, and so can accept heavier threads or a combination of threads. You may have difficulty using some of the more delicate threads in the needle, such as rayon and metalic threads.

TEXTURIZED NYLON

Texturized nylon is a stretchy untwisted nylon thread. It was originally sold under the name "Woolly Nylon" by *YLI*. Now several companies have similar threads. When selecting texturized nylon make sure it is fluffy and elastic. It is crimped so the individual fibers look like a zig-zag. This makes it stretchy. When it is not stretched the fibers spread out, covering edges beautifully. Therefore it is often used in the upper looper, especially for a narrow rolled edge. Since it is stretchy tensions need to be loosened. Especially when using it in the upper looper make sure tensions are loose enough so the texturized nylon "spreads" out and covers the edge well. Sometimes the stretchiness is an advantage. In the lower looper it can help a narrow rolled edge to roll over tightly. In the needle it can put extra stretch in a seam (eg. for swimwear) and reduce rippling (eg. for sweater knits). Refer to the section on "Threading," page 21, for suggestions on getting it through the needle. Since it is nylon it is strong. Since it is fine it can be combined with other threads, for example rayon (the texturized nylon gives strength and covers well, the rayon gives sheen).

RAYON THREAD

Rayon thread looks like silk and comes in a wide range of brilliant colors. It comes in two weights, 50 and 30, which are about the weight of normal sewing thread. The 50 weight is finer and more commonly available, on both tubes and cones. A thread net is almost essential for rayon thread to keep it from slipping under the spool. (refer to the section on "Special Threads," page 90). It is not as strong as conventional serger thread. If you sew slowly it can be used in the needle for seams which will not be under a lot of stress. It is generally used in the loopers for decorative effect. Especially for the 50 weight rayon the tensions may need to be tightened slightly. A store which stocks supplies for machine embroidery will carry rayon thread if your dealer does not. Monogramming machines use cones of this. You can check the yellow pages for dealers who sell or service these machines.

A heavier type of rayon thread is sold under the brand name *Decor 6*. It is a heavy untwisted rayon thread which can be used in needles or loopers. It is beautiful. You may need to get on the phone to track down a source for this. Try yarn stores and shops specializing in decorative sewing. Some sewing machine dealers are a wonderful source for this and many other decorative threads. Otherwise you can mail-order. (refer to Appendix D: Sources, page 189) You can also combine strands of finer rayon thread, perhaps combining different colors, to get a similar effect.

Pearl rayon is also available. It is heavier than *Decor 6* and about the weight of the heavier pearl cottons. (refer to section below on "Cotton Threads").

Yet another product is serger ribbon. This is a fine very flexible rayon ribbon which can be fed through the upper looper. It is heavier than the *Decor 6* or pearl rayon, and beautiful. Use it with a wide long stitch to show it off. Some fabric stores carry this, as well as craft stores. You can also try the places mentioned above for *Decor 6*.

INVISIBLE THREAD

Nylon monofilament thread is now available in a very fine weight, 80 or 90 weight. You will need to use thread nets with this thread. (refer to section on "Special Threads," page 90) This is as fine as a hair and nearly invisible. It comes in two colors, smoke and clear. This is primarily used in flat-locking and couching. (refer to the section on "Decorative Flat-Locking," page 106, and the section on "Couching," page 117) You may need to mail-order this thread. It is much finer than conventional transparent thread.

FUSIBLE THREAD

This is ordinary thread coated with fusible glue, like fusible interfacing is coated with and fusible web is made out of. It is fused after sewing, using a damp press cloth and a "wool" setting on the iron. This can be put in the upper or lower looper. It can also be used in the bobbin of a conventional machine. If the edge of a facing is serged with this it can be fused onto the garment. Hems can be fused as well. It can be used to make fusible passementerie. (refer to section on "Decorative Uses of Chain," page 136) If serging the edge of a very ravel-prone fabric you can put this in one or both loopers, then fuse it afterwards to help secure the edge. Use one of the Teflon fusing sheets to protect your iron and ironing board. If used in both loopers this may make the edge too scratchy to wear next to the skin. If used to serge the raw edges of wovens, the seam allowances can be fused flat to the garment after the seams are sewn. (Make sure the fusible thread is on the wrong side of the fabric so you can fuse it to the garment rather than the iron.) There are many other uses for this thread, such as sewing on buttons and making buttonholes: fuse after sewing to secure stitching.

Use care when fusing as heat can damage the fabric or other threads. Acrylic and nylon are easily damaged by heat. Most yarns you will be serging with are acrylic, as are many sweater knits. Invisible thread is nylon, as is texturized nylon. Either one can be damaged by heat, as can sheer tricot and other nylon fabrics. Some metallics may tarnish. If using nylon or acrylic with a fusible thread protect the other threads or fabrics while fusing by using a thick well-dampened pressing cloth. Test on a sample first to make sure iron temperatures are low enough. You may need to use a longer fusing time with slightly lower iron temperatures.

YARN

Fine acrylic or wool yarn can be used in the serger loopers, especially the upper looper. Fingering weight yarn works, or the yarn sold for standard gauge knitting machines. You can also use the yarn sold for "punch needle," which can be found in craft stores. The yarn for knitting machines is already on cones and the punch needle yarn is on tubes: this makes it much easier to use them in the serger. (refer to section on "Special Threads," page 90, for tips on handling skeins of yarn) Pull on the yarn to make sure it is strong enough. If it breaks easily when you pull on it will break in the serger. Avoid yarn with slubs or excessive texture. If you find a gorgeous textured yarn, try sewing _over_ it. (refer to section on "Couching," page 117) You will need to loosen tensions when sewing with yarn, probably increase stitch length, perhaps increase stitch width. Make sure your tensions are loose enough so the yarn can "fluff" and spread out.

METALLIC THREADS

A wide variety of metallic threads and yarns are available for the serger. The finer metallic threads can be used in the needle, although most metallics are generally used in the loopers. If using a metallic in the needle sew slowly, because these are fragile threads. For heavier metallic threads and metallic yarns check out yarn stores. Metallic threads are also sold for punch needle. Generally tensions do not need to be altered for metallic threads, but will need loosening for metallic yarns.

COTTON THREADS

In this category are pearl cotton, crochet thread, top-stitching thread, embroidery floss and fine cotton yarns. Cotton is less stretchy and generally stiffer than acrylic or wool yarns. The heavier cottons need looser tensions, plus a fairly long and wide stitch.

Pearl cotton is shiny; the *DMC* pearl cotton is almost like silk. *DMC* pearl cotton comes on small balls in two weights, 8 and 5, 8 being finer than 5. Either weight can be used: the finer weight is about the weight of the 30 weight rayon thread. It comes in many beautiful colors. It is available in stores which carry embroidery supplies. A heavier pearl cotton is also available on cones especially for sergers.

Crochet thread comes in various weights. The finest is 30 weight, slightly heavier than normal sewing thread. 10 and 20 weights are also available. The 10, 20 and 30 weights can be hard to find. The most common weight is simply called "crochet thread." It is about the weight of top-stitching thread. Crochet threads are harder twisted and stiffer than pearl cotton. Colors are generally more limited.

Top-stitching thread comes on spools, which only hold a small amount. It is similar in effect to crochet thread or heavier pearl cotton.

Fine cotton yarns are put up on cones for use on knitting machines. If they do not have slubs they can be used on the serger. The effect is similar to pearl cotton.

6-strand embroidery floss is difficult to feed into the machine, but comes in a wide range of beautiful colors. Individual strands of different colors can be combined for beautiful effects. (refer to the section on "Special Threads," page 90, for tips on feeding into machine)

100% cotton machine embroidery thread, is a very fine thread which comes in a wide range of colors and has a nice sheen. It comes on spools. It is wonderful for combining strands of different colors, or for combining strands of variegated thread. If you are combining threads from several spools, here is a way to feed them all together into the serger. Put all your spools onto a straight piece of metal, such as a skewer or a section of stiff coat hanger wire. String your spools onto the holder so they unwind in alternate directions. Put a metal washer or piece of plastic between each spool, so they can turn freely. Put two piles of books behind the serger and stick one end of the skewer into each pile (see Figure 5-2), so you can feed the thread ends into the serger. Make sure your tension is loose enough.

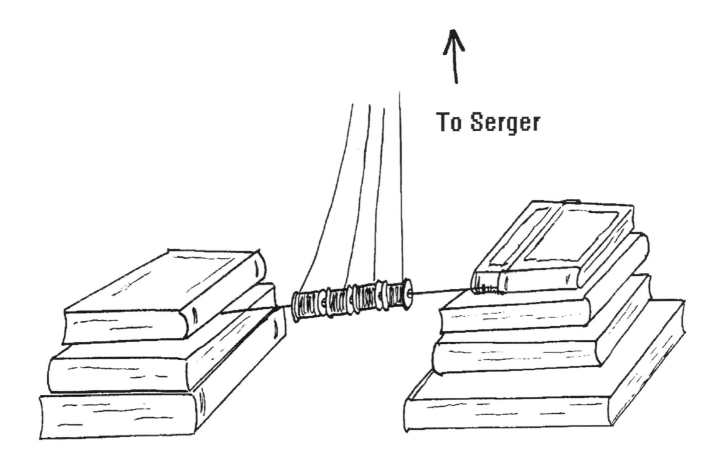

Figure 5-2: *Cotton: Feeding multiple spools of thread*

CHAPTER 6
DECORATIVE EFFECTS

There are many fascinating decorative techniques for the serger. However even the most basic stitch can be dressed up with a special thread. As you learned in the chapter on "Thread" your serger will accept a wide variety of threads, even fine yarns and ribbons. When working on a specific project or just for the fun of it, sit down and play with different threads, settings and techniques. After a while you will find yourself using techniques in new ways, or even inventing new techniques. If there is a certain effect you want to get, think about different ways you could get that effect. Or, think about different ways you could use a given technique. Make notes for future reference: on an 8.5 X 11 piece of thin cardboard or heavy paper note settings, fabric, threads, amounts used of certain special threads, any observations or ideas for other uses. Then staple on a sample of the stitch, and perhaps a sample of a special thread. You can put these in a 3-ring binder labeled, "My Bag of Tricks." (Another option for storing your samples is plastic sleeves or pouches, 3-ring punched, available at stationary supply stores.)

Be playful: glitz can be artistic and beautiful. Or if you wish you can be elegant, delicate, romantic, dramatic, playful, whatever. As you are reading this chapter try to picture different effects you can get with these techniques. For example, strings of fine pearls on a wedding dress has a very different effect than strings of sequins on a gold lame and black velvet jacket, yet both use the techniques for attaching beads. Or you could use the same techniques for attaching a fine chain to weight the bottom of lace or sheer curtains.

Generally you will be happier with your results if you sew more slowly while doing decorative serging. You can watch more carefully how you are positioning the fabric, plus anything else you are attaching. Also, the serger will perform better. You will always want to try these techniques on scraps first. That way you can get the settings right, make sure you like the effect and practice any unfamiliar techniques.

The serger has two advantages over a conventional machine for decorative effects. It is much faster, and it will accept heavier decorative threads. Yet a serger stitch must be formed over the edge of the fabric. So, many of the following techniques are done over a fold in the middle of a garment section, to get decoration wherever you want it. Mark the lines where you want the decoration, fold the fabric along one of the lines, and start serging. It is relatively easy to turn corners and follow gentle curves, but tight curves can be a problem. The following sections detail the different decorative serging techniques you can use. If you have a 2-thread chainstitch and can disable the overlock stitch (refer to section on "2-Thread Chainstitch," page 143) you can put a decorative something in that looper and sew in the middle of garment sections without folding.

In this chapter I assume you are familiar with the material in chapters 1 through 5, particularly chapters 1, 2 and 3. However, if you need some information from an earlier chapter to do one of these techniques, the section and page number is given so you can quickly look it up.

DECORATIVE CONSTRUCTION TECHNIQUES

Decorative serging is quick and easy, and can be used whenever making seams or finishing edges. This chapter is full of special techniques, but any stitch can be dressed up with a special thread.

Various edge finishes are easy and attractive, including couching trims, attaching lace, corded edges and the narrow rolled edge. (refer to relevant sections in this chapter) Even a plain serger stitch is wonderful with a decorative thread. When finishing edges with decorative serging you generally want both sides to appear finished. The narrow rolled edge, wrapped stitch and blanket stitch will always do this. Both sides of the balanced stitch will appear the same if the same thread is used in both upper and lower looper. Lighter weight decorative threads, such as metallics, texturized nylon or rayon can be used in both loopers for a balanced stitch. Sometimes, if you sew slowly, heavier threads can be used in both loopers. Or, you can do the wrapped stitch with the heavier thread in the upper looper only. Experiment with stitch width and length. You will get a more pronounced effect with a wider stitch and shorter stitch length. However, you may prefer the more open look of a longer stitch length. If you are concerned about protecting the edge from raveling you can fold a strip of sheer nylon tricot over it before serging then trim the tricot to the edge of the stitching afterwards. Or you can serge the edge with a matching or invisible thread before doing the decorative serging.

Flat-locked seams are naturals for displaying a decorative thread. Here are some more ideas.

Exposed seams

Exposed seams (sewn wrong sides together) are decorative, especially when they are made with a decorative thread and/or are lettuced. If the decorative thread is only in the upper looper, the seam can be top-stitched flat with an invisible or matching thread. Use a zig-zag stitch on knits.

Piping look

Narrow strips of ribbing or interlock cut on the crossgrain can be folded and sewn into seams of knit garments for a piping look that is easy and fashionable (see Figure 6-1). Some machines have an accessory, called a tape/piping guide, which will fold and guide a bias strip of woven fabric into the middle of a seam, producing this effect.

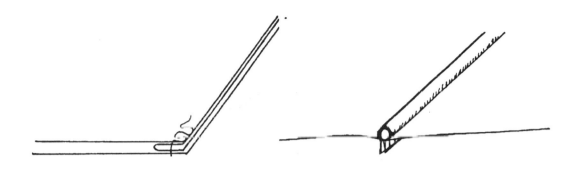

Figure 6-1: Strip of fabric folded into the seam

Top-Stitched seams

Serged seams sewn right sides together can be pressed to one side and top-stitched on a conventional machine. This helps secure the seam. It can also be used to accentuate style lines.

Both raw edges can be finished with a decorative thread before the seam is made. Then the seam is sewn with a straight stitch on a conventional machine, just outside the edge of the serger stitches, wrong sides together. Finally the seam allowances are pressed to each side and top-stitched (see Figure 6-2).

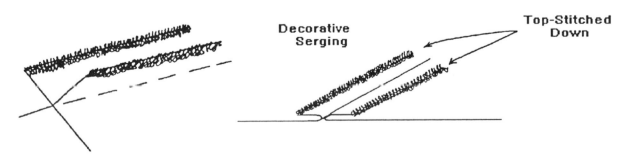

Figure 6-2: Serged Seams Top-Stitched

Facings

Facings can be attached to the garment with a decorative edge (see Figure 6-3). Put a decorative thread in the serger, place the facing on the garment wrong sides together and serge. You can also use the techniques for attaching beads, attaching lace or couching. (refer to relevant sections) This is a quick attractive finish.

Figure 6-3: *Facings attached with decorative serging*

Reverse Facings

The serger is a natural for reverse facings (see Figure 6-4), which are wonderful for such things as cardigan jackets. Instead of ending up on the wrong side of garment edges, the reverse facing is turned to the right side with the inner edge of the facing top-stitched onto the garment. Decorative serging is a natural way to finish the inner edge of a reverse facing before it is top-stitched. The facing can be in matching or contrasting fabric. Instead of the smooth edge of a normal facing, the inner edge of a reverse facing can be curved or scalloped as desired. Also, the reverse facing can be made wider than a normal facing. The first step in making a reverse facing is deciding if you want to change the inner edge of the facing. If you wish to make it more decorative, copy the facing pattern onto another piece of paper and draw the desired style line for the new facing. Cut out the facing sections and interface if necessary. Sew the facing sections together and finish the inner edge with decorative serging. Assemble

Figure 6-4: Reverse Facings

the garment sections except for the facings. If you wish a decorative serged edge on the outer edge of the garment, place wrong side of the facing to the right side of the garment and serge together. If you wish a plain edge, place right side of the facing to the wrong side of the garment, serge, turn and press. The last step is to top-stitch the inner edge of the facing to the garment. Use a matching or invisible thread.

GUIDING FABRIC

When serging a seam or finishing an edge the knives can be used as a guide for accurately positioning fabric. If you wish to avoid cutting something while you are serging it you can move the knife as far to the right as possible, thereby increasing stitch width. However I do not recommend swinging the knife out of cutting position. Not only does it serve as a guide, it also ensures nothing will go too far to the right and collide with the upper looper. For most tasks you can accurately guide fabric just to the left of the knife. If you do swing the knife out of the way, watch carefully what you are doing and move it back into position as soon as possible.

Decorative techniques often require positioning "stuff" (yarn, cord, trims, lace, ribbon, etc.) somewhere to the left of the knife. Often a fold of fabric must be guided to the left of the knives, with or without attaching stuff. The description of each decorative technique in this chapter details where fabric is to be guided, plus where to guide anything that is being attached to it. This section details _how_ to guide the fabric and stuff.

Accessories are available which facilitate guiding fabric plus anything being attached to it, and these are described in the section on "Special Attachments," page 153. Here are two techniques which can be used on any machine without special accessories.

> For many techniques it is necessary to guide a fold of fabric accurately between the knives and the needle. To do this you can put a long piece of tape on the bed of the machine just in front of the presser foot. Make sure the tape does not touch the feed-dogs. Mark lines on the tape slightly to the right of each needle. You may also want a line halfway between the right needle and the knives. It may help to make these marks different colors. Use a ruler to draw these lines accurately and position the tape accurately. (It is easier to guide the fabric if you have a longer line.)

> For some techniques you need a mark on the presser foot. You can use nail polish, acrylic paint, typing correction fluid, whatever is handy. You can use the marked presser foot instead of the tape for any technique, but it is nice to have the longer guide line of the tape when possible. Mark both needle positions on the foot. This is useful on the standard foot, the beading foot and the narrow rolled edge foot (if your machine has a special foot for this stitch).

Whatever tools you are using, you can always look down on top of the presser foot, and see where the needle is sewing. Edges of folds can be guided very accurately this way, and this method can be used along with another tool such as a blind hem foot.

Guiding Fabric Without Attaching Anything

Many techniques involve guiding a fold of fabric just to the right of the needle without attaching anything else to it. These include pintucks, flat-locking over a fold, serger lace and fagoting. The tools for these techniques are the tape (as described above), blind hem foot, seam guide or cloth guide accessory. Some machines offer a optional "cloth guide accessory" which is fastened to the bed of the machine in front of the presser foot and can adjusted sideways: fabric is guided along it. A magnetic seam guide functions similarly and can be used on most machines. A blind hem foot is available for most machines, and is the most accurate way to guide a fold of fabric. Accuracy is particularly important for flat-locking over a fold. However, many blind hem feet will not accept a wide flat-lock while most flat-locking over a fold is done with a wide flat-lock. This is because many blind hem feet only accept the right needle. Refer to the section on "Special Attachments," page 153 if you have this problem. Although you can also use the tape (as described above) for guiding fabric to the left of the knife, it is not as quick and easy to be accurate with it.

Guiding Fabric While Attaching Something

Light cording or fishline is sometimes incorporated into a stitch. This can be used for gathering heavy fabrics but is most commonly used with the narrow rolled edge stitch. (refer to section on "Decorative Narrow Rolled Edge," page 125) Some presser feet have a guide for light cording. Lacking this, an elastic foot with the clamp tension loosened can be used, or a foot with a tape guide. Some standard presser feet have a slot for tape in the front of the foot. Pull the cord gently to the right if using the elastic foot or tape guide, to keep the cord to the right of the needle. If you do not have a foot with a guide for cording you can put the cord over the front of the presser foot and to the right of the needle, then under the back of the foot. Hold the cord in place for the first few stitches until it is caught in the stitching. Then hold it to keep a little tension on it and sew slowly enough to make sure it stays in the stitching.

Often twill tape, lace, ribbon and various trims are positioned to be caught by the needle. Sometimes this is used to stabilize a seam, sometimes for couching or applying lace. There are several techniques and tools available to do this. If guiding something so just the right edge is caught by the needle, you can use a blind hem foot with whatever you are attaching being guided just to the left of the blade. Move the blade further to the right than you would have it for blind hemming, so you are more certain to catch the edge of your trim on every stitch. When you wish the right needle to catch just the right edge of a lace or trim but accuracy is not critical you can guide the lace or trim so it is just on the edge of the opening in the presser foot for the knife. Or, you can use a marked presser foot, as described above. If your elastic foot is open on the left you can use it for guiding wider trim and lace just to the left of the knife:

loosen the clamp tension completely. A foot with a tape guide can be used for guiding narrow ribbon or twill tape under the needle.

Sometimes when couching you want to guide narrow ribbon or yarn to the right of the needle. You can guide the ribbon or yarn just to the right of the blade on the blind hem foot. Another option is an elastic foot with the clamp tension loosened. Some feet with a tape guide are adjustable, so narrow ribbon can be positioned to the right of the needle and the left of the knives.

Many techniques involve attaching medium to heavy cord to fabric. These techniques include couching and serger piping. The best tool for these techniques is a beading foot. Some cords can be guided to the right of the blade on a blind hem foot. Medium weight cord can be guided over the front of a standard foot and under the back. Another option for lighter cord is a foot with a tape guide. Heavy cord can be tricky to guide without a beading foot, because there is a tendency for it to get caught in the stitching. If you do not have a beading foot here are some techniques you can use. If your machine has the upper knife coming up from below (refer to section on "Stitch Width and Knives," page 37) you can hold the cord and guide it over the top of the upper knife. If your machine has the upper knife coming from above, try putting the cord to the right of the knife: open the front door, feed the cord to the right of the knife, under the upper looper if it is on top of the stitch, and under the back of the presser foot. Then close the door and begin sewing, guiding the cord and keeping a little tension on it so it is being pulled slightly away from the needle. If the cord is too heavy for this use just the left needle, perhaps with a wrapped edge stitch if you cannot do a left needle narrow rolled edge. (refer to section on "Decorative Narrow Rolled Edge," page 125, for information on the left needle narrow rolled edge) Set the stitch width as wide as possible.

Refer to section on "Attaching Beads," page 112, for suggestions on attaching beads and sequins. Sequin strings may be guided over the front of a standard foot or to the right of the blade on a blind hem foot if you lack a beading foot.

DECORATIVE FLAT-LOCKING

(refer to section on "Flat-Locking," page 51, for information on flat-locking techniques) Flat-locking is wonderful for decorative effects. The upper looper will accept a wider variety of threads than the lower looper or needle. Many decorative threads, such as yarns or serger ribbon, only work well in the upper looper. With flat-locking this upper looper thread can be boldly displayed in the middle of the fashion fabric. (What about a pair of black dressy pants with a gold metallic stripe down the outseam?) If you are emphasizing the upper looper thread you will generally de-emphasize the needle and lower looper threads: they can match the upper looper thread or the background fabric, or they can be the new invisible thread. (refer to section on "Invisible Thread," page 94) In any case they would be a finer weight than the upper looper thread. Sometimes a decorative thread is put in the needle and the "ladder" side used as the right side. Another option is to use a matching or invisible thread in the needle and loopers. After flat-locking and pulling flat you can thread a yarn needle with something interesting (perhaps a richly textured yarn) and thread it through the ladder: catch only every third or fourth stitch so the something can stand out.

The technique of flat-locking over a fold offers many possibilities (see Figure 6-5). A line of decorative stitching can be placed anywhere on the garment, beginning and ending wherever desired. It can even be worked over gentle curves. (Mark the curve with chalk and sew slowly, adjusting as you go.) You can also turn corners. (refer to section on "Serging Corners," page 62) Flat-locking over a fold can be used in a garment with flat-locked seams to provide additional accent lines. The two seams are indistinguishable in appearance. The flat-locking over a fold can begin or end in the middle of the fabric. The thread chains can be pulled apart and threaded to the inside of the garment for knotting or left exposed as another decorative element.

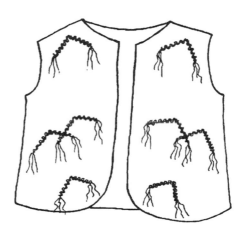

Figure 6-5: *Flat-locking over a fold*

Another flat-locking technique is having the upper and lower looper threads join down the middle of the looper side of the stitch. Begin by adjusting tensions for a normal flat-lock. Then tighten the upper looper tension as you loosen the lower looper until they meet in the middle of the stitch (see Figure 6-6). This stitch has virtually unlimited stretch. It can be used for attaching ribbing: sew wrong sides together so the looper side of the flat-lock stitch shows on the right side, and secure if necessary by top-stitching with a zig-zag stitch on a conventional machine after pulling flat.

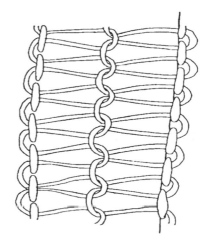

Figure 6-6: *Flat-locking with looper tensions balanced*

FLAT-LOCKED FRINGE

Flat-locking can be used to secure a fringe, as on a shawl or scarf. Cut the fabric to the finished dimensions, making sure all edges are on the straight of grain. Decide how deep the fringe is to be, for example three inches. You will need to mark a line that distance in from the edge, on all sides to be fringed. You can mark this line by pulling one or more threads, or with chalk and a ruler. Fold the first side to be fringed along this line. If you will be fringing all four sides of a rectangle, begin at the intersection of two of these lines. Using the techniques for flat-locking over a fold, flat-lock until you get to the next intersection. Using the techniques for turning outside corners (refer to section on "Serging Corners," page 62), clear the stitch finger, refold so the next side is ready to sew and flat-lock the next side. Continue, using the techniques for squares and rectangles described in the section on "Serging Corners." (see Figure 6-7)

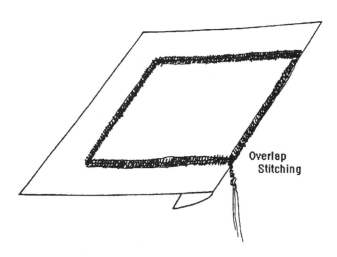

Figure 6-7: *Flat-locked fringe overlap stitching*

Sometimes you want to fringe a single edge, for example on a scarf, vest or skirt. Start at one side and flat-lock to the other (see Figure 6-8). For garment sections, make the fringe before sewing side seams. Secure the ends of the stitching with a straight stretch stitch on a conventional machine. If the side seams will be serged, you can use the techniques in the section on "Securing Seams," page 60, to secure and conceal the flat-lock chains. Use the techniques for beginning at a corner (refer to section on "Beginning at a Corner," page 62) to conceal the chain from the seam serging. For a scarf you may wish to fringe just the ends, but serge the sides with the same decorative thread: turn corners as described above.

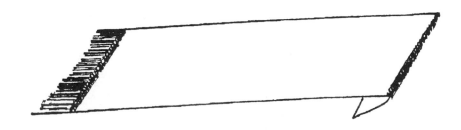

Figure 6-8: *Flat-locked fringe scarf*

When finished flat-locking, make the fringe by pulling out threads up to the line of flat-locking. If the fabric does not ravel readily, cut slashes in from the edge to the flat-locking every three inches.

If you wish you can couch a decorative something while flat-locking. (refer to the section on "Attaching Beads," page 112, and the section on "Couching," page 117) Or, you can use a decorative thread while flat-locking. What about a fine gold thread on a black challis shawl? Or delft blue yarn on a white wool scarf? Or fine beads couched around a fringed chiffon shawl?

FAGOTING

Flat-locking can be used to produce a fagoted seam. This is a space filled with lacy threads between two pieces of fabric. Finish each raw edge with a balanced stitch. Fold back edges about 1/2" and press with an iron. Place folded edges together and flat-lock using techniques for flat-locking over a fold. Pull apart. In order to get an open lacy effect use a long stitch length, and very loose needle and upper looper tensions. Set the tensions on a scrap of fabric so they hang off the edge of the fabric. Use a prominent decorative thread such as pearl cotton or metallic thread. The closer the folded edges of the fabric are to the needle the wider the stitch will be, especially if you are using a wide flat-lock. (refer to section on "Guiding Fabric," page 104) In order to keep the thread tensions from pulling in the edge of the stitch and making it narrower, you can put one or more strips of water soluble stabilizer under the fabric and next to the knives. Dissolve the stabilizer with water after sewing. (refer to glossary under "Water Soluble Stabilizer" for more information)

There are several ways to deal with the fabric edges. They can be secured by top-stitching on a conventional machine, perhaps with a decorative stitch. They can be flat-locked. (refer to section on "Flat-Locked Hemming," page 55: do not serge raw edges before fagoting) They can be secured by putting a narrow strip of fusible web between them and the fabric and fusing. Or they can be secured by using fusible thread when serging the raw edge then fusing in place. (refer to section on "Fusible Thread," page 94)

Fagoting is nice for attaching lace to tricot, for example at the bottom edge of a slip. No raw edges need to be secured, so the fagoting need not be done over folded edges. In order to get sufficient stretch, loosen the lower looper and tighten the upper looper tensions, as described in the section on "Decorative Flat-Locking," page 106.

A beautiful effect can be achieved by combining fagoting with spaghetti tubing. (refer to section on "Spaghetti Tubing," page 110 for directions on making and turning the tubing) Use fagoting to join the tubes together into lacy fabric. Press the tubing flat, put two strips of it under the needle and fagot, pull flat, put the next strip of tubing on top of one of the strips already fagoted, fagot those two strips together, and continue. You will end up with the strips of tubing joined by lacy bands of fagoting.

SPAGHETTI TUBING

Spaghetti tubing can be made on the serger. Silky, slippery fabrics are much easier to turn: allow a slightly wider opening if turning a non-slippery fabric. Cut a strip of fabric 1 and 1/4" to 1 and 1/2" wide. Fold it in half, right sides together, with a strand of crochet cord or something similar inside the fold. Let the cord extend out 6" on both ends (see Figure 6-9). Place the raw edges next to the knives and sew with a balanced stitch, making sure not to catch the cord in the stitching. Tie one of the thread chains to the cord with an overhand knot (a square knot will tend to pull out while turning the tube), trim the ends of the knot to 1" and pull on the other end of the cord to turn right side out. An accessory is available on some machines which can assist this process. It is called a tape/piping guide. It will guide a cord into a folded strip of fabric while the edges of the fabric are being serged together. The fabric strip should be 1 and 1/4" wide. Another technique is to make a thread

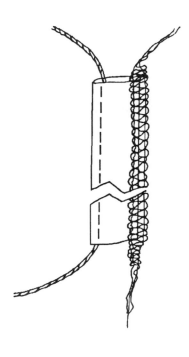

Figure 6-9: *Spaghetti tubing*

chain 6" longer than the strip of fabric. Leave the chain attached to the machine but place into the fold of the fabric as described above. Sew and turn, making sure not to catch a loop of the chain in the stitching. This is not as easy as with the crochet cord, because the chain tends to get caught in the stitching.

Here is a technique for cording the tubing (see Figure 6-10). If you want the tubing to be firmly corded make the fabric strip just wide enough to pull over the cord. Sew samples until you get the right width. You will need a piece of cording at least twice the finished length of tubing, plus some extra for hanging onto. Normally you will

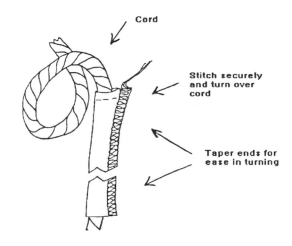

Cord

Stitch securely and turn over cord

Taper ends for ease in turning

Figure 6-10: *Corded Spaghetti Tubing*
Method I: Sew over heavy cord

not cut this length from your skein or ball of cording until the tubing is turned. Let us say your finished length of tubing will be 30". Then you fold your strip of fabric, wrong side out, around the cord beginning 30" from the end. Serge close to the cording, but not too close: you have to be able to turn the tubing. You will need to use a piping foot if your cord is heavy. However, the piping foot may sew too close to the cording: only use the right needle, and a wide stitch width if possible. On a conventional machine, secure one end of the fabric to the cord. Then turn fabric over cording and trim off excess cording. The tape/piping guide described above will make it easier to guide the cording and fabric, but may not feed a heavy enough cord or a wide enough strip of fabric to turn over your cord.

If you do not have a piping foot and are having problems guiding the heavy cord next to or under your presser foot, here is another technique (see Figures 6-11 and 6-12). Make your tube as if you were not cording it, with just the strand of crochet thread inside it. Taper out both end of the tube, to make it easier to turn over the heavier cord. Leaving the crochet thread in the tube, insert the end of the cording into one end of the tube, and tack in place on a conventional machine. Secure the crochet cord by tieing it to the chain as described above then turn fabric over cording.

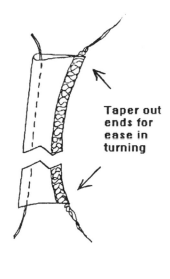
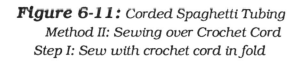

Taper out
ends for
ease in
turning

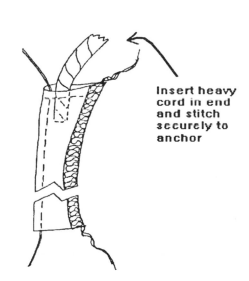

Insert heavy
cord in end
and stitch
securely to
anchor

Figure 6-11: *Corded Spaghetti Tubing*
Method II: Sewing over Crochet Cord
Step 1: Sew with crochet cord in fold

Figure 6-12: *Corded Spaghetti Tubing*
Method II: Sewing over Crochet Cord
Step 2: Insert heavy cord and turn

MAKING CORDS

Decorative cords can be attached by couching, or made into piping for sewing into a seam. (refer to the section on "Serger Piping," page 114, and the section on "Couching," page 117) To make your own cording, get an assortment of interesting threads: pearl cotton, metallics, serger chain, fine ribbon, yarn, embroidery floss, whatever. Lay them together and come up with an interesting combination that is about the weight you want. Remember, the serger will have to be able to form a stitch over it. Next decide if you want to braid or twist your cord. If you want to twist it, re-evaluate how thick your combination of threads is because the twisting process will double the thickness. Decide how long you want the finished cord to be, allowing some extra for experimenting with stitch tensions. (If worst comes to worst, you can always rip out faulty stitching, but you do not want to have to: refer to section on "Ripping Out a Serger Stitch," page 83.) If you will be twisting your cord, cut lengths of your ingredients somewhat more than twice your finished length. Put the cords together and tie each end of the bundle to a pencil. Get a friend to hold one pencil or secure it some way. Holding the other pencil and keeping the bundle taut, begin twisting. When you have twisted enough, put both pencils together, pull the midpoint of the cord away from the pencils, and let it roll up together. Tie the ends of the cord together to keep it from unrolling. If you want a machine to do the twisting for you, you can tie one end to the blade of a kitchen mixer (a hand-held one works best) or tighten it into the chuck of a drill. If the cord is too tightly twisted you will lose the character of the individual threads.

ATTACHING BEADS

A serger can be used to sew strings of beads, pearls or sequins to a garment edge or fold. By serging beads or sequins to a fold they can be attached anywhere on a garment. If attaching beads or sequins in the middle of garment sections, mark where the beads are to be attached with a washable or chalk marker. Fold along these lines while attaching the beads. If attaching beads or sequins to the edge of a garment the edge must be finished before attaching the beads, generally with a narrow rolled edge or a blind hem.

In the bridal department of fabric stores you can often find strings of pearls _molded_ onto a string. Also available are crosslocked strings of glass beads. Either will work, as will strings of sequins. Any beads to be attached by serger must have an even space between the beads for the serger stitch to go. Measure the distance in millimeters from the beginning of one bead to the beginning of the next, usually about 3 mm. Set your stitch length for this number.

Some machines have a special foot, called a beading foot or a pearls and sequins foot. These feet make the process of attaching beads much easier. Some beading feet permit you to adjust the guide for the beads sideways: this helps ensure the needle clears the beads whichever needle you are using. If you have a cloth guide for your machine you can use that for guiding the fabric. Mark the positions of both needles on the foot, so you can guide fabric accurately just to the right of whichever needle you are using. If you do not have a beading foot but your upper knife comes up from below you can probably guide the beads over the top of the knife and under the back of the presser foot. Use a blind hem foot and guide the fabric just to the left of the blade. Move the blade to the right, to make a more secure edge. The beads must be fine enough to go under the back part of the presser foot. Sew slowly. If your knife comes down from above you may be able to sew the beads on by swinging the knife out of the way and using the blind hem foot to guide the fabric. On some machines you may have to remove your presser foot and guide the beads and fabric manually. Sew very slowly, making sure one stitch falls between each bead.

The conventional way to sew on beads is with a wide flat-lock, using the techniques for flat-locking over a fold if attaching beads or sequins in the middle of garment sections. This is best for strings of sequins. However I find the narrow rolled edge stitch finger and tensions produce a finer seam when attaching beads, particularly on the edge of the fabric. The narrow rolled edge stitch finger allows the stitches to pull in tightly around the beads, whereas the normal stitch finger makes them looser and loopier. Tightening the lower looper tension pulls the threads in between the beads and makes a nearly invisible seam. A 2-thread narrow rolled edge makes a finer edge if your machine can do it. If your machine has a special needle plate for the narrow rolled edge you may not be able to use the left needle with it. This means you will have to watch carefully where you place the beads in relation to the needle. If you cannot get this to work use just the left needle with the regular needle plate, but use the narrow rolled edge tensions. Some beading feet are adjustable: if so, use the narrow rolled edge stitch finger and position the guide as far to the right as necessary.

Use an invisible or matching thread, and the widest stitch width. Place the fabric in the machine so it will be just to the right of the needle, and run the machine until it has made a few stitches onto the fabric. If you have a seam guide or cloth guide, use it to guide the fabric. Lift the presser foot, guide the beads over the front and under the back of the foot, then drop the presser foot. (Notice that you anchor the fabric in the machine before you place the beads: it is easier to do one thing at a time.) If you are using a blind hem foot, it may work better to guide the beads under the front part of the foot, next to the blade.

SERGER PIPING

The serger can be used to make piping, which is then sewn into a seam on either the serger or conventional machine. There are actually two different types of piping which can be made on the serger. One type is made by folding a bias strip around a cord, then inserting it into a seam. The other type is called serger piping and is unique to the serger: basically, a narrow rolled edge stitch is done over a heavy cord which is sewn onto a strip of fabric at the same time. Not only is it much quicker than cutting bias strips, this type of piping can be made in any color or texture you have thread for. The disadvantage is that the piping must be sewn on very close to the edge of the cord, so the strip of fabric does not show.

Some sergers have a piping foot. This foot can be used to make piping with bias strips. This foot can be used to insert either type of piping into a seam. If you do not have this foot use your conventional machine to insert the piping.

There is an accessory available on some machines, called a tape/piping guide. It can wrap the bias strip around the cord and guide it under the needle. With this accessory plus a piping foot you can make the piping and insert it into the seam in one step (with some practice). Begin by threading the cord and bias strip through the guide. Fasten the guide to the machine, feed the bias strip and cord under the needle and make a few stitches. Then lift the presser foot, position the two pieces of fabric around the piping, drop the presser foot, and begin sewing. (An easy way to get the cord and bias strip started through the guide is with a hand sewing needle: sew through the ends of the cord and the bias strip, leaving a long thread attached to each one. Use the looper threader to feed these long threads through the guide. Another option is to sew across their ends with the 2-thread chainstitch, leaving long enough ends to feed through.) Making and applying the piping in one step only works on straight and slightly curved seams. When applying piping around curves or corners make the piping, then apply as described below. You can still use the tape/piping guide plus piping foot to make the piping. An attractive option is "shadow piping": enclose a strand of brightly colored cord, such as tubular rayon ribbon, in a strip of sheer fabric such as sheer tricot.

You can buy regular piping cording for serger piping, but I prefer to get a cord in a color close to the thread color. The yarn used for plastic canvas works quite well, because it is flexible yet firm. It is generally available where craft supplies are sold. Another more pricey option is rayon tubular ribbon. Regular yarn compresses to almost nothing in this process and does not work well. To get various weights of piping you can also use a number of strands of pearl cotton or crochet thread.

For the fabric strips use a matching color if possible of a lightweight fabric, preferably cut on the bias. Often you can use strips of the fabric you will be attaching the piping to. This will not work if the fabric is too ravel-prone or has too bold a print. Cut the strips about 3/4" wide so you do not have to watch exactly how you feed them in; let the machine trim off a little on the edge. Another option is to use strips of sheer tricot.

If you want a different effect you can cut wider strips of fabric, about 1 1/2" wide, and fold them over the cord before serging. The color of the cord need not match the thread. An interesting fabric can be covered with a stitch long enough to display it, for example red rayon or a gold metallic thread over black silk. Do not use the beading foot with this technique. Fold the fabric around the cord and guide it so the raw edges are to the <u>left</u> of the needle. (If you want to make conventional piping you can use the piping foot, fold the strip of fabric over the cording, and guide it so the raw edges are to the right.)

When selecting an upper looper thread for piping you are looking for both coverage and decorative effect. You may want to use texturized nylon in the upper looper for better coverage, perhaps combining it with another thread for decorative effect. You may want to combine several strands of fine thread such as machine embroidery cotton. Use a loose enough upper looper tension so the threads spread out. Other decorative possibilities include metallic yarns or rayon ribbon or pearl cotton or embroidery floss or ...

Set your serger for a narrow rolled edge with as short a stitch length as possible, just long enough so the fabric will feed. You will probably need to loosen the upper looper tension, especially when sewing over thicker cords: this allows the lower looper thread to lie in a straight line so it is scarcely noticeable. Experiment to get the tensions right. Put the fabric under the foot and sew a few stitches into it to secure it. If you have a beading foot for your machine use it. Put the cording into the beading foot, over the front of the foot, under the upper looper if it is on top, and under the back of the foot. If you do not have a beading foot, it can be difficult to keep the needle from sewing into the bulky cord. If your machine has the upper knife coming up from below, you can hold the cord and guide it over the top of the knife, pulling slightly to the right. If your machine has the upper knife coming from above, try threading the cord <u>between</u> the upper knife and the front of the machine; in other words, open the front door, thread the cord to the right of the upper knife then close the front of the machine. Then feed the cord under the upper looper and under the back of the presser foot. (refer to section on "Guiding Fabric," page 104) Make some stitches over the cord to secure it. Then begin sewing, slowly, guiding the fabric strip with one hand and holding the cord with the other hand. Another option for heavier cords is to use just the left needle, especially if you can do a narrow rolled edge with the left needle (wide narrow rolled edge stitch). Otherwise, set up your machine for a left needle (wide) wrapped stitch.

The same techniques can be used for making piping out of a decorative cord. Lengthen the stitch length and use a matching or invisible thread. (refer to section on "Invisible Thread," page 94) Use twisted together strands of pearl cotton, or the rayon tubular ribbon, or an interesting yarn, or whatever you wish. (refer to section on "Making Cords," page 112) The tension of the serger stitch will compress the cord so do not expect it to end up looking thick unless it is firm. You can also use beads. (refer to section on "Attaching Beads," page 112) This is the way to get beads or a nice cord attached to a seam, for example on princess seams, a collar edge, or finishing a faced garment edge such as a neck opening.

Piping is sewn into a seam in two steps (see Figure 6-13). First it is pinned or basted to the right side of one piece of fabric, raw edges together. When applying piping to corners or curves make sure it is loose enough to curve around without pulling when it is turned right side out, but not so loose it ripples. While pinning or basting it on, turn the seam allowance in to check if there is enough fullness. A better way to get the piping on right is to fold in the garment seam allowance by folding along the seam line, pin or baste to secure, then press. Then pin or baste the piping to the edge of the fold, raw edges together. It will be easy to see how much fullness is necessary for smooth corners and curves. Remove the pins or basting that is holding the seam allowance folded. Clip the piping seam allowances as necessary so they lie flat for stitching. Then sew the piping to the fabric. Use a piping foot on a serger or

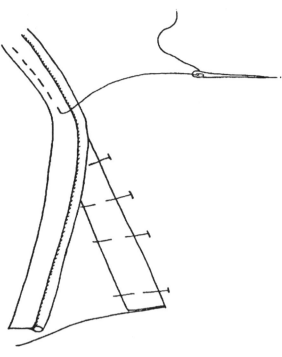

Figure 6-13: *Piping basted to seam allowance, after seam allowance is turned in, pinned and pressed*

conventional machine if you have it. Use a zipper foot on a conventional machine if you do not have a piping foot. Next, put the other piece of fabric right sides together with the piece that has the piping on it. Sew with the piece that has the piping already sewn to it on top so you can follow the stitching line. Sew on or to the left of the previous line of stitching. (Often piping is used where seam allowances will be trimmed to 1/4". A straight stitch on a conventional machine will be less bulky, but the serger seam will protect raw edges from fraying. The ideal is to sew the first seam, which attaches the piping to one piece of fabric, on a conventional machine: the straight stitch reduces bulk plus you can leave pins in place until they are almost up to the needle. Then sew the second seam on the serger to protect all the raw edges at once. You will need a piping foot for your serger.) If piping inside corners or curves, clip the piping seam allowances after stitching so they will lie flat when turned.

COUCHING

In couching the serger stitch is used to attach yarn or trim directly to the fabric. A wide variety of decorative ribbons, yarns and trims can be attached (couched) with the serger, and a wide variety of techniques can be used. Refer to the section on "Applying Lace," page 129, and the section on "Attaching Beads," page 112, for additional couching techniques. Refer to the section on "Guiding Fabric," page 104, for techniques to position fabric and trim accurately.

A balanced stitch is generally used when couching things to garment edges. In the middle of garment sections, a balanced or wrapped stitch can be used to produce a tuck with the decorative something incorporated in it. When you want the fabric to lie flat, use the techniques for flat-locking over a fold. Fold the fabric and serge over the fold, attaching whatever you are couching. When couching in the middle of a garment section you can follow curved or straight lines, beginning and ending wherever you wish.

Couching Yarn

You will want a long wide stitch to display the yarn. Generally the serger threads will be either a matching color or invisible thread. Yarn will be compressed by the serger stitch, so choose a yarn with plenty of texture and perhaps variegated colors. A plain yarn will not show up well, whereas a heavy yarn such as rug yarn will be too stiff. Mohairs work well, as do many boucles and slubs. Stores specializing in yarn generally have the best selection of unusual textured yarns. For example, get a skein of "pigtail" yarn, which has 2" strands of thread hanging down from it every 3". Carefully pulling the loose strands to the left so they do not get caught in the stitching, flat-lock rows of this randomly to a vest, using the techniques for flat-locking over a fold. When couching yarn in the middle of garment sections the couching need not go from one edge of the garment to the other. It can begin and end in the middle of a garment section, perhaps with ends of yarn hanging out, perhaps with beads or bows tied on the ends. As you are couching you can also leave loops of yarn hanging out from the stitching. When couching yarn with a flat-lock you can put the yarn on top of the stitch so it ends up under the looper side of the stitch. You can also put it _inside_ the fold so it ends up under the ladder side of the stitch. Generally this is the less noticeable side of the stitch, which means the yarn can show up better. For heavy yarns, it may work better to use a yarn needle, and thread the yarn through the stitching after it is serged.

Couching Narrow Ribbon

Narrow ribbons can be placed to the right
of the needle (see Figure 6-14). Use a long
stitch, wide enough to cover the ribbon.
You may want to use a contrasting color
thread, for example red thread over a
narrow gold ribbon. Generally you will use
matching or transparent thread. Slightly
wider ribbons can be placed to the right of
the left needle but under the right needle,
which secures them and keeps them from
twisting. What about a blue satin ribbon
with a wide stitch in white rayon thread?
Do this with a balanced stitch, perhaps
over a fold, to finish the edges of a white
robe, then use flat-locking to add strips
across the yoke. If you want a ribbon

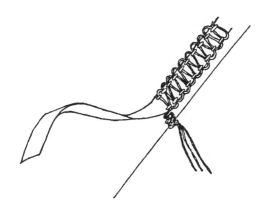

Figure 6-14: *Couching Narrow Ribbon*

under the ladder side of a flat-lock you may need to thread it through after
stitching, depending on the width of the ribbon and weight of the fabric.

Couching Cords

A narrow rolled edge or wrapped stitch in a
long stitch length is nice for couching
cords to the middle of garment sections or
garment edges. Use a narrow rolled edge
stitch for finer cords. For heavier cords
use a left-needle narrow rolled edge if your
machine can do this: otherwise use a
wrapped stitch. These stitches make the
cord more prominent. When attaching
cord to the edge of fabric that ravels easily
you can use a shorter stitch length. This
protects the edge but covers up the cord.

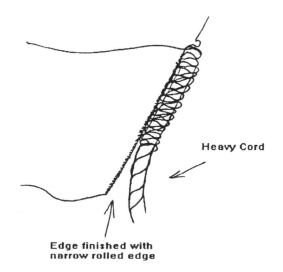

Heavy Cord

Edge finished with
narrow rolled edge

Figure 6-15: *Edge Finished with Narrow Rolled Edge*

Another option is to finish the edge with a
balanced stitch or narrow rolled edge then
couch the cord with a wider stitch over the
previous stitching (see Figure 6-15). Or,
you can blind hem the edge and couch over the fold.

For heavier cords loosen the upper looper tensions as much as necessary to
keep the lower looper thread lying in nearly a straight line.

When couching cord in the middle of garment sections guide the fold of fabric
just to the right of the needle. For finer cords you can use a cording foot if you

have one. The beading foot is wonderful for couching heavier cords. Mark both needle positions on the beading foot so you can guide the fabric accurately. Another option is the blind hem foot: guide the fold of fabric just to the left of the blade and the cord just to the right of it.

There is a tendency for heavier cords to get caught by the needle, especially if you do not have a beading foot. If the upper knife comes up from below on your machine, you can hold the cord and guide it over the top of the knife, pulling slightly to the right as necessary to keep the cord from getting caught in the stitching. If your machine has the upper knife coming from above, open the front door, guide the cord to the _right_ of the knife then close the front door. Place the cord under the back of the presser foot and sew a few stitches to secure. (refer to illustration in section on "guiding Fabric," page 104) In order to reduce the tendency for heavy cords to get caught by the needle, use a left needle (wide) narrow rolled edge if you can on your machine, or a left needle wrapped stitch.

You can often find decorative cords in home decorating departments. (Make sure they are not too heavy.) Otherwise you can use a combination of threads and cords you twist together yourself, spaghetti tubing you made from an interesting fabric, rayon tubular ribbon, slender braids, etc. (refer to the section on "Making Cords," page 112, and the section on "Spaghetti Tubing," page 110)

Couching Wide Trims

You can find a large selection of trims in the trim section of your fabric store. You can also use strips of fabric. If not couching both edges the unattached fabric edge(s) can be decoratively serged or left unfinished to ravel. One or both edges can be gathered before couching, or the strips can be folded in half and gathered along the fold. (refer to section on "Gathering," page 126) Since the needle always sews into wider trim, it is an excellent way of stabilizing garment edges. Here are some suggestions:

For trims with a woven pattern you may want to catch just the edge of the trim in your stitch. Use your blind hem foot as a guide to position the trim. When flat-locking over a fold, align the edge of the trim with the fold of the fabric as you place it next to the guide on the blind hem foot. (If you cannot do a wide flat-lock with your blind hem foot, refer to the section on "Guiding Fabric," page 104.) When using a balanced or wrapped stitch place the edge of the trim next to the guide and let the edge of the fabric extend to the knives. Sew slow! It may help to baste or pin the trim first. If pinning, place pins parallel to the edge and about 3/4" from it.

If you want the stitching to extend to the edge of the trim when you are flat-locking over a fold, put the trim right side down next to the knives with the folded fabric on top and the fold next to the guide on your blind hem foot. If you cannot do a wide flat-lock with your blind hem foot, refer to the section on "Guiding Fabric," page 104. Make sure you do not cut the trim.

On some elastic feet the slot for elastic is open on the left. This type of elastic foot is excellent for guiding trim just to the left of the knives when using a balanced or wrapped stitch, so the knives do not cut the edge. Loosen the screw on the foot so the clamp is open and not pinching the trim.

If couching a wide trim in the middle of a garment section you can use a balanced stitch over a fold to create tucks framing your trim (see Figures 6-16, 6-17, and 6-18). Any tucks will make a garment section smaller, so decorate the garment section before cutting it out. (refer to the section on "Pintucks," page 122) If you use the techniques for flat-locking over the fold your trim will lie flat.

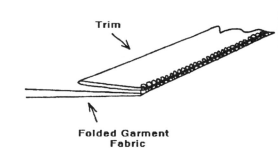

Figure 6-16: Step 1

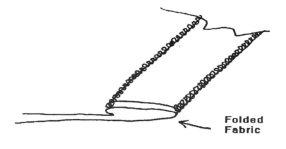

Figure 6-17: Step 2

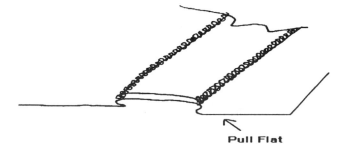

Figure 6-18: Step 3: Finished View after pulling flat

Couching wide trim in the middle of garment section with balanced stitch, making tucks.

You can attach a wide woven trim to the edges of a heavier fabric such as coating, polar fleece or boiled wool. This finishes and stabilizes the edge. Then secure the other edge of the trim to the garment by flat-locking over a fold or by making a tuck with a balanced stitch. You can use a decorative thread in your looper as well.

Another way to use wider trims is to fold them in half and attach them in the middle (see Figures 6-19, 6-20, and 6-21). This works best with softer trims such as satin ribbon or fabric strips. This can be done along a garment edge, or over a fold in the middle of a garment section. If you want to attach the trim to the middle of the fabric you can flat-lock over a fold, or sew it with a balanced stitch or wrapped stitch to produce a tuck.

Just one edge of the trim can be attached, leaving the other edge loose. (refer to section on "Applying Lace," page 129) This can be done along garment edges or in the middle. For example, lines of purchased fringe can be couched on a western style top. One edge of a strip of lace or fabric can be gathered then couched.

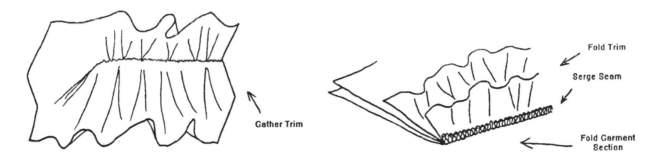

Figure 6-19: *Step 1: Gathering fabric strip*   **Figure 6-20:** *Step 2: Couching gathered strip*

SHIRRING

Shirring is parallel lines of stretchy elastic stitching on a garment section, for example at the wrist or waist. If you have a 2-thread chainstitch on your machine you can use it for shirring. Use as long a stitch length as possible, loosening the needle tension as necessary. Tightening the looper tension will increase shirring. (refer to section on "2-Thread Chainstitch," page 143) Otherwise you can shirr by couching rows of elastic thread, 1/8" elastic or 1/4" clear elastic. Use the techniques for flat-locking over a fold, with a long stitch length and a wide stitch. Fold the fabric and use a blind hem foot, with the fold of the fabric just to the left of the blade and the elastic just to the right. Use the techniques for sewing in a circle. (refer to section on "Sewing in a Circle," page 62) Do not overlap the lines of stitching: end the

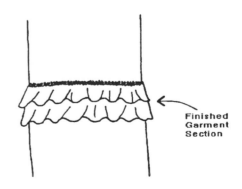

Figure 6-21: *Step 3: After pulling flat*

stitching right next to the beginning of the stitching. Leave long ends of elastic at both ends of the stitching. When all the rows have been sewn draw up the elastic to the desired amount and tie knots to secure. Make sure all the strands of elastic are the same length by drawing up the same amount on each one. If you wish the serger stitch to be a decorative element, you can put the elastic inside the fold before flat-locking so the looper side of the stitch shows. When using the 1/4" clear elastic you may need to thread it through after the stitching is completed. Use a large blunt needle such as a yarn needle or tapestry needle with an eye large enough to accept the elastic.

PINTUCKS

The rolled edge can be used to produce lovely pintucks. Set up your machine for a narrow rolled edge. Fold the fabric on the line where the pintuck is to be and press lightly with an iron. Guide the fold halfway between the needle and the knife. Narrower pintucks (closer to the needle) give a softer look, wider ones (closer to the knives) are more noticeable. (refer to section on "Guiding Fabric," page 104) Rayon thread in the upper looper adds an attractive sheen. Matching or contrasting color thread can be used. See how a longer stitch length looks: a longer stitch gives a softer look and a shorter stitch gives a more defined accent, especially in a contrasting color or with texturized

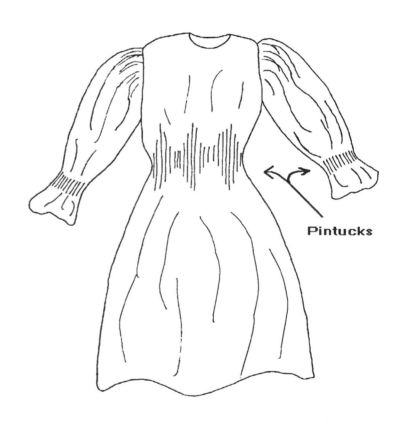

Figure 6-22: *Dress showing Pintucks*

nylon. Once you have properly adjusted tensions for a narrow rolled edge you can loosen the needle tension slightly for a softer pintuck.

These pintucks can go from one edge of the fabric to the other. If using pintucks on a garment section, cut out a piece of fabric several inches larger than the pattern piece. An example would be a blouse front. Sew all the tucks then lay pattern piece on top and cut out. Another option is released tucks. This means beginning the tucks in the middle of the fabric and going to the edge. (refer to section on "Serging Corners," page 62, for securing the stitches; use the technique for beginning at a corner) This is a wonderful technique for shaping yokes or bodices: begin the tucks just above the bust or the hips and extend to the top edge of the garment. Or the tucks could go from above the hips to below the bust, to shape the waist area. Another possibility is at the wrists of sleeves. Also, the edge of the tucks can follow a slanted or curved line as well as a horizontal one. Sketch the desired line on the fabric piece, keeping in mind that any curved or slanted line will become steeper as you make the tucks (see Figure 6-22).

Yet another possibility is crossing one set of pintucks with another set. This only works on lightweight fabric with fine thread (not texturized nylon). Use a longer stitch length and/or narrower tucks to make the pintucks less stiff and bulky. Sew the tucks going in one direction, press flat, then sew the tucks going in the other direction. These can be done diagonally in a diamond pattern or horizontally and vertically.

Another possibility is making wider tucks using a balanced stitch, 3-thread or even 4-thread. A wrapped stitch can be used as well.

LETTUCING

The narrow rolled edge makes a wonderful lettuce edge. Lettucing looks somewhat like the frilly ruffled edge of a leaf of lettuce. It can give a dressy effect in chiffon, a romantic effect in sheer tricot lingerie, or it can give a light-hearted effect when edging ruffles on a child's skirt. Use the cross-grain of a stretchy knit, or the bias of a woven. Do a rolled edge, stretching as you sew. If you wish stiffer lettucing, fold the fabric and do the rolled edge over the fold then trim to the stitching. (refer to section on "Guiding Fabric," page 104) Another option is using a balanced stitch with a short stitch length, especially if the fabric is too heavy for a narrow rolled edge.

It can be difficult to get the amount of stretching and lettucing even. First, have the machine do as much of the work as possible. If you have differential feed set it for as small a number as possible. Increase your presser foot pressure. Use as short a stitch length as possible. (On some machines and with some fabrics, too short a stitch length will keep the fabric from feeding properly. Lengthen stitch length only as much as necessary.) Texturized nylon in the upper looper helps too. For additional lettucing press the fabric against the needle plate in front of the needle with your fingers as you guide the fabric with your other hand. Another technique is to squeeze it between the thumb and forefinger of the right hand. These techniques make it fairly easy to gauge the amount of pressure you are applying and keep it consistent.

Lettucing can also be done over a fold in the middle of a garment section. The closer the fold is to the needle the softer the lettucing will be, the further away it is the stiffer it will be. Lettucing over a fold is frequently done on ribbing, especially at the neck. Lettuce the ribbing before joining it to the garment. Sometimes two or more parallel rows are made. It can also be done over a curved fold, for example around a "yoke" on a knit top or "scallops" on a skirt. Mark your fold with chalk or by pressing lightly with an iron. Lettucing over a fold can begin or end in the middle of the fabric. The wiry thread chain of the narrow rolled edge can be left as an accent, or the ends can be finished as described in the section on "Serging Corners," page 62, for beginning and ending at a corner.

Seams can also be lettuced. On most fabrics you will need to use a balanced stitch rather than a narrow rolled edge. Sew wrong sides together. If lettucing vertical seams sew a sample to see if the fabric will lettuce enough on the lengthwise grain. Lettuced seams can be wonderful on a gored skirt, flared near the hem: the hem can be lettuced too (see Figure 6-23). The fabric will lie relatively smooth over the hip and lettuce much more near the hem, where the seams are closer to the cross-grain. Another idea is to insert a strip of contrasting fabric in the middle of sleeves and lettuce the insert seams (see Figure 6-24). Raglan sleeve seams can be lettuced, along with numerous lines of lettucing over a fold

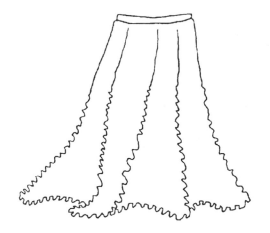

Figure 6-23: *Lettuced Gored Skirt*

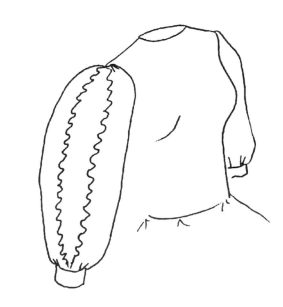

Figure 6-24: *Lettuced Sleeve Insert*

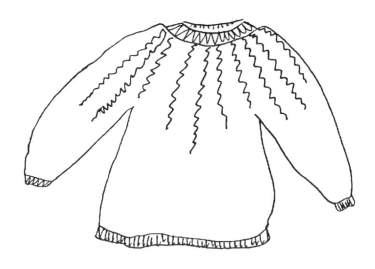

Figure 6-25: *Lettuced tucks on raglan sleeved top*

radiating from the neckline (see Figure 6-25). Lettucing over a fold will make garment sections smaller. Use a pattern with generous ease. Or, cut oversized pieces, do lettucing over a fold, then lay pattern piece on fabric and cut to size. If the seams will be lettuced with a balanced stitch do the lettucing over a fold with the same stitch. Refer to section on "Pintucks," page 122, for more ideas.

DECORATIVE NARROW ROLLED EDGE

The narrow rolled edge is usually done on an exposed edge, and is usually more or less decorative. It becomes much more decorative with a prominent thread in the upper looper. Texturized nylon (refer to section on "Texturized Nylon," page 93) gives a wonderful effect, fluffing out to both cover the edge and make the line of stitching appear thicker. Metallics, rayon or the finer cottons are other possibilities. The heavier threads do not work well for a narrow rolled edge.

A corded edge can be produced by doing a rolled edge over a heavier thread such as crochet thread or even rayon tubular ribbon. Guide the thread to the right of the needle so that it gets rolled into the stitch. Some presser feet have a guide for doing this. Use the beading foot for heavier cord. (refer to section on "Guiding Fabric," page 104) Another possibility is using fishline, 20# to 50# test, and guiding it to the right of the needle. This is usually done on the edge of a ruffle made of lightweight fabric, before gathering the other edge. This makes the edge stand out in stiff curves. This can also be done on the crossgrain of a knit or the bias of a woven, and lettuced. Unless you have a cording guide in your foot it is difficult to stretch the fabric for lettucing and guide the fishline at the same time. Leave a long length of fishline at both the beginning and the end of the seam. Do the machine settings for lettucing (refer to section on "Lettucing," page 123) but stretch the fabric after the seam is sewn. Knot the ends of the fishline to preserve the lettucing.

If your machine will permit you to use the left needle with the narrow rolled edge stitch finger, you can do a 4-thread narrow rolled edge with it. Some machines convert to the narrow rolled edge stitch finger by sliding away or removing a part of the stitch finger, so the left needle can still be used. If your machine has a special needle plate and/or foot for the narrow rolled edge, odds are it will not accept the left needle. Some machines with a special narrow rolled edge needle plate have a hole for the left needle in the plate. Some machines which convert to the narrow rolled edge by changing just the presser foot have a narrow rolled edge foot which will not accept the left needle, but their beading foot will accept the left needle and do a narrow rolled edge. If your machine uses a double needle to do a 4-thread overlock, you may be able to do a 4-thread narrow rolled edge with the narrow rolled edge needle plate and standard presser foot. However you manage to finagle it, set up the machine as for a normal narrow rolled edge, but leave both needles in and threaded. A wider edge with a double corded appearance will be produced. This gives extra security and a more pronounced decorative effect. A narrow rolled edge produced with the left needle only (wide narrow rolled edge) can be nice for doing a narrow rolled edge on heavier fabric, or for attaching beads and heavy cords. (refer to the sections on "Serger Piping" on page 114, "Attaching Beads" on page 112, "Couching" on page 117, and "Decorative Uses of Chain" on page 136)

The narrow rolled edge can be done on the edges of netting. This technique, called tracing, gives a nice effect on bridal veils. Lingerie thread gives a finer effect if desired.

GATHERING

Some industrial sergers are designed for gathering; they can gather one piece of fabric and attach it to another piece in one operation. The amount of gathering is even and consistent. The domestic serger gathers beautifully too. With your assistance or proper attachments it can also gather and attach at the same time. Serger gathering is quick and easy, the raw edge is finished, just about any fabric can be gathered, you can get as much fullness as you want, and you can adjust it easily without threads breaking. If you have differential feed on your machine you can get up to a 2 to 1 gather on lightweight fabric with it. The following techniques will gather much tighter, and work on most machines with a 3-thread overlock stitch. If you have differential feed you can use it with these techniques to get even more gathering.

The serger is wonderful for gathering lace: the stitching is scarcely visible and the lace does not shift around while being gathered. Use the techniques below but with a narrow 3-thread stitch and the narrow rolled edge stitch finger. Guide the edge of the lace just to the right of the needle.

Set your machine up for a 4-thread overlock if you have it, otherwise use a 3-thread overlock. Use balanced looper tensions and the longest stitch length. Loosen the presser foot pressure. Make a thread chain several inches long. Put your fabric under the needle. Tighten the needle tensions. Usually tightening them halfway produces a 3 to 1 gather in light fabric, but it is easy to pull out extra fullness _if_ you have long enough thread chains at the beginning and end. Sew **slowly** until the end of the fabric is under the needle. Return needle tensions to normal and chain off, leaving a long thread chain. Note that you must have fabric under the needle when the needle tensions are tightened. If the fabric is gathered too much and you left a long enough tail at both ends you can remove the extra fullness by pulling the extra fullness out towards the ends with your fingers. If you want more fullness you can pull the needle threads out from the thread chain and pull up on them. After you have the right amount of gathering knot the chains at each end of the seam to secure it.

For very heavy fabrics an alternate method is to serge over a heavy thread, placing it to the right of the needle and making sure that the needle does not pierce it. After stitching pull up on the thread. The problem with this method is that it can be more difficult to get the gathers evenly distributed.

For slight gathering, for example easing in a curved hem, use differential feed or slightly tightened needle tensions. Another option for gentle gathering if you do not have differential feed is holding a finger firmly on the fabric just behind the presser foot while you sew. The fabric will bunch up and be gathered slightly.

Here is a method for determining how much to gather your fabric. Let us say you are sewing a ruffle with a 2 to 1 gather (100" long ruffle onto a 50" skirt edge: 100 divided by 50 equals 2). Take a long scrap of your garment fabric and mark lines on it 2" apart, starting about 1" from the end. Start sewing at the end, and before you get to the first line, tighten your needle tensions to what you think will be the right amount. Sew until at least two of your lines are behind the presser foot. Then stop and measure the distance between the two lines. If they are now 1" apart you have a 2 to 1 gather. If they are more than 1" apart increase your needle tensions, if they are less than 1" apart decrease them. Keep sewing until you have another segment you can check. If you want a 1.5 to 1 gather make your lines 1.5" apart. It is important to measure accurately, so you may want to measure two or three spaces instead of one. Three spaces should measure 3".

Attaching the Gathered Piece

After gathering you will generally be attaching the gathered piece of fabric to a straight piece. Pin the ends and middle of your gathered piece of fabric onto the other piece. If the gathered piece is a little short remove the extra fullness by pulling the gathers out towards the chain. If you need more gathering you can pull the needle threads out from the thread chain and pull up on them. When the fabric is the right length knot each thread chain next to the fabric to secure. Distribute the gathers evenly and finish pinning. (Remember not to serge over pins!)

If gathering one knit onto another, for example a skirt onto a bodice, the resulting seam must stretch. Yet, the gathering stitching will not stretch. When serging a gathered knit onto another knit cut off the gathering stitches as you join them. Especially when trimming off the gathering stitches it is easier to join a gathered piece of fabric onto another piece if you leave one seam open so you are sewing one straight piece of fabric onto another. Pin the two pieces together and sew with the gathered fabric on top. Position the fabric so the left-hand edge of the gathering stitch is just to the right of the knife. As you sew arrange the fabric so the gathers are evenly distributed. Support the gathered fabric so the weight of it will not pull out the gathers after the stitching is cut off. After attaching the gathered piece of fabric sew the last seam. Due to the bulk of the gathered fabric the seam will tend to flare or stretch out. You can correct this by sewing on some elastic, preferably the clear elastic, as you attach the two pieces of fabric together. Make sure the needle sews into the elastic. Refer to the discussion on rippling in the section on "Knits," page 67. (For fullness in knits, a flounce works much better than a straight piece of fabric. Refer to the section on "Flounce" in the glossary, page 195.) Another option is to make a virtue of necessity: sew wrong sides together, stretching the shorter piece of knit as you sew. Use a short stitch length to get a more pronounced lettuce effect.

If for some reason it would be better to sew a circular piece of a gathered knit into a circular opening, use the following techniques. Position the fabric as described above. Do not cut out a notch, as you normally would for sewing in a circle. Start at the edge of the gathered fabric and angle in your line of stitching until you are trimming off the entire gathering stitch. Then sew straight. Trim off this angling-in portion as you finish the seam, then finish as for sewing in a circle. (refer to section on "Sewing in a Circle," page 62) If you have gathered over a cord as described above you can attach the two pieces of fabric together without trimming anything off. After sewing cut the cord in one or more places and pull it out of the seam. The seam will be somewhat stiffer due to the line of gathering stitches in it. Yet another technique is to sew a *second* seam, trimming off the first one as you do. In effect, the first seam functions as basting for the second.

Gathering and Attaching in One Step

Here is a technique specifically for gathering a piece of fabric onto a knit. The gathered fabric need not be a knit, but it should be fairly light weight. Set the machine for the longest stitch length. If you have differential feed set it to 2. Reduce the presser foot pressure. Working with scraps of your two fabrics, make a sample to determine approximately how much gathering you can get and whether you want less gathering. Put the two pieces of fabric right sides together with the fabric to be gathered next to the feed dogs. Sew until the needle has started sewing into the fabric. This will anchor it as you stretch the top layer (the knit). Guide both pieces of fabric but pull on the upper layer while allowing the lower layer to feed freely. The amount of gathering you get will depend on how stretchy the knit is and how strongly you pull on it. Do not pull too hard or you may bend the needle. It is important to choose a knit with good recovery, or the seam will tend to flare out rather than pulling in firmly. If this is a problem you can incorporate some elastic into the seam, preferably the clear elastic. This technique works well with ribbing, and a band of ribbing can be used to gather in the waist of a dress. Since it is difficult to calibrate accurately how much you are stretching the upper layer, this technique is easier if you are not attempting to set a circular piece of fabric into a circular opening. Cut the strips of fabric extra long, and cut off the excess after gathering. If it is necessary to set a circular piece into a circular opening or for some other reason accurately control how long each piece of fabric is, use pins or clothespins to quarter and then eighth the openings, as described in the section on "Ribbing and Elastic," page 72. If desired for decorative purposes you can do this wrong sides together so the seam shows on the right side, perhaps with a decorative thread in the loopers.

If you are gathering onto a woven fabric you can use the same technique as described above for knits, but you will need to hold the upper layer of fabric more firmly. Use differential feed if you have it, set to 2. If the layers of fabric have a lot of texture, they will resist sliding over one another and make this technique difficult. Correct this problem by inserting a layer of water soluble stabilizer between the two layers of fabric.

There are attachments which assist with gathering and attaching in one step. Industrial machines have a special gathering attachment with a knee activated control, so gathering can be engaged or disengaged even in the middle of a seam. Some can also insert piping at the same time. Also, the feed dogs have differential feed but with the division between the front and back half at the front end of the presser foot rather than by the needle. Differential feed makes gathering and attaching in one step much easier on domestic machines too: set it to 2.0 if you have it. On domestic machines you can put the upper layer of fabric into the clamp on your elastic foot. Adjust the clamp pressure to control the amount of gathering. This only works on elastic feet that have the clamp open on the left side. Some domestic machines have an optional foot or accessory called a fabric separator, gathering plate or shirring foot: it is used along with differential feed for gathering and attaching in one step. It covers the front half of the feed dogs. The fabric to be gathered is placed under the guide, so the differential feed is gathering it. The other piece of fabric is placed on top of the guide, so it is unaffected by the differential feed. These attachments will give about a 2 to 1 gather, although tighter gathering can be achieved by holding onto the top layer of fabric, as described above. Gathering can be started or stopped in the middle of a seam by adjusting the differential feed.

APPLYING LACE

There are a variety of techniques for applying lace with the serger. The strip of lace can be gathered before applying.

When applying lace to itself or to the edge of a fabric which does not ravel use a narrow flat-lock with a short stitch length and the narrow rolled edge stitch finger. This is a good technique for tricot lingerie, since it does not ravel. If you use a 2-thread flat-lock the seam will have a lot of stretch. Around the bottom of a tricot slip the stretch of the 2-thread stitch can be handy, but make sure the lace stretches as much as the fabric. Stretch the fabric while attaching the lace, or use stretch lace. Otherwise the lace is liable to tear.

You can also apply lace to an edge and finish the edge at the same time. Use the blind hem foot. Place the fabric next to the knives and the lace just to the left of the guide, right sides together. Position the guide just to the right of the needle so only the edge of the lace will be caught. You can also use this technique to attach lace while making a narrow rolled edge. Set the machine up for a narrow rolled edge. Use the blind hem foot to guide the lace if you can do a rolled edge with the blind hem foot on your machine. (This does not work on machines which convert to the narrow rolled edge by changing only the presser foot: these machines have a wide stitch finger on the blind hem foot which prevents you from doing a narrow rolled edge. On these machines make a mark on your narrow rolled edge foot to indicate where to guide the lace.)

Lace can be applied to a fold, using a narrow flat-lock or a narrow rolled edge stitch. When lace is attached to a fold with a rolled edge, the lace will be pointing toward the garment and away from the fold (tuck). When attached with a flat-lock the lace will end up lying flat on the surface of the fabric. When using these techniques to apply horizontal lines of lace to a garment make sure the lace is pointing downward (see Figure 6-26).

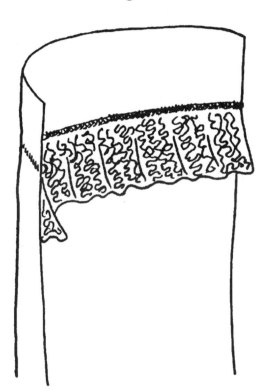

Lace can be flat-locked to an edge or pintuck previously sewn with a narrow rolled edge. If flat-locked to an edge or pintuck the lace will end up pointing away from the garment. The narrow rolled edge can be done in matching thread and the flat-locking in matching or contrasting thread.

Figure 6-26: *Lace flat-locked to fold then pulled flat*

(make sure lace is pointed down)

A decorative thread can be used when applying lace. Use fine threads when doing a rolled edge, and heavier threads if desired when flat-locking.

Another option is to couch when applying lace. For example, place narrow ribbon to the right of the needle when flat-locking lace. Sew wrong sides together so the ribbon ends up on the right side. Another option is pearls (see Figure 6-27). (refer to section on "Attaching Beads," page 112)

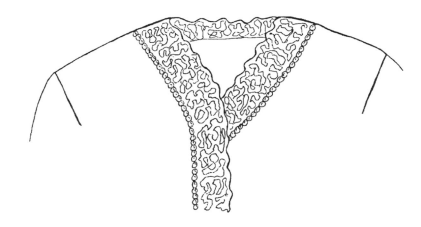

Figure 6-27: Applying Lace with Couching

HEIRLOOM SEWING

Heirloom sewing, or "French hand sewing by machine," produces delicate lovely garments out of lace and tucked or gathered strips of fabric. Although originally done by hand, these beautiful garments can be produced on the serger in a fraction of the time, using the techniques for gathering, pintucking and applying lace. The serger quickly makes the many seams required to produce these garments, finishes the seams beautifully, and even make the narrow rolled edge finish on the fabric ruffles. (refer to relevant sections) There are several good books available describing how these garments are made and showing many beautiful examples. In the most popular form of this art "fabric" is created by combining laces, strips of fabric gathered on both sides called "puffing," strips of plain, embroidered or pintucked fabric, and a special trim called entredeux. Entredeux looks like a line of satin stitch with little holes down the middle of it. It is traditional and pretty, but not necessary. It can be purchased from stores specializing in fine sewing or made on some conventional machines. The fabric used for heirloom sewing is traditionally batiste, in white or pale pastels. (refer to Appendix D: Sources, page 189, for information on mail ordering heirloom sewing supplies and books)

Let us say you wish to make the front of a blouse using these techniques. Choose a simple loose fitting style without darts or pleats, preferably one which opens in back. Trace another copy of your blouse front pattern so you have a pattern for the full front. Assemble a collection of laces and fabric strips, and begin laying out your design on top of the blouse front pattern. You will want to make your layout 4" to 6" longer than the pattern piece. For puffing strips gather both sides of 1 1/2" to 3" wide strips of fabric. Make the gather about 1 and 1/2 to 1 or more, depending on preference and fabric. Include these in your design. You may also wish to include strips of pintucks. On strips of fabric 2" to 6" wide make the pintucks. A longer stitch length gives a softer appearance, and rayon thread in the upper looper gives a delicate sheen. Include these strips in your design too. You can also have strips or areas of plain fabric, or plain fabric embroidered with decorative stitches on your conventional machine. When all is decided begin assembling the pieces, working from the center out. When joining lace to lace you will use a narrow flat-lock and the narrow rolled edge stitch finger. Except for that, your seams will be the narrow rolled edge or short narrow overlock stitch, either right sides together or wrong sides together. (refer to section on "Applying Lace," page 129) When attaching the puffing strips, cut off the gathering stitches by having the left edge of the gathering stitch to the right of the knives. (refer to section on "Gathering," page 126) Depending on fabric weight, you may have difficulty attaching the puffing strips with a narrow rolled edge. If so, use a narrow balanced stitch with a short stitch length. When all is finished, lay your pattern piece on your "fabric" and cut it out. To secure the ends of your stitching serge the edge immediately, perhaps even cutting it out on the serger. To do this, mark your cutting line on the fabric then cut it out and serge the edges in one step. Turn corners as described in the section on "Corners," page 62. Since these garments are not subject to heavy wear this should be sufficient to secure the edge. If not, bind the edges with strips of sheer tricot or use the second technique in the section on "Securing Seams," page 60.

SERGER LACE

Serger lace is a quick lovely finish for edges, although it can also be done over pintucks. (Imagine rows of this edging ruffles down the front of a blouse, with matching ruffles around the collar. Wash with care because this stitch is subject to snagging.) Set your machine for a wide long balanced stitch. Use a prominent decorative thread. Remove the right needle. When setting your tensions on a scrap of fabric, loosen the looper tensions so the loops hang off the edge of the fabric. Guide fabric just to the right of the needle and sew. (refer to section on "Guiding Fabric," page 104) When finished, make the next row by serging into the edge of the first line of serging. Continue as desired. Water soluble stabilizer will help keep the stitching even. Every row position one or more strips of the stabilizer so that it goes from the left of the needle to the right of the knife: the knife will trim off the excess. After you finish sewing dissolve it with water. (refer to glossary under "Water Soluble Stabilizer" for more information) Different rows can be different threads, for example a row of metallic between rows of pearl cotton. Another option is using different shades of the same thread, for example rayon threads ranging from light to dark pink. After sewing you can pull on the lace to spread and ruffle it. Looser needle tensions will permit more ruffling. If you watch carefully you can swing the edge of the previous line of stitching to the right and left, so the needle alternately catches it and does not catch it. This will make open spaces in your lace. When finished do not cut thread chains; thread them through the stitching with a crochet hook or yarn needle. If sewing in a circle simply spiral out, then run the beginning and ending thread chains through the stitching. Serger lace is subject to snagging, so treat it gently. To secure serger lace, zig-zag over the inner edge of every row before washing out the water soluble stabilizer: this is not possible unless you have used stabilizer.

FABRIC FLOWERS

Fabric flowers can be made by finishing one edge of a strip of fabric, tightly gathering the other edge (refer to section on "Gathering," page 126), then rolling up the gathered edge and securing it (see Figures 6-28, 6-29, and 6-30). The strip of fabric is usually about 30" to 36" long. The more tightly it is gathered the more "open" the flower will be. Shorter and narrower strips can be a little more loosely gathered and used as "buds." With lightweight fabrics the fabric strip can simply be folded in half and the two raw edges gathered together. The finished width of the strip is generally 2" to 4". A folded edge can be left plain or decorated.

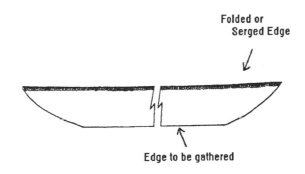

Folded or Serged Edge

Edge to be gathered

Figure 6-28: *Prepare fabric for fabric flower*

Figure 6-29: *Gather the edge*

Decorate the strip before you gather it. There are many ways to decorate the ungathered edge, whether folded or raw. Here are a few ideas:

A narrow rolled edge in matching or contrasting thread with or without cording

Yarn or ribbon couched with a balanced or wrapped stitch

A narrow rolled edge with a wide long balanced stitch over it done with fine gold thread in both loopers

Making serger lace along the edge

A string of fine pearls attached to the edge (refer to section on "Attaching Beads," page 112)

Figure 6-30: *Roll strip up and secure into a rose*

Sew tiny charms, beads or buttons along the edge.

A flower made out of lace, or an edging of lace flat-locked to a narrow rolled edge (refer to section on "Applying Lace," page 129)

Lettucing (if bias of woven fabric or crossgrain of knit)

The fabric can be satin, chiffon, tricot, ribbing, interlock, etc. Soft fabrics can be interfaced or left soft and floppy.

Generally the gathered edge is secured by hand stitches as it is rolled up but it can be hot-glued for such things as hair ornaments. For additional decorative effect, centers can be added to these flowers before rolling up and sewing them together. Possibilities include loops of yarn or knotted narrow ribbon (see Figure 6-31), a small circle of fabric (perhaps metallic, perhaps embroidered) stuffed with a bit of fiber fill and gathered around the edge, circles or bias squares of contrasting fabric tacked on through the center(s), a small tassel made from rayon thread, etc.

There is another way to gather and fold a strip of fabric to make a flower. The folded edge is so pretty you probably would not decorate it. Cut a piece of fabric as shown in Figure 6-32 and fold it in half from point to point, pulling gently on it. Notice how the fold has diagonal wrinkles in it. Gather along the raw edges, gathering both raw edges at once. Keep both raw edges next to the knife so both get caught in the stitching: if necessary guide the fabric

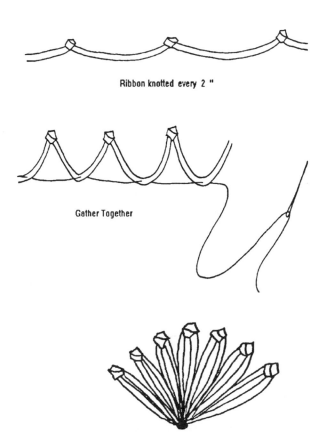

Ribbon knotted every 2 "

Gather Together

Figure 6-31: *Knot thread to make flower center*

so you are trimming something off. The fold will be curved at the ends. Do not worry if the gathering stitching is not perfectly even because it will not show. If you have trouble gathering both edges together without losing the diagonal folds you can gather each edge separately. Fold in half and baste the gathered edges together, then construct as described above.

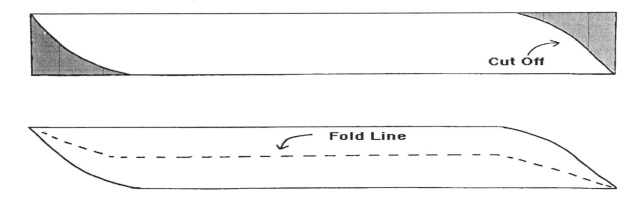

Figure 6-32: *Fabric Flowers*

You can make leaves for your flowers. You can cut out suitable shapes and serge around with a short narrow wrapped or balanced stitch. If the fabric permits you can do a narrow rolled edge. If the fabric has a definite wrong side or if it needs additional stiffening, fuse two layers of "leaf" fabric together with a fusible web. Cut out shapes and serge around the edges. Make the "veins" with a satin stitch on a conventional machine. Another option for leaves is to make circles of leaf fabric, fold into quarters, gather the raw edge tightly, and attach (see Figure 6-33). If you wish you can make stems out of spaghetti tubing. If you plan to couch the "stems" cord the tubing so it will keep its shape. (refer to section on "Spaghetti Tubing," page 110)

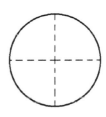

Circle of Leaf Fabric

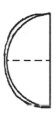

Fold in half

Fold in Quarters and Baste along Raw Edge

Gather Along Raw Edge to Form Leaf

Figure 6-33: *Fabric leaves*

You can cover a hair band with a tube of fabric then attach one or more flowers, perhaps with "leaves" and/or "stems," perhaps with some gathered lace. (refer to section on "Gathering," page 126) You can make the tube normally and turn (refer to section on "Spaghetti Tubing" but use a wider strip of fabric), or you can make it by taking a strip of fabric folded wrong sides together and serging the edges together, then serging along the fold. Use a wide decorative stitch or a narrow stitch.

Another nice hair band is made by threading a strip of wider elastic, like 3/4" wide, through a tube of fabric. Make sure the tube of fabric is big enough to go comfortably around the wearer's head with some ease. Make the elastic about 1" shorter than the distance around the wearer's head. Sew the elastic into a circle after it is threaded through the fabric tube, then tack the ends of the tube together. Wear this end under the hair in back.

Fabric flowers are also wonderful on ponytail holders and barrettes. I hand sew the flower to a fabric covered rubber band. These come in two sizes, and are sold with other hair care items such as brushes and barrettes. I get the smaller rubber bands. The wearer uses another rubber band to secure the ponytail then puts the flower decorated rubber band on top. If she wants a flower barrette she wraps the rubber band a few times around a barrette.

DECORATIVE USES OF CHAIN

The serger chain can be used decoratively. When flat-locking, lettucing or tucking in the middle of the fabric the beginning and ending chains can simply be left as a decorative element.

Serger chain can be made without fabric in the machine then stitched down for monograms or as a type of passementerie (see Figure 6-34). Lift the presser foot when making long lengths of chain unless you have fabric in the machine: this saves unnecessary wear on the bottom of the presser foot from the feed dogs. You can use the 2-thread chainstitch chain for fine serger chain or a right needle 3-thread balanced stitch for heavier chain. For a balanced stitch use a short narrow stitch with fusible thread in the lower looper and a decorative thread in the upper

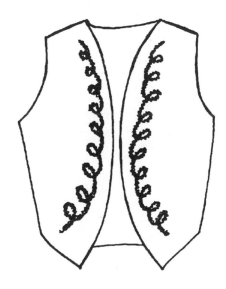

Figure 6-34: *Passementerie*

looper. (refer to section on "Fusible Thread," page 94) Unless using a firm thread and narrow stitch width, you will want to serge over something to give the chain more substance. You can put yarn, cord or narrow ribbon to the right of the needle and serge over that. The short stitch length and narrow stitch width should cover completely whatever you are serging over. Another option is to serge over a strip of fabric such as sheer tricot then trim the other edge of the fabric to the stitching. With fabric a wide stitch width can be used. If you want a wider trim you can serge the other edge of the fabric, making sure the edges of the two lines of stitching meet. Using a wide stitch on both edges will produce a wide decorative trim. If you will be serging both edges of a strip of fabric, make sure the strip of fabric is wide enough so you are trimming something off on the second edge: it makes it easier to handle.

Pull the chain gently from the rear of the serger as you sew. Arrange and pin on garment as desired, fuse in place with an iron, then top-stitch with conventional machine, using a zig-zag or straight stitch. If any of your threads are nylon or if you are serging over sheer tricot, use a thick damp pressing cloth to protect the nylon from excess heat when fusing. Test a sample to check iron temperatures.

SERGER RIBBON

Ribbon can be made on the serger. For plain ribbon just finish both edges of a strip of fabric with a narrow rolled edge. This is a nice way to get matching hair ribbons for a child's dress. Use two layers of fabric if the dress fabric has a noticeable wrong side. Serger ribbon can also be made by serging both edges of a fabric strip with a wider stitch, using a decorative thread. Serge one edge then turn and serge the other edge, perhaps so the lines of serging meet in the middle. The second line of stitching can be a narrow rolled edge if you wish a narrow fancy ribbon. Make sure the strip of fabric is wide enough: narrow strips are easier to handle if you are trimming something off on the second edge. Remember that generally a ribbon will be seen from both sides. The wrapped edge stitch looks the same from both sides. If using a balanced stitch use the same thread in both loopers. Cord, yarn or beads can be couched to the edge.

Instead of having the lines of stitching meeting you can make a wider strip and leave a space in the middle, to be filled with decorative flat-locking or couching, or with decorative stitches on your conventional machine, or with a pattern in decorative 2-thread chainstitch. Two layers of wide serger ribbon, curved or straight, can be interfaced and joined to make a nice belt.

SERGER APPLIQUE

The serger can be used to finish the edges of appliques. (refer to chapter on "Securing Edges") Avoid small intricate shapes. The serger allows you to use a decorative thread for edging the applique shapes. In one technique you serge around the applique piece with a decorative stitch then sew it on with a zig-zag stitch on a conventional machine. Another option is to use flat-locking to sew on the applique, after fusing the applique to the background fabric. To do this, cut out your applique pieces and sew around them with fusible thread. (refer to section on "Fusible Thread," page 94) Either put it in the bobbin of a conventional machine and zig-zag around the edges or put it in one looper with thread that matches the fabric in the other looper and serge around with a balanced stitch. Fuse the applique pieces in place. Finally, serge around them using the flat-locking over a fold techniques with a decorative thread in the upper looper. The easiest technique is to put fusible thread in the lower looper and decorative thread in the upper looper. After serging the edge with a balanced stitch the pieces can be fused to the background fabric then attached with a conventional machine. The fusing makes it much easier to sew.

These same techniques can be used to make patch pockets. Serge around the edges of the pocket with a decorative thread. Top-stitch in place with a conventional machine.

PIECING QUILTS

Use a serger to piece your quilt tops. (refer to section on "Securing Seams," page 60) It is quicker, plus your seams are more secure. The 1/4" piecing seams are subject to abrasion even within the quilt, particularly when washed, and do sometimes fail if they are not protected by serging. Another advantage of the serger is that it facilitates accurate seam allowances: if you set the machine for a 6.3 mm stitch width and guide the fabric edges so the knife is skimming them, you have <u>exactly</u> 1/4" seam allowances. In order to allow for "turn of cloth" you may wish to make the seam allowance <u>slightly</u> less. If you cannot adjust the cutting width on your serger, refer to section on "Guiding Fabric," page 104.

You have more control over a serger's speed if you select a machine which has an electronic foot control. Some machines also have a half speed or "Sew Slow" control.

All piecing seams are pressed to one side, usually towards the darker fabric. A serger seam prefers to lie with the upper looper thread on top and the lower looper thread next to the fabric. When piecing, put the darker fabric next to the feed dogs so that the seam lies a little flatter when pressed towards the darker fabric. When crossing one seam with another, refer to the section on

"Securing Seams," page 60. Make sure the seam allowances are turned in opposite directions.

It is desirable to reduce the bulk in piecing seams. Make sure your stitch length is not too short, or about 2.5 to 3.0 mm. Use an extra-fine thread, especially in the loopers. (Refer to section on "Basic Thread," page 89). A slightly heavier batting makes a bulkier seam allowance less apparent.

There are many books available on machine piecing techniques that can give you valuable shortcuts and tips. Many of these are based on cutting strips of fabric, serging them together, cutting these sections of fabric apart into strips, and combining these strips into blocks. Sometimes they suggest cutting strips on an unthreaded serger. I do not recommend this: I do not feel it saves time over using a rotary cutter, it is not as accurate, and it is unnecessary wear-and-tear on your serger. Do not feel you have to follow traditional patterns with hundreds of pieces. Some of the most beautiful Amish quilts are quite simple. I made a quilt by framing a large center panel of a nice print with panels of other fabrics. Simple, yes, but much appreciated.

CHAPTER 7

STITCHES

Most of this book has dealt with the overlock stitch. There are several other types of stitches. A listing of the various types of stitches is in the section on "Stitch Codes" at the end of this chapter. The most common stitches are described in detail below.

2-THREAD OVEREDGE STITCH

This is stitch 502 or 503. (refer to the section on "Stitch Codes," page 148) The first home sergers were 4/2-thread machines, making a 2-thread overedge stitch and a 2-thread chainstitch. Although few domestic 4/2-sergers are now sold, many industrial machines still use this configuration. These machines have one looper for the chainstitch and one looper for the overedge stitch. The newer domestic machines that offer a 2-thread overedge stitch actually use two loopers to form the stitch. They are basically overlock machines which can be converted to make a 2-thread overedge stitch. The thread is removed from the upper overlock looper and a small guide is swiveled or snapped into place so that the upper looper can catch the lower looper thread and carry it up over the top so the needle can catch it. The needle thread may have a different threading path for the overedge stitch. Check your manual.

For most applications, the 2-thread overedge stitch is adjusted so the looper thread lies on top of the fabric and the needle thread on the bottom (see Figures 7-1 and 7-2). Their loops join along the edge of the fabric, neither pulling it in nor hanging loose outside it. When rethreading the lower looper, you need to clear the needle thread as described in the section on "Threading," page 21.

The 2-thread overedge stitch cannot be used to make a seam.

The 2-thread overedge stitch does not protect a raw edge from fraying as well

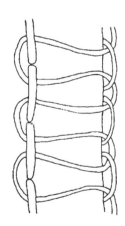

Figure 7-1: *2-Thread Overedge Balanced Stitch - Top*

as a 3-thread overlock stitch, despite the fact that it uses nearly as much thread. However, on fine silkies it will make less of a mark through to the right side when seam allowances are pressed flat.

The 2-thread overedge stitch has a great deal of stretch, due to the fact that both the looper and the needle threads are zig-zagging back and forth. Therefore it is wonderful for sewing elastic to the edge of knits before turning and top-stitching.

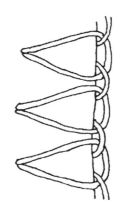

The 2-thread overedge is nice for a blind hem. There is plenty of stretch for the stretchiest interlock, and the hem lies flat and is therefore less noticeable. It does not protect the raw edge from raveling as well as a 3-thread blind hem. After stitching

Figure 7-2: *2-Thread Overedge Balanced Stitch - Bottom*

pull the hem flat. You will notice it has become about 1/4" narrower than what you pinned up: this is the width of the stitch. Allow for this when pinning up your hem.

A 2-thread narrow rolled edge is finer and lighter than a 3-thread narrow rolled edge, and appears the same on both sides. Tighten the needle tensions to convert from a balanced 2-thread overedge to a 2-thread narrow rolled edge, plus use the narrow rolled edge stitch finger and stitch length. Do not use as short a stitch length as you might for a 3-thread narrow rolled edge. (refer to section on "Narrow Rolled Edge," page 46) The 2-thread narrow rolled edge is not quite as secure as a 3-thread rolled edge on heavier fabrics.

The 2-thread overedge is already a flat-lock, and generally no adjustment of tensions is necessary. One nice feature is that the extra looper thread is gone, making both edges of the stitch completely symmetrical. If the overedge stitch is made with overlock loopers, as described above, any decorative threads must be placed in the lower looper then carried over the top by the upper looper. This is a more difficult threading path for heavy threads.

For the wrapped stitch loosen the looper and tighten the needle. The 2-thread wrapped edge looks finer than a 3-thread wrapped edge, but has the same problem with heavy decorative threads that the 2-thread flat-lock has if made with converted overlock loopers. Experiment: it may work fine on your machine.

A 2-thread stitch makes a better blanket stitch than a 3-thread stitch. (refer to section on "Blanket Stitch," page 57) For the blanket stitch tighten the looper and loosen the needle.

2-THREAD CHAINSTITCH

This is stitch 401. (refer to section on "Stitch Codes," page 148) The 2-thread chainstitch is made with a needle and a chainstitch looper. It is most commonly found on 5-thread machines, along with an overlock stitch. Domestic 5-thread machines generally offer the option of a 3-thread overlock with or without a 2-thread chainstitch, or a 4-thread overlock without the chainstitch. Industrial 5-thread machines are not convertible to a 4-thread overlock stitch. Some domestic 5-thread machines also offer a 2-thread overedge. On 5-thread domestic sergers the same tension disk is used for either a chainstitch needle thread or an overlock stitch needle thread. Check your manual for any differences in the threading paths. (Sometimes people wonder why they cannot have a 2-thread chainstitch with a 4-thread overlock. This would be a 6-thread stitch, but the poor machine only has 5 tension disks.)

On the top of the seam the 2-thread chainstitch looks much like a straight stitch on a conventional machine. On the bottom of the seam the looper thread loops forward and backward in the stitch such that it is triple thickness (see Figures 7-3 and 7-4).

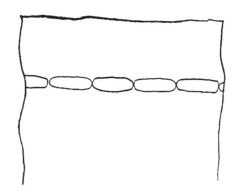

Figure 7-3: *2-thread chainstitch - top*

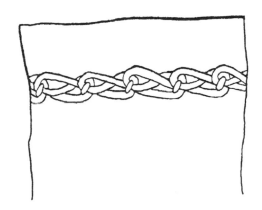

Figure 7-4: *2-thread chainstitch - bottom*

The chainstitch need not be made over the edge of the fabric. Therefore some domestic machines offering this feature provide a means of disabling the upper looper and swiveling the upper knife out of the way so a flat piece can be inserted into the machine to the right of the needle, making a larger sewing area.

The chainstitch can be raveled out, starting at the end of the seam (not the beginning). Pull on the loose end of the looper thread. There are two ways to prevent the end of a seam from raveling out. The easiest way is, when ending a seam, pull the fabric away from the machine slowly while continuing to press on the foot control. This will ensure that the chain continues to form. Then just cut the chain in the middle. If you pull too hard on the work as you are removing it from the machine, you will notice where the chain stops forming and you just get two separate threads. Cut the threads and stick a pin through the ending loop of looper thread. Pull on the loop so you pull it through the last stitch: this will keep the chain from raveling out.

On some domestic and most industrial machines the tensioning device for the chain stitch looper thread is hidden behind the left door.

When rethreading the chainstitch looper you can have the same problems as when rethreading the lower looper for the overlock stitch. (refer to section on "Threading," page 21) Either clear the needle thread or re-thread the needle after threading the lower looper. Once the needle and chainstitch looper are threaded, you must sew with fabric in the machine in order to bring the chainstitch looper thread up through the needle plate. Use a stitch length of at least 2.5, or longer if using heavier thread in the looper.

In a properly adjusted 2-thread chainstitch the needle thread goes all the way through the fabric and around the chainstitch looper thread. On the bottom of the seam the needle thread should be visible as a tiny dot of thread on the chainstitch looper thread. If it is too loose it will form loops on the bottom of the seam and the seam will pull apart. If it is slightly too tight the seam will be stiff. If it is even tighter the seam will pucker. The loops of the chainstitch looper thread should not extend too far past the ends of the stitch nor should they pull so tight they pucker the seam. The chainstitch looper thread should curve smoothly and snugly around the dots of needle thread.

This stitch is rarely used for knits, because an overlock stitch is sufficient for most knits and because with normal settings the chainstitch has little stretch. Loosening the tensions will give a stitch that stretches. You will probably need to loosen the looper tension, and may need to loosen the needle tension. Another alternative is to use texturized nylon or elastic thread in the lower looper. Loosen the looper tension and check the needle tension. Using the 2-thread chainstitch with the overlock stitch results in a wider and more secure stitch on loose ravel-prone knits.

This stitch is often used to seam wovens. Since it is a serger stitch, it is sewn much faster than a straight stitch on a conventional machine. Also, any raw edges can be finished at the same time with the overlock stitch. Therefore it is wonderful for home furnishings or production sewing. It is also wonderful anytime you do not wish to press seam allowances flat after every washing. If desired the seam allowance can be pressed to one side and top-stitched: this is nice on the outseam of casual slacks.

Since the chainstitch need not be sewn over an edge, its needle is placed to the left of the overlock needles on a 5-thread machine and a wider seam allowance results. This provides extra security for sewing wovens. (refer to section on "Woven Fabrics," page 76)

The chainstitch can also be used for decorative top-stitching. Larger threads can be used in the looper than can be used in a needle. In addition the looper thread is triple density (see Figure 7-4) so any decorative thread has a pronounced effect. To get the looper thread on the right side of the fabric, decorative top-stitching must be done upside down. On some machines a clear plastic foot is available so decorative chainstitch stitching can be accurately positioned. Using normal serger thread, this can be used where normal top-stitching would be used, for example around garment edges. With heavy decorative threads, top-stitching can be used for a variety of effects, from wearable art to elegant embellishments.

A 2-thread chainstitch is often used for shirring. Put elastic thread into the chainstitch looper, lengthen stitch, loosen tensions, then gradually tighten the looper tension as you test. Make sure the needle tension is just loose enough to allow the seam to stretch as much as the fabric. Small loops of needle thread may be visible on the bottom of the seam. The longer the stitch length the more shirring you can get.

Here is a fun technique if you have a domestic 5-thread machine which allows you to disable the overlock stitch. Put a heavy decorative thread in the chainstitch looper and a matching or invisible thread in the needle. Lengthen the stitch to allow for the heavy thread, and loosen tensions so there is no puckering. Now you are ready to stitch on a water soluble stabilizer. If the weather is humid and the stabilizer is too limp, iron the stabilizer with a dry iron. Fold it so you have a double layer and pin it to the finished edge of a piece of fabric, perhaps a placemat or vest. Sewing slowly and guiding your work under the presser foot, take one stitch onto the edge of the fabric and then about 4-6 off of it, another stitch onto the fabric and so on. A lovely scalloped edge will result. This can also be done over a fold, so the scallops end up in the middle of the garment section.

On some machines there is an attachment available so you can attach bias binding with the 2-thread chainstitch.

MULTI-THREAD CHAINSTITCH

The multi-thread chainstitchs are only available on industrial machines. The codes are 402, 406 and 407. (refer to section on "Stitch Codes," page 148) They consist of two or three needle threads, with a looper thread joining the needle threads on the bottom. These stitches need not be formed over an edge. On the top they look like parallel lines of top-stitching, and on the bottom the looper thread goes back and forth between the needle threads. They cannot be used to make a seam.

Stitch 402 has two closely spaced needle threads with a looper thread on the bottom. It is called a "cording stitch." With the looper tension tightened enough to make a ridge, it is used for permanent crease lines on pants and for tucks. The pintuck does not end up as tight as it would if made over a fold with an overlock stitch. (refer to section on "Pintucks," page 122)

A machine which can produce a coverstitch, codes 602 or 605, can also be used to produce these multi-thread chainstitchs, if the cover thread is not used. If the coverstitch machine has 3 needles, for producing a 605 stitch, one of the needles can be dropped out as well, to produce a 406 or 602 stitch.

Stitch 406 has two needle threads with a looper thread on the bottom (see Figures 7-5 and 7-6). It is similar to stitch 402 except the needles are further apart and the looper tension is loose enough so the stitch lies flat. It is called a "cover seaming stitch." This stitch is used to flatten and secure seam allowances after a seam is sewn, for example shoulder seams or ribbing seams. After serging the seam is pulled open and top-stitched from the right side with the cover seaming stitch. It is also often used for hemming knits. When hemming knits check tensions and stitch length to make sure there is enough stretch: a hem is on the crossgrain (the stretchiest direction) plus it gets stretched a lot. This stitch is imitated by a double needle sewing a straight stitch on a conventional machine. (refer to section on "Blind Hemming," page 44)

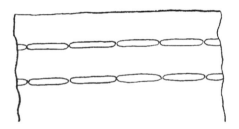

Figure 7-5: Stitch 406 - cover seaming - top

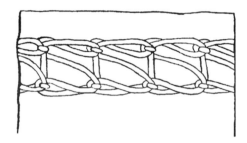

Figure 7-6: Stitch 406 - cover seaming - bottom

Stitch 407 has three needle thread plus a looper thread. It is used for applying elastic and it is called an "elastic stitch" (see Figures 7-7 and 7-8).

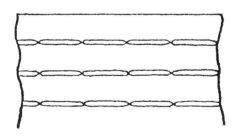

Figure 7-7: Stitch 407 - elastic stitch - top

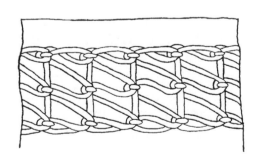

Figure 7-8: Stitch 407 - elastic stitch - bottom

COVERSTITCH

The coverstitches are only available on industrial machines. The codes are 602 and 605. (refer to section on "Stitch Codes," page 148) They consist of two or three needle threads, with a looper thread joining the needle threads on the bottom and a cover thread on top. These stitches need not be formed over an edge. The top and bottom look very similar, with the cover thread going back and forth on the top of the stitch while the looper thread does the same on the bottom. Stitch 602 has two needle threads (see Figures 7-9 and 7-10) and stitch 605 has three needle threads (see Figures 7-11 and 7-12). These stitches are used for flattening and securing seam allowances, for example around ribbing. They are also used for hemming: make sure tensions are loose enough to allow sufficient stretch. They cannot be used to make a seam. The flat-lock stitch is used to imitate them, but is not as secure.

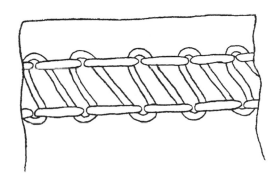

Figure 7-9: Stitch 602 - coverstitch - top

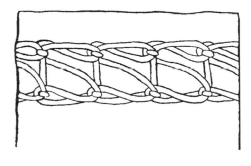

Figure 7-10: Stitch 602 - coverstitch - bottom

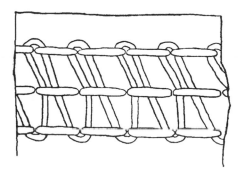

Figure 7-11: Stitch 605 - coverstitch - top

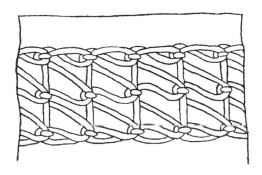

Figure 7-12: Stitch 605 - coverstitch - bottom

FLAT-SEAMING

The flat-seaming stitch is only available on industrial machines. The code is 607. (refer to section on "Stitch Codes," page 148) This stitch need not be formed over an edge. Two pairs of needles are used, a left pair and a right pair, making four in all. A looper thread joins the needle threads on the bottom and a covering thread secures the top of the seam (see Figures 7-13 and 7-14). The top and bottom look very similar, with the cover thread going back and forth on the top of the stitch while the looper thread does the same on the bottom. This stitch is used to make flat seams in knits. With the four needles, this is a wide secure stitch. The raw edges of the fabric are butted together or overlapped slightly, and the seam is actually made by top-stitching. This makes a very flat seam for activewear, underwear and baby clothes. It is imitated with the flat-lock, although the flat-lock with zig-zag top-stitching more closely duplicates the security of the covering stitch.

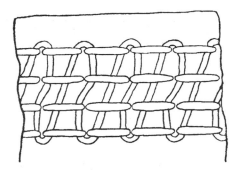

Figure 7-13: *Stitch 607 - flat-seaming - top*

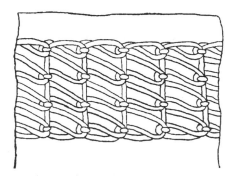

Figure 7-14: *Stitch 607 - flat-seaming - bottom*

STITCH CODES

The United States government has published specifications for sewing machine stitches, assigning a code to each type. This is the federal standard 751-A. It also includes codes and specifications for various seam configurations. It can be ordered from: General Services Administration, Specifications Activity, Printed Materials Supply Division, Building 197, Naval Weapons Plant, Washington, D.C., 20407

Stitches on industrial machines are often referred to by these codes. Here are the code numbers and descriptions of some commonly used stitches. (Unless you are in the market for an industrial machine you can blissfully ignore these codes.) In preceding sections of this chapter I described some of these stitches in detail.

100 Single thread chainstitch: All these stitches are made with a single needle thread.

> **101 Chainstitch:** used for basting, attaching buttons, etc.

> **103 Blindstitch:** This is the stitch used on blindstitch machines.

300 Lockstitch: This is the stitch made by a conventional sewing machine. It is made with one needle thread and one bobbin thread.

> **301 Straight stitch lockstitch**

> **304 Zig-zag stitch**

400 Multi-thread Chain Stitch

> **401 2-thread chainstitch**, as described in the section on page 143

> **402 Cording stitch for permanent creases:** Two needles, closely spaced, with a looper thread on the bottom, three threads in all.

> **406 Cover seaming stitch:** Two needles with a looper thread on the bottom, three threads in all.

> **407 Elastic stitch:** Three needles with a looper thread on the bottom, four threads in all.

500 Overedge and safety (overlock) stitches: These are what are most commonly referred to as "serger" stitches. Some of these stitches are formed the same way as others but receive different codes because of the way their tensions are adjusted.

> **502 2-thread overedge with the needle tension tightened and the looper tension loosened**, as described in the section on "wrapped stitch," page 57.

> **503 2-thread overedge with the needle and looper threads balanced** as described in the section on "2-Thread Overedge Stitch," page 141.

> **504 3-thread overlock stitch**, with tensions adjusted for a "balanced stitch."

> **505 3-thread overlock stitch with the needle tension loosened and lower looper tightened** so they meet on the edge of the seam, as described in the section on "Flat-Locking," page 51.

512 4-thread overlock with upper looper thread only caught by right needle thread, also called a mock safety stitch.

514 4-thread overlock with upper looper thread caught by both needle threads, also called a safety stitch.

515 safety stitch seaming: 2-thread chainstitch (stitch 401) plus 2-thread overedge (stitch 503), produced on what is sometimes called a 4/2-thread machine.

516 safety stitch seaming: 2-thread chainstitch (stitch 401) plus 3-thread overlock (stitch 504), produced on what is sometimes called a 5-thread machine.

519 safety stitch seaming: 2-thread chainstitch (stitch 401) plus 4-thread covering stitch (stitch 602).

521 4-thread overlock stitch with both needle tensions loosened and lower looper tightened so they meet on the edge of the seam, as described in the section on "4-Thread Flat-Lock," page 54. This stitch is sometimes called a hosiery stitch.

600 Coverstitches and flat-seaming stitch

602 4-thread coverstitch: two needles, one looper thread on the bottom and one cover thread on the top.

605 5-thread coverstitch: three needles, one looper thread on the bottom and one cover thread on the top.

607 Flat-seaming stitch: four needles, one looper thread on the bottom and one cover thread on the top. Used for flat or butted seaming.

CHAPTER 8
HARDWARE OPTIONS

INDUSTRIAL SERGERS

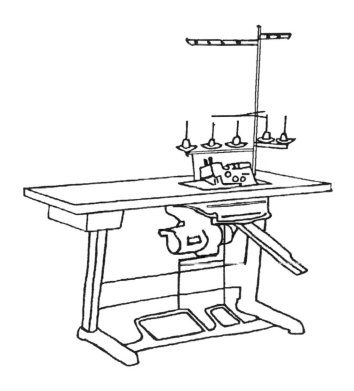

Figure 8-11: *Industrial Serger*

Industrial sergers are workhorses. Although they cost at least twice as much as a home serger they last many times longer, often 15 to 30 years of full-time daily use. Their stitch is even and consistent on a variety of weights of fabric. They can sew extremely fast, although they can sew slowly too if necessary for control. They can handle heavier fabrics and heavier threads. All controls, including the presser foot lift, can be operated by knee or foot, leaving the operator's hands free to manipulate fabric. They are set into a worktable along with a heavy motor, and are anything but portable. A flexible arm light is attached to the worktable, providing excellent light on both the machine and the fabric. They can be set up for 110 volts (normal household current) or 220 volts.

One of the advantages of industrial sergers is the wide variety of attachments available. These attachments make it quick and easy to do such things as blind hemming, gathering, piping, taping seams, automatically cutting the chain, and automatically pulling it into the beginning of the seam. There are also special attachments for such things as sewing denim or removing the curl when seaming knits. As necessary, these accessories are engaged and controlled by knee or foot action. Also, a machine can be customized for a particular task or type of fabric by changing the needle plate, feed dogs and/or presser foot.

In commercial settings sergers are often set up for one specific task, with a rule that operators do not change any of the settings. If operators are allowed to change settings it is a good idea to leave a sample of the fabric and stitch last used in the machine, so the next user knows how the machine is set. If the machine is tailored for a particular type of fabric it is a good idea to so label the machine, especially if there are a variety of machines in the same shop. If there are any attachments on a machine it should also be so labeled.

Make sure the machine has enough oil, as indicated in the sight glass. Especially if working in a dusty environment, change the oil periodically. Periodically clean the tension disks, and clean out the lint behind the front door. Adjust the light so your work is well lighted. If your light plugs into the motor, it probably takes a special low voltage bulb. These bulbs are available from your dealer. Do not plug the light into a wall plug, or you will blow the bulb.

Selecting an Industrial Serger

It is particularly important to find a qualified dealer when purchasing an industrial machine. You need knowledgeable assistance in selecting the proper machine and accessories for your needs. You also need prompt competent service in the event of any breakdown. Some things to look for in a dealer are how long the dealer has been in business, whether the repair people are trained on your machine and how large the dealership is (larger dealers are likely to have had more experience in solving different types of problems). You should also ask around to find out which dealers people have had good or bad experiences with.

The stitch codes described in the section on "Stitch Codes" on page 148 are widely used for describing industrial machines. Each machine is assigned a long code, part of which indicates the type of stitch it produces. Other parts of this code indicate features which can be changed, such as special attachments or another type of feed dog. In other words, adding a gathering attachment or changing the presser foot will change the code, and what the machine is set up to do best. Many of these changes can be done on site. The company brochures, available from your dealer, describe their codes in detail. Some brochures may use the term "bight" or "overedging width" for stitch width.

The first step in selecting an industrial machine is to define exactly what you will be using it for. Bring along samples of your fabric to the dealer, and list any special functions you would like to be able to perform. If you will be doing more than one type of sewing you may want to be able to change the machine: look for a machine which is easy to convert. Check how easy the machine is to thread and adjust. Look at and sew on a variety of machines. Refer to Appendix C: Selecting a Serger, page 177, for additional tips. Many of the numerous features mentioned there will not be relevant, but the rest of the material will be useful.

SPECIAL ATTACHMENTS

There are not as many attachments and presser feet available for domestic sergers as there are for domestic conventional machines. Also, there is less standardization, so a foot made for another machine probably will not fit yours. If your machine has snap-on feet, it is possible that another machine's foot will fit. Different manufacturers may have different names for some of these special feet. Ask to see the foot, and ask what it is used for. Some machines also have special attachments which can be fastened to the bed of the machine.

Blind Hem Feet

On most domestic sergers a blind hem foot is available as an optional extra. The blind hem foot has a long blade to enable you to guide a fold or edge of fabric accurately (see Figure 8-2). This foot is useful for many things besides blind hemming. It is the best tool when you need to accurately position one edge or fold of fabric on top of another. This is necessary for blind hemming, applying lace and some couching. In order to attach lace or trim to a fabric edge while finishing the edge at the same time, place the lace or ribbon to the left of the guide so the needle just pierces the edge of the lace or ribbon while the edge of the fabric is finished. On machines which do not have a special foot for the narrow rolled edge, the blind hem foot can be used while doing a narrow rolled edge. This means lace can be applied to a narrow rolled edge in one step, as described in the section on "Applying Lace," page 129. The guide can also be used for positioning things for couching, whether for going to the right of the needle or for going under the needle. Position the guide as necessary. Another advantage of the blind hem foot is that you can guide fabric very accurately with it. Accuracy is particularly important when flat-locking over a fold, which is usually done with a wide (left needle) flat-lock. Unfortunately, the blind hem foot for most machines limits you to a narrow flat-lock because it will only accept the right needle. If your blind hem foot does not have an opening for the left needle, see if you can get a friendly someone to cut an opening for you, using your regular foot as a guide. Make sure the edges are finished smooth.

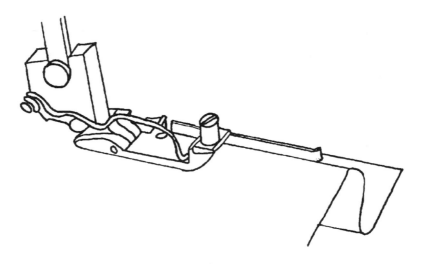

Figure 8-2: Blind hem attachment

Elastic Guides

Many machines have an optional foot or guide for sewing on elastic. The feet for sewing on elastic are sometimes called elasticators or gathering feet. The guides or feet have an adjustable spring loaded clamp that you feed elastic through so it can be sewn into the seam (see Figure 8-3).

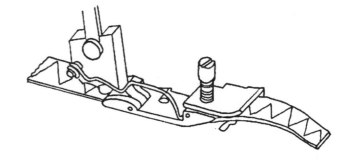

Figure 8-3: Elastic foot

In order to know how tight to set the clamp for sewing elastic you must sew samples until you get the proper degree of gathering for a given type of elastic, and it must be reset when you change elastic or are attaching elastic to a different garment edge. For this reason the elastic attachment or foot will probably not save time when sewing elastic onto one of a kind garments, although it can be a great timesaver in production sewing. In addition the elastic must be sewn onto a flat piece of fabric. After applying the elastic the last seam is sewn including the ends of elastic. This is not as secure as overlapping the elastic 1/2" and sewing it together, then sewing it into a circular opening.

The elastic attachment or foot can also be used for gathering. In one method, an edge is gathered by sewing on elastic. This is perfect for some soft furnishings, such as bed ruffles. Another gathering technique only works with elastic feet which have the guide open on the left. The fabric to be gathered is placed under the foot next to the feed dogs while the other piece of fabric is placed into the clamp. The fabric under the foot, if it is lightweight enough, is then gathered onto the fabric in the clamp in one step. Use with differential feed if you have it. This can be a real timesaver when doing large amounts of gathering. (refer to section on "Gathering," page 126 for more information on gathering)

With the clamp tension loosened the elastic feet or guides can be used for guiding ribbon or tape so the knives do not cut the edge. If the guide on the elastic foot is open on the left, wide trim or lace can also be guided. (refer to section on "Guiding Fabric," page 104)

Tape/Piping Guide

There is an accessory, available on some machines, which is called a tape/piping guide (see Figure 8-4). However, it bears no resemblance to the tape guide described below. It is fastened onto the body of the machine and is used for folding a wide strip of bias fabric and inserting it into the middle of a seam, as a sort of uncorded piping. This look is common in sports clothes and active wear. There is also a hole for guiding cording through the middle of the bias strip. It can be used with a piping foot to make piping.

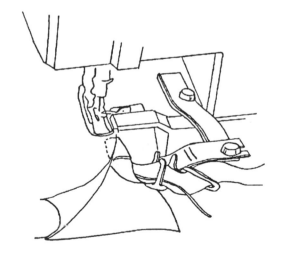

Figure 8-4: *Tape/Piping Guide*

Tape Guide

Some standard feet have a guide for feeding narrow tape under the needle. Generally this does not work for feeding tape to the right of the needle, although often it can be used for guiding cord or fine yarn to the right of the needle. This guide is useful for feeding a stabilizing tape while serging a seam. Some machines offer an optional tape foot for this purpose. On some tape feet the guide can be adjusted for different widths of tape, and can be positioned left or right to control the position of the tape relative to the needle. Some machines have a separate tape guide attached to the bed of the of the machine, which can be positioned left or right as necessary.

Cording Guides

Some machines offer a means of guiding fine cord to the right of the needle. Some machines have this guide on the narrow rolled edge foot, some have it on the regular foot. Some machines offer an optional foot or guide for cording. Sometimes this guide is adjustable, so it can accept slightly larger cord. Some machines have one or more additional cord guides on the machine to facilitate feeding the cord.

Beading Feet

There is a beading foot available on some domestic sergers, sometimes called a pearl and sequin foot (see Figure 8-5). Sometimes the blind hem foot converts for guiding beads. This greatly facilitates the process of sewing strings of pearls, cross-locked beads or sequins onto a piece of fabric. It also makes it much easier to make serger piping and couch heavier cording. (refer to the sections on "Piping" on page 114, "Couching" on page 117 and "Attaching Beads" on page 112) If you have a beading foot, mark the positions of both needles on it: when using this foot you are usually guiding a fold or edge of fabric just to the right of one needle.

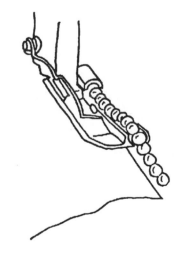

Figure 8-5: *Beading foot*

Piping Foot

With a piping foot you can make conventional piping, and sew either conventional or serger piping into a seam (see Figure 8-6). This foot can also be used for serging on zippers, though the regular foot works well too. If zipper teeth are quite large, the piping foot makes it easier to attach the zipper.

Bias Binding Attachment

The bias binding attachment uses the 2-thread chainstitch on a 5-thread machine to double fold a bias strip and attach it to the edge of a piece of fabric.

Cloth Guide

Some machines offer an adjustable cloth guide (see Figure 8-7). This is useful for many decorative techniques, although the elastic or blind hem foot can be used in lieu of it.

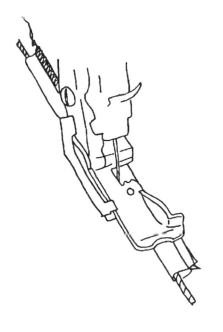

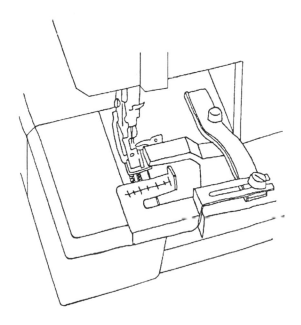

Figure 8-6: Piping Foot

Figure 8-7: Cloth Guide

Clear Plastic Foot

Some machines offer a clear plastic foot. At present this is only used with the 2-thread chainstitch. The clear plastic permits accurate positioning of top-stitching and decorative stitching. Since the foot just has a single opening for the chainstitch needle, it holds the fabric more securely than the standard foot.

Gathering Plate

Also available on some domestic machines is an accessory called a fabric separator, gathering plate (see Figure 8-8) or shirring foot (see Figure 8-9). It is used with differential feed to gather one piece of fabric onto another. (refer to the section on "Gathering," page 126, for more information)

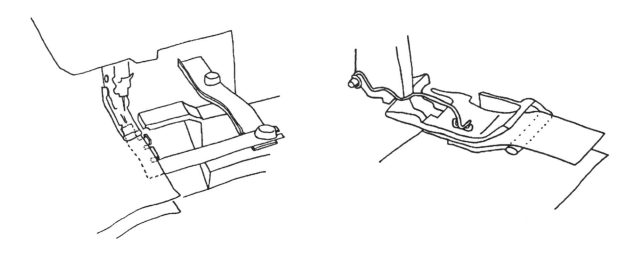

Figure 8-8: Gathering Plate   *Figure 8-9:* Shirring Foot

APPENDIX A
TROUBLESHOOTING
GUIDE

Here is a detailed troubleshooting guide. If none of these suggestions resolve a problem, take the machine to your dealer along with samples of the problem. It may help to also bring along this book, so you can tell him or her what you have checked.

SKIPPING STITCHES

Make sure the needle is inserted all the way into the machine. Check both needles if using a 4-thread overlock: the left needle will be slightly higher. (If the needle is hanging down too far it cannot catch the upper looper thread.)

Check for a damaged needle. (Refer to section on "Needles," page 19)

If your machine uses round shank industrial needles make sure the long groove is facing directly forward.

Make sure you are using the proper type of needles. There are several different types of industrial needles. If your machine uses conventional needles try to use the same kind that came with your machine. Use a size 11 or 14 (75 or 90).

If sewing a thick layer of fabric, refer to section on "Bulky Fabrics" in Appendix B: Dictionary of Fabrics, page 169.

Check tensions: extremely tight tensions can cause skipping stitches.

If the problem only occurs with a decorative thread, your machine may not accept that thread. Try loosening tensions and/or increasing the stitch length. It may work in the upper looper if you use regular serger thread in the lower looper.

Check your loopers for burrs, particularly the lower looper. Move the looper with the balance wheel so you can run your fingers along it to feel for any roughness. Smooth with crocus cloth, which is available at a hardware store.

Make sure all guides are properly threaded.

Make sure all needles and loopers are threaded. Often when a thread breaks its end gets caught and carried out with the other threads. All appears normal, except no stitch is formed and the eye of the needle or looper is not threaded.

If all else fails, bring your machine in for service.

THREAD KEEPS BREAKING

If the thread breaks immediately after rethreading, refer to section on "Threading," page 21.

Make sure none of the tensions are too tight.

Checking every guide, make sure machine is properly threaded. Sometimes the lower looper thread gets caught around something while threading the left-hand end of the lower looper.

Check to see if a thread is caught under the edge of a cone or the thread stand. Use the thread nets as described in the section on "Adjusting Tensions," page 32.

Change the needle. A worn needle can cause thread breakage. If the needle is too small for the thread this can also cause thread breakage. Make sure the needle is properly inserted.

Check your machine for burrs. Move the lower looper all the way to the right with the balance wheel and feel along it with your fingers. Feel along the upper looper. Visually check the needle hole on the needle plate. If in doubt, use a fine soft thread to check it. Pull a loosely twisted thread from a piece of light fabric, such as silk or acetate. If you can, remove your needle plate from the machine. If you cannot, remove the presser foot and use a floss threader to run the thread through the needle hole. Keeping it loose, gently pull the thread up and down to see if it catches anywhere. Smooth any burrs with a strip of crocus cloth.

Old thread tends to become brittle and break easily.

THREAD TANGLES

If the thread tangles right after rethreading a looper, rethread that looper. Make sure to avoid catching another thread, as illustrated in Figure 1-8 on page 12.

If the thread tangles when beginning to serge, you may not have remembered to pull the chain back and to the left before you began. Rethread, and remember next time.

NEEDLE BREAKS

Do not pull on fabric behind the needle while sewing. This can cause the needle to collide with the lower looper.

Put in a new needle and see if problem persists. You may have had a damaged needle. If sewing heavy fabric use a larger size needle. Make sure needle is properly inserted into machine.

Make sure tensions are not excessively tight.

Sew more slowly if using a difficult fabric that resists needle penetration.

Use proper type of needle for your machine. Check your manual to be sure.

Many scrgcrs do not have an opening for the left needle in the narrow rolled edge needle plate and/or presser foot. If you try to sew with the left needle when one of these machines is set up for a narrow rolled edge, the needle will break.

NEEDLE HOLES IN FABRIC

Make sure your needle is not too big for your fabric.

Check your needle for damage, as described in section on "Needles," page 19.

If sewing with knits, you can try a ballpoint needle, as described in the section on "Needles," page 19.

If you are getting needle holes when blind hemming, move the guide slightly to the right and loosen needle tensions slightly. Sew a sample.

Prewash the fabric using fabric softener. It makes the threads more flexible so they can more easily move out of the way of the needle.

Make sure needle tensions are not too tight.

RIPPLING SEAMS

Use differential feed set greater than one. Lengthen the stitch length and/or loosen presser foot pressure. Refer to the section on "Knits," page 67, and the section on "Sweater Knits," page 174, for more information.

PUCKERING SEAMS

If you have differential feed use it with a setting of less than 1.

Loosen needle tension slightly. If the lower looper tension is tight, for example when doing a narrow rolled edge or a flat-lock, loosen it slightly.

Shorten the stitch length.

Increase pressure foot pressure.

Check to see if a thread is caught somewhere. If sewing with a slippery thread a loop may have slipped under the cone. This can be corrected with thread nets, as described in the section on "Special Threads," page 90. Sometimes, when lifting the thread telescope to begin sewing, a loop of thread will get caught under the base of the thread stand. A quick check for caught threads is to feel each thread as it goes into its tension disks: if a thread is caught it will feel very tight.

FABRIC NOT FEEDING EVENLY

Adjust the pressure foot pressure. Use a heavier pressure for firmly woven or thinner fabrics. Use a lighter pressure for thicker fabrics or stretchy spongy fabrics.

Allow knives to trim off at least a narrow strip of fabric.

Make sure presser foot is down.

FABRIC JAMS UP UNDER PRESSER FOOT

If you already have a jam you can cut the stitches with a seam ripper. Remove the presser foot if you can. Carefully lift up on the seam ripper as you cut so you do not scratch the needle plate or presser foot.

Make sure presser foot is down.

If sewing without fabric in the machine, pull gently on chain from the back of the machine.

Lengthen stitch length and/or loosen tensions. Too short or too tight a stitch will jam up.

If a spongy and/or thick fabric jams up, loosen the presser foot pressure.

On some machines you can get a jam if you have just put on a narrow rolled edge presser foot but not removed the left needle. The narrow rolled edge foot has a hole for the left needle, but no opening behind the hole to allow the stitch to slide off. Get the needle as high as it will go, pull extra needle and looper thread through, remove the presser foot, and carefully use a seam ripper to cut the stitches off the foot.

Sometimes a loop of thread gets caught around the presser foot. Lift presser foot and check that nothing is caught. To prevent this, make sure the thread chain is pulled under the presser foot and to the back of the machine before beginning sewing. If rethreading, make several stitches while pulling the threads to the back before inserting fabric.

OTHER STITCH PROBLEMS

If the left needle is in the machine and not threaded, there will be loops of the upper looper thread on the left edge of the stitch.

If tensions are inconsistent, make sure that every guide is threaded. Refer also to the section on "Adjusting Tensions," page 32.

If the needle thread tension is too tight the stitching may break under stress, particularly on knits. If either the needle or lower looper tensions are too tight the seam may pucker. If the looper tensions are too tight the seam may be stiff rather than flexible. (refer to section on "Adjusting Tensions," page 32)

If the needle thread tension is too loose loops will show on the bottom of the seam. In most cases the seam will pull apart. (refer to section on "Adjusting Tensions," page 32)

Sometimes a thread will be excessively loose because it is sitting on top of or beside its tension disks rather than being squeezed between them. Make sure each thread is pulled securely into its tension disks.

If the stitch length is too short the stitching may bunch up or bind under the presser foot. Stretchy knits may ripple.

If the stitch length is too long the seam may pucker. If the fabric is a knit the seam may have insufficient stretch. (refer to section on "Knits," page 67) Even if the seam has sufficient stretch, a seam under stress will not be as strong. If a seam pulls apart at all a longer stitch length will make it more noticeable, making it less attractive from the right side. Some fabrics may not be sufficiently protected from raveling.

If the stitch width is too wide on a light-weight fabric the seam will not drape properly and may even show from the right side. If the stitch width is too narrow on a fabric that ravels the fabric may fray and pull out of the seam.

SEAM BREAKS

If the stitching is pulling out at the ends of the seams refer to the section on "Securing Seams," page 60.

If the stitching is breaking in the middle of seams on a stretchy fabric, refer to the section on "Knits," page 67. This covers how to make the stitch sufficiently stretchy and how to secure the shoulder and crotch seams.

If the seam is subject to heavy wear use a heavier needle thread and/or reinforce the stitching with a line of stitching on your conventional machine.

Use a wider stitch width, using a 4-thread or even a 5-thread stitch if appropriate. With most wovens, a wide seam allowance is necessary for security.

A seam will fail if the fabric frays within the stitch. Woven fabrics fray more than knits, loosely woven fabrics fray more than tightly woven fabrics, and fabrics with slippery threads fray more than fabrics with unslippery threads. A properly selected stitch will minimize this fraying. If the stitch length is too long, the fabric may fray because of stuff rubbing on it between the threads of the stitch: a shorter stitch length protects better against this type of fraying. If the looper threads are too loose this same type of fraying can occur, plus the looper threads can be snagged and even break. If the stitch is wide it needs a needle thread going down the middle to secure the looper threads to the fabric: this prevents the fabric from rubbing around within the stitch and fraying. This is why a 4-thread overlock is more secure than a 3-thread overlock of the same width. For example, I use a narrow 4-thread overlock for finishing the edges on lightweight silky fabrics. The lightweight fabric would move around inside a wide 4-thread stitch, yet a 3-thread stitch would not be as secure.

UNEVEN SEAM ALLOWANCE

When guiding fabric watch where knife is cutting rather than where needle is sewing.

On some fabrics the only way to get an even edge is to let knives trim off at least a narrow strip of fabric. Support fabric in front of and behind the needle so it does not feed crooked.

Adjust the pressure foot pressure. If a light-weight slippery fabric has been shifting around, increase presser foot pressure slightly.

If the knives cut a ragged edge on a variety of fabrics you may need to replace one or both blades. If you have notched a knife blade by sewing over a pin you will need to replace it. If the knives are simply dull, replace one blade as described in your manual. One blade is made of softer steel than the other, and your attachments kit generally has a replacement for this blade.

Make sure upper knife is properly positioned.

If sewing heavy or bulky fabrics, refer to section on "Bulky Fabrics" in Appendix B: Dictionary of Fabrics, page 169.

MACHINE IS SLUGGISH

Clean and oil, as described in the section on "Maintenance," page 27.

If your machine has a "sew slow" mode, check to see what position the control is in.

You may be asking too much of your machine if sewing a thick layer of densely woven fabric. Check out an industrial machine if you need to do this type of sewing. Otherwise finish the raw edges on the serger then construct on a conventional machine, making sure it is strong enough for the job. Sew slowly.

Disable the knife and see if the problem persists. If the problem goes away when the knife is not cutting the problem is in the knife. Check to see whether the upper knife is properly positioned against the lower knife. If not, bring the machine in for service. It may also be that you locked the upper knife as described in the section on "Stitch Width and Knives," page 37 then tried to increase stitch width without loosening the set screw.

Change the needle, and see if that fixes the problem. A damaged needle may not penetrate fabric easily.

If the problem persists, and especially if the machine makes strange noises, bring it in for service.

NOISES

Some brands of sergers are noisier than others. All machines run quieter if they are cleaned and oiled. If the table the machine is on is not sturdy and vibration-free put the machine on some sort of vibration absorbing pad.

If a machine makes a clicking noise the needle is probably hitting the lower looper. Try running it without a needle then with a replacement needle. If it does not make the sound without the needle but does with a new needle bring it in for service. If changing the needle eliminates the noise, check the lower looper for burrs. Move it all the way to the right and run your finger along both edges.

If the machine makes a laboring sound, you may be asking it to sew too heavy a layer of fabric.

If the machine still makes a noise that sounds unhealthy bring it in for service, especially if it seems to be laboring or is not sewing right.

APPENDIX B

DICTIONARY OF FABRICS

Chapter 4 has general information on sewing with knit and woven fabrics. This appendix contains information specific to certain types of fabrics. Use this information together with the relevant sections in chapter 4. Chapter 2 describes the different types of stitches, and should be referred to for any questions about flat-locking or the narrow rolled edge.

Bias Fabrics

On woven fabric, the bias is the diagonal between the lengthwise and crosswise threads. When a piece of woven fabric is cut on the bias it can stretch. Loosely woven fabrics such as challis will stretch more than tightly woven ones, and drape better on the bias. The advantages of working on the bias are drape, fluid movement, and stretch or ease. (The bias ease is not like the stretch of a knit, because bias does not stretch or recover like a knit. It moves and drapes like a bias, wonderfully elegant in the right style and fabric.)

Narrow strips of fabric cut on the bias can be used for binding garment edges. Wider bias strips can be used decoratively, as described in the sections on "Decorative Narrow Rolled Edge," "Lettucing", and "Fabric Flowers." Sometimes just a section of a garment is cut on the bias. For example, bias sleeves are more comfortable than slim sleeves cut on the straight of grain.

An entire garment can be cut on the bias, as is sometimes done for lingerie, but fitting and assembly require special techniques. Choose a simple flowing pattern without a lot of seams, darts or gathering. On each major pattern piece draw a new straight-of-grain line 45-degrees away from the original one (see Figure B-1). All pattern pieces should be cut from a single layer of fabric. If a pattern piece is supposed to be laid out on a fold, make a copy of it and tape the two pieces together so you can do all your layout on a single layer of fabric. Since the suitable fabrics for bias are shifty, make sure you lay out the fabric so the crossgrain is perpendicular to the selvedge. If necessary, pull a thread to find the crossgrain. A gridded cutting table makes it easy to lay out the crossgrain at a right angle to the selvedge. Layouts on the bias generally require more fabric. Cut the pieces with extra wide seam allowances and let hang on the bias for 24 hours before sewing: a clip type

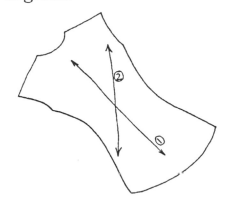

Figure B-1:

1. Original Grainline
2. New Bias Grainline

skirt hanger works well. Lay pattern pieces on fabric to see how much it has stretched and if it has stretched evenly. If the threads going in one direction are heavier or closer together than those going in the other direction the fabric is likely to stretch unevenly: you want to catch and compensate for this before assembling the garment. Mark any changes on the fabric. Baste or pin together and try on for fit.

Bias seams must be able to stretch and move. Since bias edges ravel very little, a narrow stitch is usually sufficient and will drape better. A 3-thread overlock stitch will give stretch and allow the fabric to move fluidly. Use a 4-thread stitch if the fabric is very loosely woven. (If you want to get really fancy, bias garments will drape better if bias seams do not cross each other. Sew the first seam in two sections, ending each section a seam's allowance from the edge (see Figure B-2). Then sew the second seam in two sections, ending each seam at the same point where the first seam sections ended (see Figure B-3). For precision sewing like this, a conventional machine is easier. Use a short stitch length for stretch, or a very narrow zig-zag.)

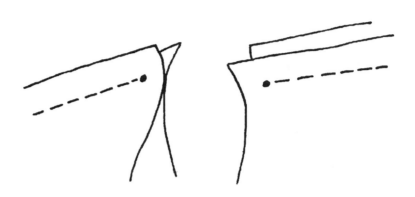

Figure B-2: *Sew First two Seams end at Dot*

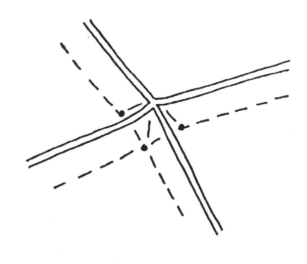

Figure B-3: *Sew last two Seams end at Dot*

Garment edge finishes should be light on bias garments so the fabric can drape and move. Consider replacing facings with other finishes such as flounces, seam binding, narrow top-stitched hem, or a narrow rolled edge.

Bias can be wonderful, but it requires time for experimentation. Volume 21 of "Threads" magazine has a wonderful article on Madeleine Vionnet, a master of bias. Bias can be a subject in itself!

Bulky Fabrics

This includes quilted fabrics, boiled wool, melton, polar fleece, chinella, etc. They have a spongy texture. Although some are knitted most have limited stretch. For bulky knits that ravel easily also refer to the section on "Sweater Knits" in this appendix, page 174. For bulky wovens which ravel easily also refer to the section on "Wovens, Medium to Heavy Weight" in this appendix, page 176. Use a wide 4-thread stitch and a stitch length of about 3 to 3 1/2. Check your stitch: you will probably need to loosen tensions. The bulk of these fabrics may "choke" the knives on some machines, so it is better to cut out your pieces with 1/4" seam allowances. You may need to loosen the presser foot pressure slightly to get proper feeding. If you are having problems with skipping stitches reduce stitch width slightly so the upper looper thread has a better chance to clear the edge of the fabric and be caught by the needle. Another option is to put a strip of sheer tricot or a strip of water soluble stabilizer between the fabric and the presser foot. This will help compress the fabric as you sew. If using sheer tricot, trim the excess off after serging. (refer to glossary under "Sheer Tricot" or "Water Soluble Stabilizer" for more information) Or, you can zig-zag the edge of the seam on a conventional machine to compress the layers, then serge over the zig-zagging. Clothespins are handy if you need to "pin" the fabric before sewing. Sometimes the layers will tend to shift, with the lower layer feeding faster than the upper. Loosening the presser foot pressure will help. Also, use the clothespins to align the layers, then use your fingers to slightly force the upper layer under the presser foot so the two layers feed together. When blind hemming you will probably need to move the guide slightly to the right so the needle catches the fold of fabric properly.

Coated Fabrics

These are usually nylon with a coating for waterproofing, and are intended for outdoor wear. The coating virtually eliminates any problems of raveling. For garments you can use a 4-thread serger seam. Use a long stitch length and a fine needle to reduce needle holes, since needle holes reduce waterproofness. Loosen needle tensions as necessary to control puckering. If desired a liquid is available which can be painted on the seams after sewing to seal any holes and restore waterproofness. Another option is gluing a tape over the seam on the inside: this is often used in ready-to-wear. Use clothespins or paper clips instead of straight pins for holding seams together while sewing. If the fabric coating is sticking to the needle plate and/or presser foot, fold a strip of water soluble stabilizer over the edge of the seam while serging. An alternative is to use a wide strip of sheer tricot. Seams Great is sometimes sold in wider strips than the normal 5/8" width: the extra width is necessary to cover both sides of the seam completely and prevent sticking. (refer to glossary under "Sheer Tricot" or "Water Soluble Stabilizer" for more information) Sometimes you can purchase adhesive backed *Teflon* for applying to presser feet: this reduces sticking. If using the heavier weights of coated fabric, serge the raw edges then construct on your conventional machine if it can handle the load.

Fake Furs

There is a wide variety of fake furs and shaggy fabrics on the market. Many have a resin coating on the back, making them stiff and scratchy: these fabrics need to be lined. Also, they generally require dry-cleaning. Other fake furs have a soft knitted backing, and are suitable for such things as an unlined cardigan. When selecting fake furs, check the pile density by pulling apart the pile on the right side. A sparse pile will not look nice or wear well.

When cutting out fake furs lay the fabric out pile side down. Adjust your pattern for 1/4" seams: this makes it possible to push the pile out of the seam as you sew, resulting in nearly invisible seams. (see below) Cut only a single thickness of fabric at a time. When cutting out pieces that are laid on the fold, cut out one half then flip the pattern piece over and cut out the other half. Or, you can make a duplicate of the pattern piece, tape together and use to cut out fabric. Using the tips of the scissors or a razor blade, cut through just the backing of the fabric without cutting the pile.

Use a long stitch length, about 3 to 3 1/2. Check tensions: you will probably need to loosen them. You may need to reduce presser foot pressure to get the fabric to feed properly.

Sew right sides together, pushing the pile to the left between the fabric layers as you sew. This keeps the pile from getting caught in the stitching. After sewing the seam pull it flat and check the right side to see if any of the pile got caught in the stitching. If some of the pile is caught it can be pulled out. Scratching at the caught pile with a finger nail usually pulls most of it clear. If necessary, a darning needle can be used to pull it out.

When sewing the fake furs which do not have a resin backing use a wide 4-thread balanced stitch.

For the resin backed fake furs a wide flat-lock seam works well. Let the stitches hang off the edge, using the techniques for flat-locking over a fold. If you are using the blind hem foot as a guide, move the blade as far to the right as possible, so the fabric layers overlap slightly when they are pulled flat.

If you are having problems with skipping stitches, reduce the stitch width slightly so the upper looper thread has a better chance to get over the edge of the fabric and around the needle. If still having problems, zig-zag along the seam on a conventional machine to compress the layers, then serge over the zig-zagging.

Clothespins make it easier to hold fabric layers together while sewing. As with bulky fabrics, sometimes the layers will tend to shift, with the lower layer feeding faster than the upper. Loosen the presser foot pressure. Also, use the clothespins to align the layers, then use your fingers to slightly force the upper layer under the presser foot so the two layers feed together.

Interlock

This is technically a double knit, meaning each row or course is knit from two separate threads. It is knit from fine threads, either cotton or a polyester/cotton blend. It is smooth on both sides and does not curl on the edges. It has a great deal of crosswise stretch, often 100%, and very good recovery. It is widely available. It is most commonly used for turtlenecks and casual summerwear. It can also be used as a light to medium weight ribbing, because of its stretch and recovery and because it is readily available in a wide variety of colors. Because it is a double knit it has a somewhat spongy texture, although the fine threads it is knit from obscure this fact. It is subject to needle holes when blind hemming. The section on "Blind Hemming," page 44, discusses solutions to this problem. Even though it has excellent recovery, because of its spongy texture it tends to ripple. Refer to the section on "Knits," page 67, for setting tensions: you will probably have to begin with a stitch length of about 2 3/4 for horizontal seams. Use a medium width stitch, either a narrow 4-thread stitch or a 3-thread stitch. Interlock does not ravel, so a wide 4-thread stitch is not necessary. A wide 4-thread stitch would be bulky and not drape well.

Lace and Stretch Lace

Lace is easily sewn on the serger. Use a short stitch length, about 2. A fine lingerie thread makes a finer, less noticeable seam. For attaching lace to other fabrics, refer to the section on "Applying Lace," page 129. The serger is wonderful for gathering lace: the lace is gathered evenly with a nearly invisible seam. For sewing lace to itself, a narrow flat-lock produces a minimal seam. For more security use a 4-thread flat-lock. A 3-thread balanced stitch can be used as well. When seaming fine lace, the nicest way to seam it is to overlap the seam edges then top-stitch with a medium width and length zig-zag. Cut out generous seam allowances so the stitching can go around the edges of motifs, then trim the seam allowances to the stitching.

If you want to determine the right side of lace, look for a raised thread, called a cordonette. This thread is more prominent on some laces than others. The side with the cordonette is the right side.

Lame

The metallic threads in this fabric give it a very dressy appearance, and can cause problems for the sewer. The metallic threads are stiff, creating problems with the narrow rolled edge stitch. (refer to the section on the "Narrow Rolled Edge," page 46, for specific suggestions on producing a nice narrow rolled edge on these fabrics) The threads are slippery, which makes the fabric ravel easily. They can be scratchy if a fabric edge is next to the skin. A good way to control the scratchiness is to enclose the raw edges in a strip of sheer tricot. Get the wider strips of sheer tricot if possible. Fold the strip of tricot over the raw edge then serge over it, being careful not to cut the folded edge of the tricot. (refer to glossary under "Sheer Tricot" for more information) Use a wide 4-thread stitch for security, and a stitch length of about 2 1/2. Since these garments typically receive light wear, the serger can be used to seam them. Use a 5-thread stitch (2-thread chainstitch plus 3-thread overlock) if you have it.

Lycra Fabrics

Lycra, sometimes called Spandex, is an extremely stretchy fiber. It is blended in small amounts, usually about 5% to 15%, with other fibers to produce a very stretchy fabric with excellent recovery. Sometimes Lycra is used in woven fabrics to produce a fabric with some give and excellent memory. Most commonly it is used in knits. Unlike most knits, Lycra knits stretch both lengthwise and crosswise, producing "2-way" or "4-way" stretch. Most swimsuit fabric is a nylon/Lycra blend, producing a fabric that is strong, dries quickly, takes dyes brilliantly, and has the superb stretch and recovery of Lycra. Heavier weights of nylon/Lycra are used for such things as biker's shorts. Lightweight cotton/Lycra is used for leotards that are absorbant, comfortable and form-fitting. Cotton/Lycra is also wonderful for underpants and other lingerie, as well as for leggings and tights. Heavier weights of cotton/Lycra knits can be used for all sorts of comfortable casual garments. The addition of Lycra makes the cotton knit more durable, as well as ensuring it will keep its shape. However, the cotton/Lycra knit still has the softness and absorbancy of cotton.

Some Lycra fabrics stretch more than others, which can affect the fit and comfort of garments. Most garments designed for a Lycra fabric are actually cut smaller than the corresponding body dimensions, so the fabric is stretched on the body. The pattern envelope should specify how much stretch the fabric should have in each direction. If your fabric stretches less than this in one direction, you may need to add to the pattern or use a larger size. Another way to check stretch is to take a length of fabric and stretch it "some" until it feels about right, then measure how long it is before and after stretching. This will give an idea of how much smaller the pattern should be than the equivalent body measurement. Measure stretch in both directions. For the best comfort and fit, Lycra garments should be stretched only slightly in the lengthwise direction.

Seams in Lycra fabrics must stretch: refer to the section on "Knits," page 67, for setting tensions. They will commonly accept a short stitch length, of about 2. A narrower seam allowance looks sleeker, like a medium width 3-thread stitch or a narrow 4-thread. Do not use fabric softener when washing Lycra fabrics, particularly nylon/Lycra. It tends to make the Lycra threads pull back out of the edge of the fabric. The 4-thread stitch will help control this, as will wider seam allowances. Hand washing is really the best for nylon/lycras, or at least a gentle machine cycle with the tub at least half full of water and very few other clothes in the load. Lycra should be air dried because it shrinks when exposed to the heat of the dryer.

Nylon Tricot

This is typically used for lingerie. It is strong, light weight, quick drying, non-raveling. Curling is not a problem if the raw edge is not stretched. Technically it is a warp knit, meaning that the threads run vertically rather than horizontally. It comes in various weights: 15 denier is sheer tricot, 30 denier is commonly used for slips, 40 denier may be used for robes. A very narrow seam is used: use a narrow 3-thread stitch with the narrow rolled edge stitch finger. Because of the narrow stitch a short stitch length is used, 1 1/2 to 2. Lengthen stitch length if rippling is a problem. Use a fine needle, and lingerie thread if you have it. Whereas skipped stitches are often a problem when sewing tricot on a conventional machine, the narrow opening on the serger needle plate makes this uncommon when serging. If you do have skipped stitches put some silicone needle lubricant on your needle. Your dealer carries this. If puckering is a problem loosen the needle tension slightly. If you have differential feed, you can set it to greater than 1.0 to control rippling. This is a knit fabric so seams must stretch, particularly horizontal ones. Refer to the section on "Knits," page 67. The section on "Lingerie," page 82, has some ideas for using this fabric in lingerie.

Silkie and Sheer Wovens

With its long feed dogs and narrow opening for the needle, the serger does a beautiful job of sewing these difficult fabrics. Set the differential feed to less than 1.0 if puckering is a problem, and check your needle thread tension. You may want to increase presser foot pressure slightly to keep the fabric from shifting around under the presser foot. It may also help to cut extra wide seam allowances so you are trimming something off as you serge. If you can find some lingerie thread, it will give a finer stitch and permit a shorter stitch length. A short stitch length, of about 2, will help protect these fabrics from raveling. Check your tensions: they may need slight tightening, particularly the needle thread. For finishing edges use a narrow 4-thread stitch. Refer to the section on "Woven Fabrics," page 76, for various ways to use the serger on wovens. If using the serger to seam wovens use the widest 4-thread stitch, or a 5-thread stitch if you have it. French seams are wonderful on sheers and silkies: use a narrow 3-thread for the initial seam, sewn wrong sides together. After opening, pressing and turning, the second seam can be a straight stitch on a conventional machine or a wider serger stitch if your conventional machine does not handle silkies well. Although French seams work best on straight or slightly curved seam, sheer tricot seam binding is a nice way to securely finish a serged armscye seam. Fold the sheer tricot strip over the edge of the seam then top-stitch with a zig-zag on a conventional machine. The narrow rolled edge is a good way to finish exposed edges on silkies. Refer to the section on the "Narrow Rolled Edge," page 46, for general information plus specific tips on silkies.

Sweater Knits

These are knit from yarns rather than threads, and often look like they were hand knit. They are usually bulky, ravel easily, are stretchy with poor recovery, and generally can be difficult to sew. But, they are comfortable and usually have wonderful texture. Due to the rich texture, choose a simple pattern. Refer to the section on "Knits," page 67, for discussion on getting a good stitch for knits, suggestions on stabilizing shoulder seams in sweater knits, and information on selecting a pattern size. The section on "Bulky Fabrics," page 169, has useful tips for the bulkier sweater knits. Make sure you use a heavy enough ribbing for the neck, as this can stretch out of shape too. Many sweater knits have a tendency to curl when being prewashed, so fold the fabric in half and serge around the three open sides before prewashing. You may want to prewash twice to remove residual shrinkage. Cut off serging and lay flat for cutting out. You may want to cut out the bulkier sweater knits from a single layer of fabric.

Use a wide 4-thread stitch to protect against raveling. Start with a stitch length of 3. Loosen presser foot pressure and lengthen stitch length as necessary to control rippling. If you have differential feed set it to 2 to also help control rippling. If you do not have differential feed, press down firmly on the fabric just behind the presser foot with the fingers of your left hand, so the fabric scrunches up under your fingers. Make sure you support the fabric in front of the presser foot so it is not being stretched at all. You can even push up a little mound and hold it in front of the presser foot while you sew. This ensures the fabric is not being stretched by its own weight. When the mound is gone stop and rebuild it. As necessary, loosen needle tensions to ensure sufficient stretch: the fabric texture will conceal a seam that pulls apart slightly. These fabrics are generally easier to handle if you are trimming something off when you sew them together. Allow extra seam allowances when cutting out fabric. With all this fuss, remember that your pattern will have just a few pieces and your garment will go together quickly.

Sweatshirt Fleece

Although technically a knit, this fabric typically has little stretch. Take this into account when choosing a pattern size: you may want to go one size larger if using a pattern intended for knit fabrics. For crew necks you may need to trim off some additional fabric so the garment will fit over the head. This fabric does not ravel or run, so all seams can be made on the serger. A medium width 3-thread stitch is wide enough, although a 4-thread works fine too. Use a stitch length of about 3. Wide flat-lock seams work well on this fabric and are great for adding embellishments to sweatshirts, along with the other decorative techniques described in chapter 6. Sweatshirts are one place to have fun!

Tee-Shirt Knits

These are lightweight single knits. The front and back are not identical. The edges curl and some fabrics run easily. They are usually knit from a cotton thread or a cotton/polyester blend. They have good crosswise stretch with good recovery. When prewashing these, fold in half and serge together around the three raw edges: this protects the edges from irrecoverable curling in the wash. Cut off serging and lay flat for cutting out. Often the vertical lines are not perpendicular to the horizontal lines. If the fabric is striped lay out with the grain line arrows perpendicular to the stripes. If the fabric is not striped use the vertical lines (or the selvedge edge) as your reference for laying on grain. (This "biasing" or shifting of the horizontal and vertical grainlines is common in knits and is caused by an unbalanced twist in the thread the fabric was knit from. It is especially common in tee-shirt knits because they are single knits. Prewashing helps ensure that any shifting takes place before you cut your pattern pieces, eliminating twisted T-shirt seams. Better quality knits are less subject to this.) Handle gently after cutting out, because any stretching will make the edges curl. You may need to stop and uncurl the edges as you seam them, bit by bit. An easier way is to cut out with extra wide seam allowances, and cut off this extra as you sew the garment together. Spray starch also helps control the curling. For all this fuss, these are the lightest knits for lingerie or summer wear. Use a medium to wide 3-thread stitch, or even a narrow 4-thread if the fabric is loosely knit and subject to pulling out of the seam. A stitch length of about 2 1/4 to 2 1/2 is usually about right, and read the section on "Knits" on page 67 for setting tensions.

Velour and Stretch Terry

These are knitted pile fabrics, the loops being cut in velour and left uncut in stretch terry. All are washable, unlike their namesake velvet. Robe velour is a thin, closely knit fabric with little stretch. It is generally 100% synthetic fiber. Cotton velour is thicker, with a cotton pile. It may have a synthetic base. It has good stretch, as does stretch terry. Stretch terries are most commonly used for summer wear and for baby clothes. They are not always easy to find, but are comfortable and have a beautiful texture. They can snag easily. Use a medium width 4-thread stitch, and a stitch length of about 3. Cotton velours and terries can curl, so fold in half and serge the three open sides together before prewashing. Cut off serging and lay flat for cutting out garment pieces.

Wovens, Medium to Heavy Weight

In most cases, garments from these fabrics should have the raw edges finished on the serger then be constructed on the sewing machine, as described in the section on "Woven Fabrics," page 76. For casual garments which will be washed but not ironed, an alternative is the serged and top-stitched seam. Use the widest 4-thread stitch, or a 5-thread stitch if you have it. Serge the seam, press to one side, then top-stitch the seam allowance flat on a conventional machine. For more security the seam can be made on a conventional machine, the two seam allowances serged together while trimming off 1/4", then pressed to one side and top-stitched. (This gives a wider seam allowance if you do not have a 5-thread machine.) Either way, the top-stitched seam allowances do not need to be pressed flat every time the garment is washed.

For finishing raw edges, use a stitch length of about 2 1/2. If the fabric is loosely woven and subject to raveling use a 4-thread stitch. Otherwise a 3-thread stitch is sufficient for finishing edges. If the fabric is quite heavy or stiff, you may want to lock the upper knife. (refer to section on "Stitch Width and Knives," page 37)

APPENDIX C

SELECTING A SERGER

HOW TO SHOP FOR A SERGER

Carefully research all available machines before you buy a serger. Sergers are not all the same. Read the section on "Industrial Sergers," page 151, to decide if you should consider an industrial serger: use it as a guide and be particularly careful about selecting a dealer if you buy an industrial machine. Talk to your friends who have sergers, and pay particular attention to those who shopped around. Ask them why they purchased their machine, what they like about it and what they may not like. Read issues of sewing magazines which list current models of domestic sergers together with their features. "Sew News" and "Vogue Pattern Magazine" periodically have such articles. These articles will give you an overview of different machines, and they will also give you an overview of options and features to look for. ("Sew News" has stopped printing these reviews: they can be ordered by writing "Sew News," page 189.) Study this book, especially the first and last chapters and this appendix. Bring it along for reference. Take notes on your research.

Before you buy any machine, spend time sewing on every machine that interests you. Check the tensions and how the machine feeds fabric, as described below. Check how well it gathers and does a narrow rolled edge. Make sure you at least see how to change stitch width and stitch length, how to thread the machine and how to convert to a narrow rolled edge on the machine. This will show you what the machine is like to operate. If you are interested in decorative serging bring along some decorative threads to try: some machines handle them much better than others. Most machines handle texturized nylon well. Heavier threads or very fine slippery threads can be more difficult.

With your research, you should come up with a few machines to consider. If you instinctively like or dislike a machine, try to analyze why. Was it because of the way it was demonstrated or how it looks? Was it because of vibration or noise? Did it seem heftier or better made? Did it seem easier to operate? Did the tensions seem to come in easier and hold better? Look at the manual for such things as what the machine weighs, whether the internal bearings are oil sealed (or does it have oil holes on the top of the machine for feeding oil through a wick: refer to section on "Maintenance," page 27), how you adjust it to do different things, what the range of adjustment is for stitch width, any special features. Bring along a mechanically minded friend for advice; whether he or she sews is not important. Try to determine which machines the dealer likes best, and why. After listening to them, ask them why they like different machines. One may be more economical, one may have a better reputation, one may be more reliable in the dealer's experience. They may feel one is more suited for a skilled sewer and another for a novice sewer. Visit different dealers who carry a variety of machines and get their opinions. A dealer does not want an unhappy customer, although most dealers would prefer an unhappy customer to no customer.

In sergers the better quality machines do cost more. My impression is that once people get familiar with their machine, most of them use their sergers a great deal. If an expensive machine is too much initially, buy a good quality lower price machine. Choose good quality over ease of use or special options. Later on you can probably sell it (or keep it as a second machine) and buy a better machine, especially if you made a good choice initially. Dealers are sometimes reluctant to take trade-ins, but you can very likely find an individual to buy it.

SERGER FEATURES

There are many different things to look for in sergers but they fall into three basic areas; general quality, ease of use, and special options. I think of general quality as affecting the quality of the finished product, whereas special options are only used occasionally (but may be important to you). As the domestic serger market has matured, sergers have improved in all three areas, so if you have an older machine you should check out what is available now.

General Quality

Even consistent tensions are one of the major features of the better machines. Check for them when shopping for a serger. Bring along a bag with scraps of a variety of fabrics: tricot, crepe de chine, broadcloth, denim, interlock, sweater knit, polar fleece. Adjust the stitch for the different fabrics and check the stitch quality. The narrow rolled hem is an excellent test of tensions, so check it on every machine you consider, using the same fabric on every machine. A fine weave broadcloth is a good basic fabric to use. The crepe de chine may present more of a problem for some machines, so try that too. It is easiest for a machine to do a rolled edge on the straight of grain, so check how it does on the bias. While looking at a machine, loosen tensions completely and brush out between the disks as if cleaning, then return to previous settings. Does the stitch look the same? You want the tensions to come in easily and stay solid.

Check how the machine handles the variety of fabrics from your bag. How much power does it have for heavy fabrics? Does it handle slippery or delicate fabrics well? Check a very short stitch length. Try sewing across a previously sewn seam. Does the fabric feed well, without hesitating or shifting sideways? Try sewing at various speeds, and while serging around a curve. Does the stitch look the same?

You get a better quality stitch if the width of the stitch finger closely matches the stitch width as set by the knives. Some domestic machines now offer *three* needle plates, one for rolled edge, one with a medium width stitch finger for a balanced stitch in lightweight fabric, one with a wide stitch finger for a balanced stitch in heavy fabric. On some machines the stitch finger width changes as the stitch width (cutting width) is changed.

Differential feed usually costs about $150 more. It is particularly useful for gathering, preventing a narrow rolled edge from puckering, and preventing seams in knits from rippling. (refer to section on "Differential Feed," page 40) On some domestic sergers the differential feed has a range of adjustment of 0.5 to 2.0, whereas on others the range is 0.7 to 2.0. Industrial machines do not have as wide a range of adjustment.

An electronic foot control gives you the ability to sew slowly with full control and power, also to begin and end seams slowly and gracefully.

A machine with adjustable stitch width can produce a quality seam on a wider variety of fabric. I like the option of having a wide 4-thread overlock for heavy knits. A wide stitch width is necessary if you will be seaming wovens. Anything over 6.0 mm I would consider wide, and the wider the better. (Note, 2 thread chainstitch seam allowances can be very wide. They are generally not used for knits but are often useful for sewing with wovens. The chainstitch tensions can be loosened if desired for knits. Refer to section on "Woven Fabrics," page 76.) On the other hand, I like the option of having a narrow 3-thread overlock for seaming fine knits, particularly lingerie. If necessary you can guide fabric slightly to the left of the knives for a narrower seam, using the techniques in the section on "Guiding Fabric," page 104.

Some machines have a stitch finger in the presser foot, which helps compress fabric and prevent skipped stitches on very bulky fabrics.

Make sure you at least get a 3-thread overlock stitch. If you are not getting a 5-thread machine you will want to have the option of a 4-thread safety overlock. If you get a 5-thread machine you will have a more versatile machine, particularly if it can be converted to produce a 4-thread overlock.

Most machines have a means for adjusting presser foot pressure. This is sometimes necessary for getting a quality stitch on certain fabrics.

Fewer thread guides may make a machine easier to thread, but tensions may be less consistent. Pop-in guides are easier to thread, but sometimes the thread can pop out of them and this can lead to uneven stitches.

Ease of Use

Check the tension disks to see whether it will be difficult if not impossible to have a thread lying _on_ them when you think it is lying _in_ them. The vertical tension disks inset into the top of the machine are usually ok. If the tension disks are the "beehive" type check to see if they have a little hook guide on one side so the thread goes 3/4 of the way around the disk. If a machine has this design problem but you like the machine otherwise, make a mental note to check that each thread is _in_ the disks whenever changing thread.

A calibrated presser foot pressure adjustment mechanism makes it easier to get the proper presser foot pressure for each task. ("Calibrated" means you can see numbers that tell you whether the pressure is light or heavy, so you can easily adjust it and easily return it to a previous setting.) Most people are much more likely to actually use their presser foot presser adjustment if it is calibrated.

If you purchase a machine with round shank industrial needles you will need to be careful when inserting them to make sure the eye is facing directly forward.

Industrial needles generally last longer. Conventional needles are more readily available, although your dealer carries whatever needles are necessary for your machine.

Some machines have a built-in needle threader, which makes it easier to thread the needles. Some machines have slightly more room between the needle and presser foot shaft than others do: this also makes it easier to thread needles.

It is much easier to learn how to adjust tensions and replicate settings if the machine has calibrated tension dials (meaning there are numbers on them). However, once you learn how to adjust tensions you will no longer be looking at any numbers.

It is easier to learn how to use a machine if the tension dials do not go more than once around. However, in general tensions are more accurate if the tension dials make more than one turn. And again, once you learn how to adjust tensions the number of turns is not important.

The size of the opening in the knives will limit how bulky a seam you can trim. Machines do vary on this, but if your machine has too small an opening for your fabric you can cut out your pieces with 1/4" seam allowances. On some fluffy fabrics such as quilteds, you can compress the layers by sewing over them with a zig-zag stitch before serging.

Check how easy it is to convert to a narrow rolled edge, and decide how important this is to you. Check if you need to purchase additional accessories to do a narrow rolled edge.

Snap-on presser feet save you time changing presser feet.

Snap-in needle plates makes it much quicker to change needle plates.

There are two types of thread cutters, one on the back of the presser foot bar and one up on the corner of the machine. The one on the corner of the machine works better and is much more convenient.

Most machines do not offer a built-in waste collector, but it is convenient. The kind you buy that hang on the serger feet is not as good.

Check how easy it is to adjust stitch width and stitch length. External controls for stitch width, stitch length and/or differential feed save time, because you do not have to open a door to get at the control. Controls you operate with one hand are easier than controls requiring two hands. Having to loosen a set-screw will also take more time. Dials are generally easier to read than levers, because you can read them from any position. Some external levers for differential feed are positioned so it is easy to accidently hit them and change their setting.

A swingaway presser foot makes it easier to thread the needle, although on a machine with snap-on presser feet it is an easy matter to remove the presser foot while threading.

Some "self-threading" loopers make it easier to re-thread. With your handy-dandy super looper threader (Butler's "E-Z Thru Floss Threader"), most machines are reasonably easy to thread. Some machines have a narrow needle plate: this make threading easier, particularly for a chainstitch looper.

Many machines have knives coming up from below, under the presser foot. This makes it easier to thread the needle and use the presser foot lever. It also makes some decorative techniques easier, such as serger piping. On some of these machines you cannot watch where the knife is cutting because the presser foot is covering it. Until you know the machine well this can create problems for the edge finishing maneuvers described in the chapter on "Securing Stitches."

Home sergers are generally "rated" at 1200 to 1500 stitches per minute. The speed of a machine is important for some types of sewers and some types of sewing, such as long straight seams or edges.

Some machines have a computer, which can be used to memorize settings for various types of stitches. This is helpful when learning a machine. After you understand how to adjust the stitch the computer can serve as a reminder. Settings will change depending on fabric, desired effect and unknown variables (how recently the machine was cleaned and oiled, temperature and humidity, etc.). The settings in the computer can be changed to reflect your machine and the type of sewing you do.

Make sure you get a built-in light. Most machines have this now.

It is nice having accessory storage within the machine.

Special Options

The 2-thread overedge stitch and the 2-thread chainstitch are attractive options for some types of sewing. (refer to the section on "2-Thread Overedge," page 141, and the section on "2-Thread Chainstitch," page 143) The 2-thread chainstitch is available on 5-thread machines and 4/2-thread machines. Some domestic 5-thread machines and 4/3-thread machines also offer a 2-thread overedge stitch.

Some domestic 5-thread machines offer a 4-thread overlock stitch if the 2-thread chainstitch is not being used: others do not. Some require a special double needle for making the 4-thread overlock. Some domestic 5-thread machines enable you to use the chainstitch in the middle of garment sections rather than just on the edge. This is accomplished by having a mechanism for disabling the overlock loopers and knife, then inserting a section to the right of the needle to support the fabric to the right of the needle. A 5-thread machine will be more difficult to thread because of the chain-stitch looper in front of the overedge loopers. The floss threader makes this easier. Some 5-thread machines have a narrow needle plate, which makes it easier to get at both ends of the chainstitch looper.

Check to see if the upper looper thread is caught by the left needle in the 4-thread overlock stitch. If it not, there will not be much point in putting a decorative thread in the upper looper, because the upper looper thread covers such a narrow area. This limits the use of the machine for decorative techniques, because the upper looper is the customary place to put a decorative thread. Also, you cannot drop out the right-hand needle for flat-locking or a left-needle wrapped stitch. However, the upper looper uses less thread, which may be important for production sewing. (refer to section on "Stitch Codes," page 148)

You will want to get a blind hem foot, which is an optional accessory on most machines. The other accessories are used less often, but one or more may be important to you. Read the section on "Special Attachments," page 153 and decide which ones you want. Then find out which machines offer these. Most manufacturers are expanding their line of accessories, so even though the accessory you want may not be available today on a particular machine it may very well be available within a year. Ask your dealer.

Some feed dogs are a combination of the conventional saw tooth surface with a "micro edge" surface. This has a larger surface area and is designed to feed certain types of fabric better.

See if the standard foot has a tape guide and/or cording guide: these are useful for some techniques. If there is a separate narrow rolled edge foot, see if it has a cording guide. This makes it easier to do a corded narrow rolled edge.

Some machines offer an open or free arm. Some sewers like this.

See if the machine will accept the left needle when it is set up for the narrow rolled edge. Some decorative techniques use this. A 4-thread narrow rolled edge is more secure on some fabrics. (refer to section on "Decorative Narrow Rolled Edge," page 125) On some machine the narrow rolled edge foot will not accept the left needle, but a 4-thread narrow rolled edge can be done with the beading foot. Some machines cannot do a 4-thread narrow rolled edge, but can do a wide narrow rolled edge for such things as attaching beads or making serging piping.

It is handy to have a blind hem foot which will accept the left needle. (refer to section on "Special Attachments," page 153)

Various safety features are available, such as a guard around the needle or an interlock so you cannot sew with the doors open. These may be important to you.

A half speed setting is nice when learning how to use the machine, especially for children.

Some presser feet have marks on the front of them to indicate needle positions: this is useful but you can add it if necessary. Some machines have marks on the front door in front of the knife indicating where to guide the fabric for various seam allowances. You can add these if desired. (refer to "Beginning a Seam" in the section on "Starting Sewing," page 26)

CHOOSING A DEALER

Choose a dealer as carefully as you choose a machine. Once you decide on the machine you want it is worth driving an extra distance to get the dealer you want. You are dependent on that dealer for warranty service, plus any information he or she can give you on your machine. Ask who does their service, what kind of training that person has, how much they work on sergers, if they just do service. And, try to find out what they do with any machines they cannot fix. They may have an arrangement with another dealer who is an expert, they may send the machine to the factory, they may be the local expert. What you want to watch out for is a dealer who cannot fix tough problems and does not care enough to make sure they get fixed another way. If you buy a machine from some place other than a dealer, realize they will almost certainly be sending the machine out for any repairs, and the delay is likely to be at least a week and probably more. Warranty service is only free from the place you bought the machine, but you do have the option of taking it any place for repair if you are willing to pay for it.

Especially if you are purchasing an industrial machine, refer to the section on "Industrial Sergers," page 151, for more suggestions on choosing a dealer.

Find our what kind of training and support a dealer offers. Find out if a video tape is available, and if it is included in the price of the machine. Actual classes are much better if available: find out what classes are available on your machine and which are included in the price of the machine. Are there sewers working in the store who are familiar with your machine, to answer questions as they come up later? Each machine is different. Although I have tried to make this book as complete as possible, it helps to have someone point out how _your_ machine adjusts for particular operations, and what little features it has.

Ask your friends with sergers about their dealers. What kind of training and support did they get? Was the dealer willing and able to fix problems? What kind of attitude did the dealer demonstrate? While you are in the store, listen to the conversations the dealer has with other people coming in: do the customers generally seem happy with him or her? Watch the dealer's attitude while they are waiting on you. If a dealer is patronizing or uncooperative _before_ they have your money, they will only get worse after. There are wonderful dealers out there who care about their customers and treat them right. If you get one of these jewels treat them right too, and do not make unreasonable demands. This is their livelihood and they have a right to make money for providing good service. If you get a good dealer be sure to tell your friends about him or her: your friends deserve the best too!

APPENDIX D
SOURCES

SERGER BOOKS

Basic Serger Books

Sewing With an Overlock, Singer Reference Library. It has wonderful photographs of machine parts and basic stitches. It can be ordered from Cy DeCosse, Inc.; 5900 Green Oak Drive; Minnetonka, MN 55343.

Decorative Techniques and Garment Ideas

These books contain pictures of garments and other projects with descriptions of the techniques used to make them. The emphasis is on decorative techniques rather than basic construction, except for the books by Gail Brown which cover both areas.

Creative Serging, by Gail Brown, Patti Palmer and Sue Green. The publisher is Chilton Book Company.

Distinctive Serger Gifts & Crafts and *Simply Serge Any Fabric*, both by Naomi Baker and Tammy Young. The publisher is Chilton Book Company.

French Sewing by Serger and *60-Minute Heirlooms: Serging for Babies*, by Kathy McMakin. These books include many pictures of garments plus patterns. Order from Albright & CO. Publishers; P.O. Box 2011; Huntsville, AL 35804; 205-539-3288.

Innovative Serging, by Gail Brown and Tammy Young. The publisher is Chilton Book Company.

Know Your Babylock, *Know Your White Superlock*, *Know Your Pfaff Hobbylock*, etc. These are by Naomi Baker and Tammy Young. The publisher is Chilton Book Company.

The Serger Idea Book, by Ann Hesse Price. This also has an excellent section on decorative threads. It is published by Palmer/Pletsch Assoc.; P.O.Box 12046; Portland, OR 97212.

Stylish Serging, Stylish Serging II, Pattern Applications, Stylish Serging III, Fun With Variegated Threads, Stylish Serging IV, Wardrobe Coordinations, by Ervena Yu. These books can be ordered from the author at 211 Bayside Place; Bellingham, WA 98225.

Miscellaneous

Simply Serge Any Fabric, by Naomi Baker and Tammy Young. This contains specific tips for different types of fabric. The publisher is Chilton Book Company.

Owner's Guide to Sewing Machines, Sergers and Knitting Machines, by Gale Grigg Hazen. This describes how sergers work and how to take care of them. The publisher is Chilton Book Company.

Serge-A-Quilt, by Ann Person. Ann Person is founder of Stretch-and-Sew, a company specializing in patterns and books for sewing knits. If you cannot find her products in a local store you can write to Stretch & Sew, Inc.; P.O. Box 185; Eugene, OR 97440.

Serger Patchwork Projects, by Kaye Wood. This will show you how to do quilt piecing on the serger.

Update Newsletters publishes 8-page newsletters (no advertising) crammed with information for the home sewer. Each costs $3.95. Their address is: Update Newsletters; 2269 Chestnut, Suite 269; San Francisco, CA 94123. The titles relating to serging are: "Beyond finishing: Innovative Serging," "Know Your Serger," "Serged Bathroom," "Serged Gifts, in Minutes!," "Serging for Special Occasions," "Serging Lingerie," "Serging Stretch Fashions," and "Serging Sweaters." They also publish the 8-page "Serger Update," which comes out monthly and costs $36 per year. Much of this information ends up in their serger books which are the Chilton Book Co. books among the preceding serger books.

NON-SERGER BOOKS

General Construction

These books have innumerable tips on details like pockets or collars, construction methods, interfacing, modifying patterns for fit or style, etc. Sewing has changed a lot in the past ten years: if you have not updated your sewing skills recently read some of these books. If you cannot find these locally and no ordering address is included, order from one of the companies listed in the section on "Supplies," page 189.

Sew Wonderful Silk by Cheryl Arrants with Jan Asbjornsen. Order from Sew Wonderful, Inc.; P.O.Box 31928; Seattle, WA 98103.

Power Sewing and *More Power Sewing* by Sandra Betzina. Order from Power Sewing; 95 Fifth Avenue; San Francisco, CA 94118.

Sensational Silk by Gail Brown. It is published by Palmer/Pletsch Assoc.; P.O.Box 12046; Portland, OR 97212.

Innovative Sewing, by Gail Brown and Tammy Young. The publisher is Chilton Book Company.

Sew Smart, by Judy Lawrence and Clotilde. Order from Clotilde; 1909 SW First Avenue, Ft. Lauderdale, FL 33315; 305-761-8655.

Complete Guide to Sewing, published by Reader's Digest.

Speed Sewing, by Jan Saunders. This is published by Van Nostrand Reinhold Co.

Claire Shaeffer has written several excellent sewing books, including *Claire Shaeffer's Sewing S.O.S.* and *Fabric Sewing Guide*.

Simplicity's Simply the Best Sewing Book, by Simplicity Pattern Company.

The Singer Reference Library has published many excellent sewing books, including *Timesaving Sewing* and *The Perfect Fit*. They can be ordered from Cy DeCosse, Inc.; 5900 Green Oak Drive; Minnetonka, MN 55343.

The Vogue/Butterick Step-by-Step Guide to Sewing, by editors of Vogue and Butterick Patterns; Prentice Hall Press.

The Busy Woman's Sewing Book, by Nancy Zieman. Order from Nancy's Notions; P.O. Box 683; Beaver Dam, WI 53916; 414-887-0391. Nancy Zieman has also written booklets on many other topics, based on her TV show, "Sewing With Nancy." Video tapes of her shows plus the booklets are also available from this address.

Special Techniques

The Complete Book of Machine Quilting, by Robbie and Tony Fanning, published by Chilton Book Company. This book is complete and detailed. You can piece your quilt top on the serger then quilt by hand or on a conventional machine. Several other authors have written books on quilt piecing techniques.

Kwik-Sew's Sweatshirts Unlimited and *Beautiful Lingerie*, by Kerstin Martenssen. Both books include multi-sized patterns and directions for many creative variations. The lingerie book also includes basic construction methods. Order from Kwik-Sew Pattern Co., Inc.; 3000 Washington Avenue North; Minneapolis, MN 55411. Kwik-Sew also has available a catalog of their patterns, which are primarily for knits. There are several other Kwik-Sew books.

Necklines Made Easy and *Sew Splashy*, by Ann Person. Ann supplies multi-sized patterns and directions for numerous creative variations. *Sew Splashy* gives construction methods and tells how to customize the fit of a swimsuit (and control how high the leg is cut). Order from Stretch & Sew, Inc.; P.O. Box 185; Eugene, OR 97440. There are several other Stretch and Sew books available, as well as excellent patterns for knits.

The Singer Reference Library has also published many excellent sewing books on special techniques, such as their books on *Lingerie* and *Sewing Activewear*. They can be ordered from Cy DeCosse, Inc.; 5900 Green Oak Drive; Minnetonka, MN 55343.

Sew to Success, by Kathleen Spike, describes how to make money in a home-based sewing business. It is published by Palmer/Pletsch Assoc.; P.O.Box 12046; Portland, OR 97212.

Heirloom Sewing

French Sewing by Serger and *60-Minute Heirlooms: Serging for Babies*, by Kathy McMakin. These books include many color photos of garments, complete directions, and patterns. Order from Albright & CO. Publishers; P.O. Box 2011; Huntsville, AL 35804; 205-539-3288.

Antique Clothing: French Sewing by Machine, by Martha Pullen. (This is the book on heirloom sewing.) Martha Pullen spearheaded the interest in heirloom sewing on the sewing machine. She also carries all the necessary supplies: trims and laces, fabrics, books, patterns. Order from Martha Pullen Company, Inc.; 518 Madison Street; Huntsville, AL 35801. 1-205-533-9586, order desk 1-800-547-4176

French Hand Sewing for Machine, by Melissa Stone. Published by Sarah Howard Stone, Inc.; 514 Cloverdale Road; Montgomery, AL 36106.

Mildred Turner has written several excellent instruction books. They are: *Mim's Machine Heirloom Sewing*, *Mim's Heirloom Sewing Book Two*, and *Mim's Machine Magic Book Three*. They can be ordered from Mim's Smock Shoppe, Inc.; 502 Balsam Rd.; Hazelwood, NC 28738; 1-704-452-3455 or 1-704-456-7018.

Sewing Periodicals

Although I include information on subscription rates, such prices do change. If in doubt write for information on current rates.

"Sew Beautiful" specializes in heirloom sewing and smocking. It is published 5 times a year by Martha Pullen Company, Inc.; 518 Madison Street; Huntsville, AL 35801. At present the cost is $23 per year.

"Sew It Seams" is a quarterly publication with a focus on quality fit and construction. Order from P.O. Box 2698; Kirkland, WA 98083. $22 per year at last report.

"Sew News" focuses on many different facets of sewing, including information on what is fashionable and how to sew it. There is a monthly column on sergers. Order from P.O. box 1790; Peoria, IL 61656. Presently the cost is $17.97 per year.

"Sewing Update" Update Newsletters; 2269 Chestnut, Suite 269; San Francisco, CA 94123. $18 for 6 issues, bimonthly. Same 8 page newsletter format as "Serger Update" described above.

"Threads" comes out bimonthly. I often refer to my back issues, even though only some of the articles relate directly to sewing. It covers the finest and most innovative work in the various fiber arts, which you can enjoy vicariously if not directly. $24 per year from The Taunton Press; 63 South Main Street, Box 9976; Newtown, CT 06470.

The various pattern companies publish magazines showcasing their new patterns and giving some information on sewing techniques.

"Butterick Home Catalog"; 161 Sixth Avenue, New York, NY 10013. $8 for 4 issues, quarterly.

"McCall's Pattern Magazine"; 230 Park Avenue; New York, NY 10169. $10 for 4 issues, quarterly.

"Vogue Patterns Magazine"; 161 Sixth Avenue; New York, NY 10013. $12.95 for 6 issues, bimonthly.

SUPPLIES

Most stores do not carry as wide a selection of sewing accessories as are available through the mail. Especially for threads and such it is nice to be able to buy them locally if you can. Check out what your dealer carries, and what you can find in yarn shops, needle arts stores, etc. If you cannot find something locally you can probably find it through a mail-order source. Besides, it is fun and educational to peruse these catalogs and see what is available: sewing and sewing tools have changed tremendously in the last ten years, making sewing much faster and easier without compromising quality. There is a guide to mail-order sources called "The Sew-by-Mail Directory." It is available for $3.95 from Update Newsletters; 2269 Chestnut, Suite 269; San Francisco, CA 94123. There is a book, The Fabric & Fiber Sourcebook, by Bobbi McRae, which has extensive lists of all kinds of sources. It is available from "Threads" magazine, listed in the section on "Sewing Periodicals," above. Another good book is The Wholesale by Mail Catalog, by the Print Project. Ads in the various sewing publications listed above are a good source of information. "Sew News" has a monthly column with mail-order sources for difficult to find items.

The Birdhouse has a nice looper and needle threader. Write to Birdhouse Enterprises; 110 Jennings Ave.; Patchogue, N.Y. 11772.

Clotilde, Inc. She has a catalog full of tools, books, threads, etc. Write to 1909 SW First Avenue, Ft. Lauderdale, FL 33315; 305-761-8655.

DK Sports; 134 N.W. 8th; Portland, OR 97209; 503-222-9033. They carry patterns and fabric for outdoor wear.

Green Pepper carries fabric and patterns for active wear and outdoor wear. Contact them at 941 Olive; Eugene, OR 97407; 503-345-6665

Kieffers Lingerie Fabrics & Supplies. They carry fabric, lace, notions, books and patterns. Write them at 1625 Hennepin Avenue; Minneapolis, MN 55403, or call 612-332-3395.

Nancy's Notions. Her catalog includes fabric, videos, threads, tools, ballpoint serger needles, etc. Write to P.O. Box 683; Beaver Dam, WI 53916; 414-887-0391.

National Thread & Supply Corp; 695 Red Oak Road; Stockbridge, GA 30281; 1-800-331-7600. They have sewing notions, zippers, pressing supplies, etc.

Newark Dressmaker Supply; P.O. Box 2448; Lehigh Valley, PA 18001; 215-837-7500. Their catalog has a variety of items for sewing, crafts, bridal, upholstery, etc.

The Perfect Notion. Their catalog is available from 566 Hoyt Street; Darien, CT 06820; 203-968-1257. It has a variety of sewing notions.

The Rain Shed. They carry fabrics for outdoor wear. 707 N.W. 11th: Corvallis, OR 97330; 503-753-8900

Rupert, Gibbon and Spider. They have a wonderful selection of natural colored silks suitable for dyeing, and all the dyeing supplies. Rock bottom prices. If you want natural colored silk or if you have ever toyed with the idea of silk painting or dyeing, check them out. They even have silk jersey for underwear. P.O. Box 425; Healdsburg, CA 95448; 707-433-9577; orders only 1-800-442-0455; fax 707-433-4906.

Serge and Sew. They carry special threads, a good selection of tools, textile paints, books, and several lines of patterns. (Burda, Great Copy, Kwik Sew, Patterns by the Yard, Stretch & Sew). Contact them at Serge & Sew Notions & Fabrics; 13704 83 N Way; Maple Grove, MN 55369; 1-800-969-7396.

Sew-Knit Distributors; 9789 Florida Blvd.; Baton Rouge, LA 70815; orders only 1-800-289-5648; info 504-923-1260. They have a variety of ironing tools and sewing accessories. They also have machine knitting accessories, including a cone yarn winder and ball winder.

Sewing Emporium; 1087 Third Avenue; Chula Vista, CA 92010; 619-420-3490. Sewing machine accouterments, etc.

The Sewing Workshop. This is a school for gourmet sewing in San Francisco. They also mail order special notions. They are at 2010 Balboa St.; San Francisco, CA 94121; 415-221-7397.

Thai Silks; large selection of white and printed silks at affordable prices. Write them at 252 State Street; Los Altos, CA 94022; 800-722-SILK.

Thread Discount Sales carries a variety of coned thread. Write to P.O. Box 2277; Bell Gardens, CA 90201; 213-562-3438 or 213-560-8177.

Treadleart; huge selection of books on all facets of sewing with a particular emphasis on machine arts; also tools, patterns, supplies. They carry texturized nylon in a huge variety of colors. 25834 Narbonne Avenue; Lomita, CA 90717; 213-534-5122; orders only 1-800-327-4222; fax 213-534-8372.

The Unicorn, Books for Craftsmen Inc. They mail order fiber arts books and have a huge selection. They are at 1304 Scott St.; Petaluma, CA 94954; 707-762-3362.

ORGANIZATIONS

The American Home Sewing Guild is nation wide. Local chapters support neighborhood groups, arrange workshops and lectures, and publish newsletters. The neighborhood groups meet monthly, and are usually about a dozen people. They share information and inspiration, and sometimes arrange for guest speakers. If you contact the national organization they will send you information on the local chapters.

American Sewing Guild National Headquarters

P.O. Box 50976

Indianapolis, IN 46250

If you sew professionally you may find a local organization of others who do the same. These local groups can provide opportunities for networking, training and credentialing. Although there is not presently a national umbrella organization which speaks for all local organizations, your local American Home Sewing Guild office may be able to refer you to a local professional organization. The following group is working to establish local chapters across the country for sewing professionals:

Professional Association of Custom Clothiers

1375 Broadway

New York, NY 10018

SERGER COMPANIES

The first place to look for local dealers is the yellow pages. You can also write the companies directly.

Babylock U.S.A. (Tacony Corp.)
1760 Gillsinn Lane
Fenton, MO 63026

Bernina of America
534 West Chestnut
Hinsdale, IL 60521

Brother International Corp.
8 Corporate Place
Piscataway, NJ 08854

Elna, Inc.
7642 Washington Avenue South
Eden Prairie, MN 55344

Juki Industries of America
3555 Lomita Blvd., Suite H
Torrance, CA 90505

New Home Sewing Machine Company
100 Hollister Road
Teterboro, NJ 07608

Pfaff American Sales Corp.
610 Winters Avenue
Paramus, NJ 07653

Riccar America
14281 Franklin Avenue
Tustin, CA 92680

Singer Sewing Machine Company
North American Sewing Products Division
200 Metroplex Drive
Edison, NJ 08818

Viking Sewing Machine Company
White Sewing Machine Company
11760 Berea Road
Cleveland, OH 44111

GLOSSARY

5-Thread Stitch: This is a combination of a 3-thread overlock stitch with a 2-thread chainstitch. It is produced by a 5-thread serger. (refer to the section on "Types of Sergers and Stitches" on page 15 for more information)

Applique: Pieces of fabric are cut out and sewn onto another piece of fabric to make a picture or design. An excellent book on applique is Kerstin Martensson's *Applique the Kwik-Sew Way*. Refer to Appendix C: Sources, page 189, for ordering information. Simple shapes can be appliqued on the serger (refer to section on "Serger Applique," page 138).

Armscye: This is the opening on a bodice where the sleeve is attached.

Balance Wheel: This is the wheel on the right side of a serger or sewing machine that goes around as the machine moves. You can turn the balance wheel manually to make the serger move. On industrial and older domestic sergers the balance wheel generally turns in the opposite direction from conventional machines. On the newer domestic machines the balance wheel turns the same direction as we are used to from our conventional machines (counterclockwise). There will be an arrow on or next to your balance wheel, indicating which way it moves. Do not turn it backwards because threads will tangle.

Balanced Stitch: This is the most commonly used serger stitch. It is a 3 or 4-thread overlock stitch with the upper looper thread on top and the lower looper thread on the bottom, meeting at the edge of the stitch. The section on "The Serger Stitch," page 29, describes this stitch in detail.

Beehive Tension Disks: (refer to definition for Tension Disks on page 199)

Bight: This is another term for stitch width. (refer to section on "Stitch Width and Knives," page 37)

Blind Hem: A garment edge is folded up and stitched so that the stitching is almost invisible on the right side. This can be done by hand or machine. (refer to section on "Blind Hemming," page 44)

Boucle: This is a type of decorative yarn with little loops along it. It is made by twisting two strands together, with one strand much looser than the other. The looser strand makes the loops.

Bound Edge: This is a raw edge finished by seam binding.

Chainstitch: Some sergers can make a 2-thread chainstitch. On the top this looks like a straight stitch on a conventional machine. On the bottom the

193

looper thread looks thicker because of the way the stitch is formed. (refer to section on "2-Thread Chainstitch," page 143)

Checkspring: Some sergers with beehive tension disks have a little spring loaded wire hook beside one or more of the tension disks. The thread must be hooked into this wire after it goes around the tension disk. Sometimes, on the lower looper, this hook is only supposed to be used when tightening the lower looper thread for a rolled hem or flat-lock. Read your manual.

Clear Elastic: This is made from polyurethane, a plastic. It looks like a thin strip of clear plastic, and is more stretchy than normal elastic. Normally it is sold in widths of 1/4" or 3/8". It is unaffected by chlorine, making it useful in swimsuits. Try a sample: you may want to reduce the recommended length of elastic by 10%. It loses very little stretch from needle holes, unlike other kinds of elastic. It is so thin that it is wonderful for controlling rippling and stabilizing seams without losing stretch. Make sure the needle sews into the elastic rather than just having the stitch enclose the elastic.

Cone Thread Stand: You can make or buy this handy gadget. It enables you to use large cones of thread on your serger, or cones of serger thread on your conventional machine. (refer to the section on "Basic Thread," page 89)

Corded Edge: A lightweight cord such as crochet thread can be incorporated into a narrow rolled edge for extra definition and crispness. (refer to section on "Decorative Narrow Rolled Edge," page 125)

Couching: This is a method of attaching decorative stuff to fabric. Traditionally the "stuff" is yarn or cord, but lots of other things can be attached as well. (refer to section on "Couching," page 117)

Covering Stitch: This term is sometimes used to refer to a serger-like stitch which is not made over the edge of the fabric. There are actually three types of stitches made this way: cover seaming stitch, coverstitching and flat seaming. They are described in chapter 7.

Crossgrain: This is the direction on the fabric which is perpendicular to the selvedge. Most knits stretch on the crossgrain, with little or no stretch on the lengthwise grain (parallel to the selvedge). Swimsuit or exercise wear fabric stretches in both directions, but generally more in the lengthwise direction. Always lay out knits with the greatest stretch going around the body.

Cross-wound: This is the way thread is wound on cones of serger thread. It makes an "X" pattern. Thread wound this way feeds more evenly when it is being pulled from the top.

Differential Feed: Some sergers have this feature. With differential feed the front half of the feed dogs can be set to move faster or slower than the back half, easing or stretching the fabric as it is sewn. (refer to section on "Differential Feed," page 40)

Domestic Serger: This is a serger intended for home use. (refer to section on "Industrial Sergers," page 151)

Double Needle: Two needles are joined at the top into one shank, which can be inserted into a conventional machine like a normal single needle. A separate thread goes through each needle. It is used for decorative effects, including top-stitching and hemming. Because the single bobbin thread zig-zags, a double needle stitch has some stretch, especially when bobbin and/or needle tensions are loosened. Therefore it is suitable for use on knits. It duplicates the effect of the 2 needle cover seaming stitch, which has 2 parallel rows of straight stitching on the right side and a looper thread on the wrong side. Some domestic 5-thread sergers use a special double needle for making a 4-thread overlock stitch. (refer to section on "Blind Hemming," page 44 for using the double needle)

Facing: This is a method of finishing garment edges. A separate piece of fabric is sewn onto the edge then turned to the wrong side.

Fagoting: A fagoted seam has an open lacework of thread filling a space between the two pieces of fabric. Although traditionally done by hand this can be done on the serger, as described in the section on "Fagoting," page 109.

Feed Dogs: These are found on the bed of the machine underneath the presser foot. They move the fabric forward between stitches.

Floss Threader: This tool greatly facilitates the threading of sergers, especially the loopers. (refer to section on "Threading," page 21)

Flounce: This is the "other" way of adding fullness, besides gathering. A flounce is a curved piece of fabric attached along its inside edge. Unlike gathering, the seam is neither stiff nor bulky. This makes it especially wonderful for knits, such as swimsuits. The lack of bulk is also generally more attractive. An easy way to make flounces is to make circular pieces as shown in Figure G-1. The width of the flounce is the distance between the inner and outer circles, minus seam allowance and hem. The smaller the inner circle, the fuller the flounce will be.

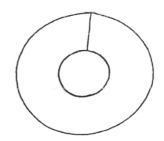

Figure G-1: *Flounce*

Seam together several circular pieces if necessary for a longer flounce. Line, or finish the edge with a serger stitch. A narrow rolled edge works well, as does lettucing. If desired, the inner edge can be somewhat gathered before attaching. Experiment with flounces of tissue paper taped together to decide on what fullness and width you want.

French Seam: This is a fine seam for lightweight wovens. It works best on straight or slightly curved seams. Make a narrow seam with wrong sides together, trim, press flat, turn so right sides are together and previous seam is enclosed. Stitch just far enough from fold so raw edges do not protrude. On a serger, make the first seam with the narrow rolled edge stitch finger and as narrow a stitch width as possible. On light or sheer wovens the second seam can be made on a conventional machine with a straight stitch. For decorative effect on heavier fabrics the second seam can be a wide flat-lock. (refer to section on "Flat-Locking," page 51)

Fusible Web: This is a type of fabric glue that melts when heated by an iron, glueing fabric together. It comes in two forms. It can be sold as a sheet by itself: this sheet is placed between two pieces of fabric and fused with an iron. Sometimes this is sold under the brand names "Fine Fuse" or "Stitch Witchery." Another form comes bonded to a piece of paper. Sometimes this is sold under the brand name "Wonder-Under." The paper-backed fusible web requires two steps: first the web is fused to one piece of fabric and the paper is peeled away. Then this piece of fabric is fused to the other piece of fabric. The two step process gives more control. Follow product directions for fusing. Sheets of plastic are sold as pressing sheets or fusing sheets. These are used when fusing because the fusible web cannot stick to the plastic. With their assistance a layer of fusible web without paper backing can be fused to one side of a piece of fabric.

Industrial Serger: This is a serger intended for commercial or industrial use. (refer to section on "Industrial Sergers," page 151)

Inset Tension Disks: (refer to definition for Tension Disks on page 199)

Interlock: This is a lightweight double knit fabric commonly used for summer casual clothes. It is very stretchy with excellent recovery. (refer to section on "Interlock" in Appendix B: Dictionary of Fabrics, page 171)

Lettucing: This is a decorative edging applied to stretchy fabrics. (refer to section on "Lettucing," page 123)

Loopers: Loopers are used on sergers instead of bobbins to carry some of the threads for the stitch. Loopers have an eye at the end like a needle. However, since they do not have to pierce the fabric, they and their eye can be much bigger. Refer to the section on "How a Serger Works," page 16, for a description of how a 3 or 4-thread overlock stitch is formed. The loopers for a 2-thread chainstitch or 2-thread overedge stitch function similarly.

Lycra: This is an extremely stretchy fiber which is combined in small amounts with other fibers to yield a stretchy fabric with excellent recovery. Sometimes it is called Spandex. (refer to section on "Lycra" in Appendix B: Dictionary of Fabrics, page 172)

Mohair: This is a type of yarn with long fibers sticking out of it.

Narrow Rolled Edge or Narrow Rolled Hem: This is a fine secure finish for light and medium weight fabrics. Generally it is used on exposed edges although it can also be used for seams in sheer fabrics. (refer to section on "Narrow Rolled Edge," page 46)

Needle Plate: This is the part of the machine that the needle goes through after it goes through the fabric. On some machines the needle plate is changed when converting to a narrow rolled edge.

Overedge: This is a serger stitch that protects a fabric edge from fraying but cannot be used as a seam. (refer to section on "2-Thread Overedge," page 141)

Overhand Knot: This is the type of knot to use when tieing on new serger threads or making spaghetti tubing. Use it instead of the square knot.

Overlock: This serger stitch both protects a fabric edge from fraying and can be used as a seam. It is the most commonly used serger stitch. It can be either a 3-thread overlock or a 4-thread overlock. (refer to section on "The Serger Stitch," page 29 for a description)

Passementerie: This is a decorative technique in which narrow braid is sewn onto a garment, generally in a scroll-like pattern or a pattern of loops. The braid is a contrasting color, often black. Although the braid can be straight stitched on, it is easier to zig-zag it on, using a conventional machine. The serger can be used to make the braid. (refer to section on "Decorative Uses of Chain," page 136)

Pintucks/Tucks: These are pleats stitched so the fold is on the right side of the garment. Pintucks are generally very narrow, tucks are wider. (refer to section on "Pintucks," page 122)

Piping: Traditional piping is made by folding a strip of bias fabric around a cord, stitching to secure, then sewing the piping into a seam so it shows from the right side. Serger piping is made as described in the section on "Serger Piping," page 114, then sewn into a seam as conventional piping is.

Polar Fleece: This is a thick, warm, comfortable pile fabric. It is washable, but one side will pill and look ratty. Chinella looks like polar fleece and is often called polar fleece. However it will not pill. If you look at a cut edge, generally the side with the thicker pile is the right side, but if in doubt wash it before cutting out. The texture will become more nubby and less plush. If it is not chinella one side will show the beginning of matting or pilling. This stuff is so cozy and comfortable you will not much care how it looks once you wear it, but it does look nice too. (refer to section on "Bulky Fabrics" in Appendix B: Dictionary of Fabrics, page 169)

Presser Foot Lift: This is the little lever, around on the back of most machines, that lifts the presser foot. If you try to get at it on a serger with your right hand you will realize this is one of the few places where lefties have a definite advantage. Some sergers have this on the front of the machine. On industrial sergers this is knee or foot operated.

Puckering: If one of the threads is too tight, generally either the needle or lower looper, a seam will pucker. This will appear as fine wrinkles perpendicular to the seam. Refer to the section on "Adjusting Tensions," page 32, for a balanced stitch and the section on "Narrow Rolled Edge," page 46, when doing a narrow rolled edge. If puckering occurs when flat-locking refer to the section on "Flat-Locking," page 51.

Recovery: In fabrics, this is an indication of how readily a knit returns to its original size after being stretched.

Ribbing: This is a stretchy knit with good recovery used for finishing the edges of garments, generally knits. (refer to section on "Ribbing and Elastic," page 72)

Rippling: If the stitch length is too short it will put too much thread into a seam, stretching it and making it ripple. Some fabrics are more subject to this than others, generally light fabrics with good recovery ripple less than heavier stretchy fabrics with poor recovery. Refer to section on "Knits," page 67, for techniques to control this.

Rolled Edge/Rolled Hem: (refer to definition for Narrow Rolled Edge)

Seam: A seam is a series of stitches used to join two or more plies (layers) of material together.

Set Screw: Tiny set screws hold the needles in the machine, and must be loosened when changing needles. A set screw may be used to lock the upper knife for heavy fabric or release it so stitch width can be adjusted. (refer to section on "Stitch Width and Knives," page 37)

Shank: This is the top part of the needle, the part which is inserted into the machine.

Sheer Tricot: Bias strips of this are sold under the brand name "Seams Great." Although normally sold in white or black, various shades are available. Since it is sheer, the color is not normally critical. The normal width is 5/8" although a wider width is available. You can also cut your own: since tricot is a knit you need not cut them on the bias. This is a wonderful way to **secure** a seam allowance in woven fabrics. Fold the tricot over the edge and top-stitch with a zig-zag. If you pull gently on the strip you will see which way it wants to fold. I use this on top of my serger stitch on very ravel-prone fabrics or in areas subject to heavy wear, such as the edges of pockets inside the garment (technically, the raw edges of the pocket bag), armscye or crotch seams in children's garments or work clothes, etc. It is also wonderful for getting a good narrow rolled edge in certain fabrics, or for controlling scratchiness in seam allowances of fabrics like metallics.

Shirr/shirring: Parallel rows of elastic are sewn to a garment to take in fullness while providing ease. Commonly this is done at waistlines and the bottoms of sleeves, although it can also be done around the neck. The section on "Shirring," page 121, tells how to do this on a serger.

Slub: This is a yarn with small lumps of fiber twisted into it. They may be matching or contrasting color.

Smocking Stitch: This stitch looks like rows of diamonds. It is available on many conventional machines. I use it for securing the ends of elastic.

Spool Caps: These came with your machine. They look like small frisbees with a hole in the middle. Whenever sewing with a spool of thread on the serger, put one of these on top of the spool to ensure the thread feeds smoothly.

Stabilization: This is an extra layer of fabric used to keep a seam from stretching, wrinkling or tearing. Most commonly this is provided by interfacing.

Stitch: A stitch is a formation of thread for the purpose of making a seam or stitching.

Stitch Finger: This is the little tongue of metal that the stitches form around. (refer to section on "How a Serger Works," page 16)

Stitching: This consists of a series of stitches used to finish the edge or decoratively stitch a single ply (layer) of material.

Stretch: This is a measure of how much a given fabric will stretch. (refer to section on "Knits," page 67)

Sweater Knits: These are loose single knits made from yarn rather than thread. They generally have poor recovery, but lovely texture. (refer to section on "Sweater Knits" in Appendix B: Dictionary of Fabrics, page 174)

Take-up Lever: The older sergers often did not have a take-up lever, the newer ones do. It helps make a better stitch. It does not move nearly as far as the take-up lever on a conventional machine. It is located directly above the needle on the body of the machine. It is generally inside a sort of metal box, so it is not obvious.

Telescope: This is the part of the machine that the thread goes through after it comes off the cone. It can be pushed down for storage, but should be pulled up as far as it will go for sewing.

Tension Disks: Each thread passes between two smooth metal disks that squeeze the thread between them. They control how the stitch looks. There are two types of tension disks. The beehive tension disks stick out from the front of the machine and are shaped somewhat like a beehive. The vertical or inset tension disks are inset into the top of the machine. (refer to section on "Adjusting Tensions," page 32)

Tension Release: Some machines have a control which completely releases all tensions. Sometimes this is automatic when the presser foot is lifted. Sometimes a separate control is used.

Texturized Nylon: This is a crimped untwisted nylon thread that is very useful on a serger. (refer to section on "Texturized Nylon," page 93)

Thread Chain: This is the serger stitch when there is no fabric is the machine. A length of serger chain is left at both the beginning and ending of every serger seam, although it may be cut off later. As long as the machine is threaded there is a length of serger chain on the machine. Long lengths of this can be produced and used for various purposes. (refer to section on "Decorative Uses of Chain," page 136)

Thread Nets: These usually come with the machine. They are stretchy tubes of plastic mesh, and are used on cones or spools of slippery thread to keep it under control. Refer to the sections on "Threading," page 21, or "Special Threads," page 90, for a description of how to use them.

Top-Stitch: This is stitching which shows from the right side of the garment. Since it is not done over the edge of fabric it must be done with a conventional machine or with a 2-thread chainstitch. (refer to section on "2-Thread Chainstitch," page 143)

Tubular Ribbon: This is a round rayon ribbon which can be used decoratively. Look for it in yarn or craft stores.

Tunneling: If a wide stitch is used on light to medium weight fabric the fabric will tend to wrinkle or fold up within the stitch. This has two causes. If the thread tensions are too tight they will pull in on the edge of the fabric, causing tunneling. This is why the zig-zag stitch on a conventional machine tends to form a ridge or tunnel, and why tensions must typically be loosened slightly for it. This type of tunneling can be partly prevented by having a stitch finger, as the serger does. Another reason for tunneling is movement of the fabric within the stitch. If you were to try a balanced stitch with just the left needle (wide stitch) on a light fabric, the fabric would be likely to fold up or crumple within the stitch unless the stitch width was quite narrow. On a conventional machine this type of tunneling is prevented by having several little stitches across the width of the seam allowance, for example the smocking stitch, or multi-step zig-zag. On the serger the right needle thread helps prevent tunneling by preventing the fabric from moving around within the stitch.

Twill Weave: Fine diagonal lines or ridges show on the right side of this fabric because of the structure of the weave. It is a strong durable fabric often used for slacks. Denim is a twill weave.

Underlining: Sometimes the fashion fabric of a garment needs extra support. Often this is accomplished by cutting another layer of fabric using the main pattern pieces, putting it on the wrong side of the fashion fabric, then treating the two layers of fabric as one during construction. A lace blouse might be underlined with beige china silk, to give both opacity and support. A silk noil might be underlined with batiste to give it enough weight for a suit. An easy serger method is to serge around both layers at once, finishing raw edges and joining them together.

Vertical Tension Disks: (refer to definition for Tension Disks)

Water Soluble Stabilizer: This looks almost like a piece of plastic food wrap. It is most commonly used for machine embroidery techniques. The magic is that, with water, it dissolves into a glob that easily washes away. Especially on humid days, pressing it with a dry iron will make it stiffer and less sticky. (refer to sections on "Bulky Fabrics," "Coated Fabrics," "Narrow Rolled Edge," "Serger Lace," and "Fagoting" for suggestions on using it) To find it, begin with stores which carry supplies for machine embroidery: many dealers carry these supplies. Otherwise you can mail order it. (refer to the section on "Supplies" in Appendix D: Sources, page 189)

POSTSCRIPT

Note to Teachers: This book is based on my experience as a teacher, on what I have found is the most effective way to assist people in mastering sergers. The book makes it unnecessary to takes notes in class, which enables people to concentrate on the material. It also is useful for additional self-study and as a reference book. As a teacher you can demonstrate the material in each section or guide students as they demonstrate it to themselves. At the end of each section solicit questions to make sure people understand the material covered so far. The material builds, so it is important to ensure students do not get left behind. I always make it clear from the beginning that questions are welcome at any point. This helps people relax, and so they learn better. I always tell my students to go home and practice, to use the techniques as soon as possible so they do not forget them.

Here is a list of the sections I like to make sure are covered in class:

For teaching the basics, I have found it valuable to present the material in this order: "How a Serger Works," "Threading," "The Serger Stitch," and "Adjusting Tensions."

All the material in chapter 1 is necessary except the section on "Types of Sergers and Stitches," and the subsection on "The Sewing Area." Some machines do not have differential feed and so those students do not need to cover that section.

In Chapter 2, the most important sections are: "Blind Hemming" and "Narrow Rolled Edge." Many students will also be interested in the section on "Flat-Locking."

In Chapter 3 the most important sections are: "Securing Seams," "Sewing in a Circle," and "Serging Corners."

The "Knits" Section in Chapter 4 is very important.

Students enjoy the section on "Gathering" in Chapter 6.

If a student has a 2-thread chainstitch or a 2-thread overedge stitch, they need to go over the relevant material in Chapter 7.

You may want to cover the "Special Attachments" section in Chapter 8, on the attachments available for the students' machines.

Beyond this you can simply point out what else the book covers. Chapter 4 has several other important sections for students to refer to as needed. Chapters 5 and 6 are mostly for decorative serging. Appendices A and B are used frequently.

This material requires only a basic knowledge of sewing, so I have not had problems with students who cannot keep up. Students certainly do come in on different levels, and some will pick up all the little details while others are getting only the basics. However they are all learning, and are able to successfully use a serger after covering the material. Many express a desire to take the class again, to get more of the details.

Note to Home Sewers: I am a home sewer myself, so I have been determined to make this book useful and easy to understand for you. If you read the introduction it tells you how to use this book for self-study. I want you to be able to produce quality work without frustration, and with that touch of your own creativity. Home sewing gives us the opportunity to get exactly what we want and at a price we can afford, to express ourselves and have a sense of accomplishment, and to enjoy the sheer magic of sewing. Growing numbers of men are discovering the fascination of sewing. I always enjoy having them in my classes: they tend to be more analytical, less constrained by practical considerations (play clothes for Johnny), and utterly delighted by sewing. I think it has been too easy for women who sew to belittle their skills, accomplishments and needs. Sewing is a marvelous skill: respect and enjoy it. Fabric and clothing are extremely ancient: for millennia women have been clothing their families, and using this opportunity to express themselves. Much has changed, but there is a wonderful sense of continuity and community through our love of fiber and fabric. Cherish your connection with generations past. And when the opportunity arises, share it with the oncoming generations.

Clothes affect how we feel about ourselves. They should not only make our bodies look good, they should also express who we are, what is uniquely beautiful and precious about us. One of my daughters has a vibrant personality: for her I make beautiful vibrant clothes. Another daughter has many quiet depths: for her I make clothes of quiet beauty. Find what makes you feel wonderful, not necessarily what is familiar. If you are a romantic, let it show. If you love nature, let it show. If you have a sense of fun, by all means share it. If you love classic elegance but have seven kids, chose washable fabrics and classically elegant lines. This, as sewers, we can do for ourselves and those we love. We are much more than our physical bodies, but that does not mean we should deny them. If we try to make clothes substitute for who we are, we will create only sorrow. But, if we let our clothes express our unique beauty, we have lifted ourselves and others. Each of us has a uniquely precious beauty which we yearn to express, and others yearn to see.

Note to Production Sewers: By understanding your machine you will improve quality and speed, and reduce your frustration. Be sure you check your tensions periodically, especially when changing fabric. Find a good dealer, one who is knowledgeable and who provides good service when you need it. Let him or her know what types of sewing you do. Find out what accessories are available for your machine, and remember that on industrial machines you can also change presser feet, needle plates and feed dogs to suit a particular type of sewing. Remember that in most cases your greatest expense is labor: having the right equipment and knowing how to use it will enable you to get the most value for your or your employees' time. Make sure you know how to use your machine and its accessories. Once you are familiar with this book ask your dealer for any additional information you might need. Especially for you, getting a good dealer is essential.

INDEX

We hope you enjoyed <u>Understanding Sergers</u>, and that it has helped you enjoy your serger more and get more value out of it. We would love to hear from you. If you wish additional copies you can order them directly from Acorn Press. Please enclose $24.95 per copy plus $2.50 for shipping and packaging. Minnesota residents please add sales tax.

Acorn Press
P.O. Box 26333
Shoreview, MN 55126